# The Rise and Fall of the Voting Rights Act

Studies in American Constitutional Heritage
Justin J. Wert and Kyle Harper, Series Editors

# The Rise and Fall of the Voting Rights Act

Charles S. Bullock III
Ronald Keith Gaddie
Justin J. Wert

University of Oklahoma Press : Norman

Also by Charles S. Bullock III and Ronald Keith Gaddie
*The Triumph of Voting Rights in the South* (Norman, Okla., 2009)

Also by Justin J. Wert
*Habeas Corpus in America: The Politics of Individual Rights* (Lawrence, Kan., 2011)

Library of Congress Cataloging-in-Publication Data

Bullock, Charles S., 1942– author.
  The rise and fall of the Voting Rights Act / Charles S. Bullock III, Ronald Keith Gaddie, Justin J. Wert.
      pages  cm. — (Studies in American constitutional heritage ; volume 2)
    "This book is a follow-up to our previous work, The triumph of voting rights in the South." — ECIP galley.
    Includes bibliographical references and index.
    ISBN 978-0-8061-5200-4 (hardcover : alk. paper)
1. United States. Voting Rights Act of 1965  2. Suffrage—United States. 3. Election law—United States. 4. African Americans—Suffrage—Southern States. 5. Southern States—Politics and government—21st century. 6. Shelby County (Ala.)—Trials litigation, etc. I. Gaddies, Ronald Keith, author. II Wert, Justin J., author. III. Title.
    KF4891.B85 2016
    342.73'072—dc23                                                    2015035116

*The Rise and Fall of the Voting Rights Act* is Volume 2 in the Studies in American Constitutional Heritage series.

The paper in this book meets the guidelines for permanence and durability of the Committee on Production Guidelines for Book Longevity of the Council on Library Resources, Inc. ∞

1 2 3 4 5 6 7 8 9 10

# Contents

# Illustrations

# Introduction

On June 25, 2013, the U.S. Supreme Court handed down a decision in the case *Shelby County v. Holder.* The early summer decision created an air of grave uncertainty in the voting rights community. In *Shelby County*, the high court invalidated a significant and powerful provision of voting rights law, specifically the coverage formula for determining if a state, county, or city would have its ability to change election practices preapproved by the national government.

The decision was the culmination of an eight-year battle over the scope and application of congressional power to regulate state conduct of elections in order to ensure fair and equal access to the ballot regardless of race. The debate took place in the halls of Congress, in the media, and in courthouses in Alabama, Texas, and Washington, D.C.

The result of this case marked the close of a long, significant act of the larger play of American politics—an act that had opened a century before in Oklahoma in the case *Guinn v. United States* (238 U.S. 347 1915), which ended the use of the "Fighting Grandfather Clause" as a registration device. *Guinn* ushered in the slow, deliberate rise of national efforts in government and society to knock down racial barriers to the ballot.

The case initiated a century-long era that saw, in fits and starts, changes that advanced voting rights and opened up the electoral process. Challenges to white primaries, poll taxes, literacy tests, slating, and discriminatory redistricting followed *Guinn* between the 1940s and 1980s. Congress created a series of civil rights acts to expand national government oversight and regulation of discriminatory practices. The law in defense of Fourteenth and Fifteenth Amendment rights moved in one direction, toward more progress. The high-water mark of the movement for equal access to the ballot was the passage of the Voting Rights Act of 1965 (42 U.S.C. § 1973), followed by the nearly half-century of successful implementation of the Act. The implementation of the law, especially its Section 5 preclearance provision, ensured that the national government had a powerful lever to wield against discriminating jurisdictions. Jurisdictions in all or parts of sixteen states, mainly in the South but also as varied as the urban boroughs of New York City and the rural boroughs of Alaska, submitted their changes in election law and practice for approval as nondiscriminatory. It was the most firm, direct regulation of states by the national government since Reconstruction a century before.

A century after *Guinn* was argued, and a half-century after the passage of the VRA, the rising tide of voting rights crested. With *Shelby County, Alabama v. Holder* the Supreme Court struck down a key provision of the law. This was first constitutional reversal of a non–campaign finance federal election law since the nineteenth century. It was also the first time the Court had overturned an act of Congress created under Congress's enforcement authority under Section 5 of the Fourteenth Amendment since 1883.[1] On any dimension, *Shelby County* was important, if only as a bookend to a long period in which the Court acted in an increasingly progressive direction concerning the interpretation of congressional authority under the Fourteenth and Fifteenth Amendments.

The case, brought by a county in Alabama, challenged Section 4 of the VRA. Section 4, referred to by voting rights lawyers and scholars as "the trigger," describes the conditions under which a state or other jurisdiction is subject to Section 5 of the Act, the "preclearance" provision. Then, Section 5 uses the authority of Congress under the Fifteenth Amendment to enact legislation appropriate to enforce the Act and freezes in place election laws and practices in areas identified by Section 4 until those areas demonstrate that changes in their election laws and practices do not make minority voters worse off than they were without the change.

The plaintiffs indirectly challenged the ongoing regulation of their elections under Section 5 by challenging Alabama's coverage under the Section 4 trigger. The Supreme Court had previously dealt with the constitutionality of Section 5 (*South Carolina v. Katzenbach*, 383 U.S. 301 1966) but more recently had signaled its concern about the constitutionality of the coverage formula in a Texas case, *NAMUDNO v. Holder* (557 U.S. 193 2009). Shelby County had been covered by the Act since 1965 and had been picked up in the initial implementation of the law and all subsequent extensions of the coverage formula by Congress. The county was not able to bail out from coverage by the Act and sought to challenge the coverage formula as a means to get out from under federal oversight.

Shelby County, Alabama, was representative of the change witnessed across the South since the 1960s, and also of lingering tensions between the South and the Voting Rights Act. The county was founded in 1818, nestled in the hilly country below Appalachian Alabama. It is historically agricultural country, but it was never a heavily black county like the old slave plantation counties to its immediate south. Nonetheless, Shelby made use of a full array of Jim Crow institutions and various mechanisms available in Alabama to keep down the black vote. As late as the 1970s, it was still a rural, farming county that maintained its Wallace Democrat voting habits. But, as Birmingham grew, towns in the northwestern part of the county became bedroom communities. Until 1980 the county had not changed significantly in terms of population or demographic profile. From 1900 to 1960 the population grew from 23,684 to 32,132, and the racial makeup of the county changed, with African American population falling from 29.5 percent to 18.9 percent. In the 1980s the county underwent a population boom, with the total jumping to 66,298 persons (a 74.3 percent growth rate). The growth rates for the next three decades were over 35 percent per decade, and by 2012 the estimated county population was over 200,000.

Shelby had become wealthy, suburban, and modern. As of 2012, it ranks among the hundred most affluent counties in the United States. Over 90 percent of county residents are high school graduates, 10 points above the state average. The average home value is above the national average and nearly one-third higher than the state average, and the average household income is similarly high.

It is still a predominantly white county. The county was, according to the 2010 census, about 79.5 percent Anglo white, 11.4 percent African American, and 6 percent Hispanic or Latino. The proportion of nonwhite population is roughly the same as in 1960, though the black share of the population has fallen.

Shelby also became a very Republican county. In the six presidential elections from 1992 to 2012, the county voted at least 68 percent Republican. In 2008 President Obama did better in Shelby County than either Senator Kerry in 2004 or Vice President Gore in 2000. Like many Deep South counties, Shelby went over heavily Republican in presidential politics in the 1980s, and heavily Republican in state politics starting in 1994.

The county government generally complied with the VRA, to our knowledge. Neither the county nor any cities or towns within it were subject to a Section 2 voting rights challenge. But the U.S. Department of Justice had objected to five electoral changes by municipalities in the county since 1965, and many of these objections illuminated a pattern of noncompliance with Section 5 by municipalities within the county. Three of these were annexations by the city of Alabaster, in 1975, 1977, and 2000 (two were subsequently withdrawn); one was a set of twenty-nine annexations by the city of Leeds, which straddled Shelby, Jefferson, and St. Clair Counties in 1987 (withdrawn in 1988); and one was a set of 177 nonsubmitted annexations and a redistricting plan for the City of Calera in 2008. These objections, among other criteria, prevented the county from requesting removal from coverage under the Act using the bailout provision.

Lacking a legal exit strategy to get out from under coverage by the Act, the county would have to invalidate the coverage formula under Section 4 of the Act or remain under Section 5. After failing in an evidentiary hearing in federal district court, the county appealed the decision and was granted petition, and the case was argued before the Supreme Court in 2013. On June 25, the high court rejected the coverage formula under Section 4 and effectively ended a half-century of close scrutiny of state voting laws across the South and in three northern and four western states.

The decision was controversial, reached on a 5–4 vote along ideological lines. The five justices in the majority were appointed by Republican presidents. Four—John Roberts, Samuel Alito, Antonin Scalia, and Clarence Thomas—constituted the conservative bloc of the court. The fifth, Justice Anthony Kennedy, was the "swing vote" on the Court, and he has most often appeared in the prevailing majority on close decisions in the Court since 2005. The four justices in the minority—Ruth Bader Ginsburg, Stephen Breyer, Sonya Sotomayor, and Elena Kagan—were appointed by Democratic presidents

and constituted a liberal bloc with whom Justice Kennedy sometimes voted.

The reaction in the wake of *Shelby County* varied from elation
among politicians in some monitored jurisdictions to emotional deva-
station among advocates for voting rights. Everyone agreed that
the decision was "significant," but terms such as "gutted," "quashed,"
"eviscerated," and "assault" were used to characterize the impact of
the ruling. Pundits and election law experts noted the quick efforts
of covered states such as Texas and North Carolina to implement
controversial voter identification restrictions and forecast backsliding in minority voter access and influence. *Shelby County* closed
the books on the national government's close scrutiny of state conduct of elections, and what followed was anxiety and uncertainty
among voting rights advocates, progressives, and many legal scholars
and observers.

This is the story of the last act in the play of the second Reconstruction, and of the Voting Rights Act.

## THE PLAN OF THIS BOOK

We explore the creation, implementation, consequences, and judicial challenges to and demise of the Voting Rights Act of 1965. This
book is a follow-up to our previous work, *The Triumph of Voting Rights
in the South*, and we incorporate some material from that volume
in this study.

In chapter 1, "Conditions Giving Rise to the Voting Rights Act,"
we describe the political and legal circumstances of the southern
Jim Crow electoral regime that gave rise to the Act. The frustrating
path of voting rights progress before 1965 is discussed. We then describe the political fight to implement the Act in the wake of the
events at Edmund Pettus Bridge in March 1965. The chapter then
documents the evolution of the Act through multiple rounds of
legislative renewal in the 1970s and 1980s.

Chapter 2, "Implementing the Act," examines the implementation of four major components of the Voting Rights Act in the
southern states: the application and evolution of the Section 4 trigger to determine coverage by Section 5 and the use of preclearance
under Section 5, including instances of objections and requests
for additional information; litigation challenges and success under

Section 2, including findings of discriminatory intent; the use of bailout to allow jurisdictions to exit coverage by Section 5; and the use of the Section 3 "pocket trigger" to extend coverage by Section 5.

Chapter 3, "A Comparative Analysis of the Impact of the Voting Rights Act in the South," examines the relative success of African American political participation through registration, voting, and election to local, legislative, state, and judicial offices. This chapter is an updated and revised version of chapter 12 of *The Triumph of Voting Rights in the South*.

Chapter 4, "The VRA, Mr. Obama, and the 2008 and 2012 Presidential Elections in the South," examines the role of the Voting Rights Act in shaping the southern political environment in 2008 and 2012. Particular attention is paid to the role of the Act in transforming the Democratic presidential primary electorate, which in turn influenced the nomination and election of Barack Obama as president. This analysis updates and extends the analysis from the epilogue of *The Triumph of Voting Rights in the South*.

Chapter 5, "The 2006 Debate and Renewal of the Act," describes the political and legal issues arising in the 2005–2006 debate over the revision and renewal of the VRA. Changes in the Act related to Sections 2, 4, and 5 are described. We discuss the efforts of conservative Republicans to alter the Act through a series of amendments affecting the coverage formula, the timeframe for sunsetting coverage and renewal, the minority language assistance provisions, and the bailout process.

Chapter 6, "Pushback," describes the forms of pushback against the Act. In party politics, pushback happened through the political environment as it continued to realign to the advantage of Republicans in the southern states, and southern Republicans moved increasingly toward states' rights conservative positions. This contributes to the race/incumbency/party structure of southern politics that increasingly institutionalizes racial political differences. Legally, pushback occurred with the filing of the *NAMUDNO* case, challenging the bailout provisions of the Act, and was later followed by followed by the *Shelby County* case. This is the first in what was an anticipated series of challenges. Procedurally, pushback came from the covered jurisdictions in the South, which pursued a strategy of "simultaneous submission" to compel the Department of Justice to go into court to defend its position that states were engaged in election changes that would lead to more discriminatory effects in voting.

Chapter 7, "*Shelby County* and Equal Sovereignty," explains the case in detail and places it in the broader context of an increasingly conservative Supreme Court. We also explore the applicability of four models of judicial politics to understand and interpret the actions of the Court.

In chapter 8, "The Voting Rights Act after *Shelby County*," we explore potential solutions to the consequences of the *Shelby County* ruling, including proposals to restore the preclearance regime. We also discuss areas of concern in voting rights that were not addressed by the 2006 renewal and consider the future of voting rights legislation and litigation.

The Rise and Fall of the
Voting Rights Act

# 1    Conditions Giving Rise to the Voting Rights Act

*I want you to write me the Goddamdest, toughest, voting rights act that you can devise.*

*—Lyndon Johnson to his attorney general Nicholas Katzenbach*

To understand the power and speed of adoption of the Voting Rights Act, one must first understand President Lyndon Baines Johnson. One must also understand the political capital he accrued in the election of 1964. Johnson had just been reelected with one of the most commanding mandates ever received by an American president. By taking 61.1 percent of the vote, Johnson actually did better than Franklin Roosevelt had in his strongest reelection bid, when the New Dealer received 60.8 percent of the vote in 1936. Johnson swept the Northeast and Midwest, losing only the five Deep South states and his opponent Barry Goldwater's Arizona.

The politically astute Johnson had won election to the House when still in his twenties, and by the time he won a full term as president he had been in Washington half of his entire life. Three decades spent on Capitol Hill as a staffer, representative, and senator had made him the most knowledgeable and effective legislator since Henry Clay. In the House he had been a protégé of and learned from legendary Speaker Sam Rayburn. His later experience as majority leader of the Senate had reinforced a lesson in Johnson: even the most popular president's command of power is fleeting. He was also well aware that, if left to their own devices, members of Congress typically respond lethargically unless confronted with a crisis. Johnson, therefore, acted to make the most of his electoral mandate by goading Congress into action on voting rights.

As a son of the South, Johnson knew firsthand the obstacles confronted by African Americans eager to exercise the franchise. Even though the Texas Hill Country where Johnson had grown up had few blacks, his work in Texas as the director of the state's National Youth Administration had given him a broader understanding of the race issue in Texas. Campaigning for the Senate had taken him into East Texas, the part of the Lone Star State with the highest concentration of African Americans as well as strong cultural and historical ties to the Deep South. Moreover, having served with southerners, especially in the Senate, Johnson fully understood the depth of resistance to a second Reconstruction. Some senators, including his mentor, Georgia's Richard Russell, adamantly opposed black political participation. LBJ knew and appreciated the lengths to which some in his native region would go to exclude blacks from the electorate. Previous efforts to advance even tepid legislation on civil rights during the Eisenhower administration had required applying all of his powers as majority leader, and the passage of the 1964 Civil Rights Act had been accomplished only through extraordinary effort by the White House and through the invocation of the memory of a charismatic, dead president.

By 1965, President Johnson and congressional leaders in both parties had observed the extremes to which the South would go to circumvent efforts to desegregate schools. Although clearly enunciating that segregated schools could not satisfy the Equal Protection Clause, the *Brown v. Board of Education* (1954) decision resulted in no school districts in the Deep South coming quickly into compliance. Throughout the 1950s, Deep South schools maintained the rigid segregation of previous generations. In the Rim South, token change had begun but most children continued to attend schools in which their race constituted the vast bulk of the student body. Rather than implement the *Brown* decision, southern state legislators took the Supreme Court order as a challenge to devise ways to avoid compliance. Legislatures came up with a stunning array of legal subterfuges to thwart the courts. The massive resistance strategy initially devised by Virginia senator Harry Byrd involved enactment of new laws each of which would have to be challenged in court, with the school district appealing the cases and doing everything in its power to delay final adjudication. At the extreme, some Virginia school districts actually went out of business. In some Virginia counties providing public education ceased to be a government function. Elsewhere across the South, legislatures enacted laws forbidding teachers from encouraging desegregation and threatening to withdraw public funding for desegregated schools. Some local school boards sold public school facilities at virtually no cost to organizers of private, white, segregation academies. By the mid-1960s, a handful of previously all-white schools in the South had capitulated, but no more than token desegregation had occurred.

In many southern districts children who entered the first grade in the fall after the first *Brown* decision graduated from schools that had taken no steps toward desegregation. As Congress turned its attention to protecting the suffrage, Johnson wanted a voting rights act that would avoid a repeat of the school desegregation in which one barrier after another had to be dismantled.

## BACKGROUND

That President Johnson had to put on a full-court press to deal with persistent discrimination against perspective black voters indicates the failing of the Fifteenth Amendment. That amendment, adopted in 1870, did succeed for a few years in opening the way to the ballot box for the newly freed slaves. In its early days the federal government aggressively prosecuted individuals who sought to prevent blacks from voting. But the protections proved short lived and, especially once federal troops were withdrawn after the 1876 compromise, federal protection of the right to vote largely disappeared. Black participation declined, although it was not until the very end of the nineteenth century that concerted efforts began to eliminate most blacks from the electorate. The final onslaught against black voting began in the Mississippi Constitution of 1890, in which the two most significant provisions directed at reducing black participation implemented a literacy test and required that voters pay a poll tax. After the Supreme Court upheld these provisions, within short order other southern states adopted one or both. By 1908 when Georgia added a literacy test to the poll tax it had collected for many years, the innovations from Mississippi had spread across the South.

The poll tax, collected in a color-blind fashion, also kept many poor whites from participating. The literacy test would have also been a formidable challenge to many whites, and so efforts were made to get illiterate whites on the voting rolls. One technique, the grandfather clause, exempted those whose ancestors had voted in the past or whose ancestors had fought for the Confederacy or served in the military forces of the United States.

Unlike the poll tax and the literacy test, which were color-blind on their faces, the white primary provided an even more effective technique for minimizing black political influence. With the exception of a few mountainous sections, by the turn of the twentieth century and the demise of the Populist Party only Democrats won southern elections. If blacks were kept from voting in the primary, then even if they managed to register and vote in the general election they had no impact on political outcomes.

The first successful challenge to a Jim Crow voting law came in a 1915 Oklahoma case that invalidated the grandfather clause as a means for whites to avoid the literacy tests. But it would be decades before another would permanently fall.[1] After a generation of legal sparring that involved four separate trips to the Supreme Court, in 1944 the white primary was invalidated in *Smith v. Allwright*.[2] Beginning in the 1930s, Congress considered outlawing the poll tax, but southern senators managed to prevent action.

In addition to laws that kept black participation low in the South, discriminatory application of the standards, especially the literacy tests, was widespread. Even some blacks who managed to register subsequently had their registration challenged.[3] African Americans brave enough and persistent enough to register might encounter still further obstacles if actually trying to vote. In some instances black voters were threatened at the polls and driven away. In 1946 the only African American who dared to vote in Taylor County, Georgia, was killed a few days later.

Despite the problems of discriminatory application of requirements for voting and intimidation, black registration began growing slowly after the demise of the white primary. From 1947 to 1950, the share of black adults registered to vote across the South grew from an estimated 12 to 18 percent. By the middle of the 1950s, black registration had continued to grow, but three-fourths of the adults remained off the registration rolls. Alabama, Mississippi, and Virginia, which required both a literacy test and the poll tax, had the lowest incidences of black registration as of 1955.[4] In the first two states, less than a tenth of the black adults had registered, and in Virginia it was less than one-fifth. Less than 5 percent of Mississippi's African Americans registered to vote. At the upper end, in Arkansas, Florida, Louisiana, and Texas about a third of black adults had signed up to vote.

It was in this context that Congress began to give serious consideration to providing federal protection for African Americans eager to exercise the franchise. Although conservative Virginia representative and chair of the House Rules Committee Howard "Judge" Smith managed to prevent adoption of a civil rights act in 1956, the next year Congress finally took the first hesitant modern steps toward protecting the suffrage. Momentum was beginning to build as civil rights became the foremost concern in the American political system.

## THE CIVIL RIGHTS ACTS

The 1957 Civil Rights Act became the first federal civil rights legislation adopted since 1875. From today's perspective, the 1957 legislation may seem modest; however, since there had been no congressional action in generations, even this first modern attempt did not come easily. The 1957 legislation facilitated legal challenges to discriminatory behavior by authorizing the attorney general of the United States to file suit against local election officials in jurisdictions that had a pattern or practice of discriminating against prospective voters. Having the attorney general provide the legal muscle eliminated the need for local citizens unjustly turned away at the polls or at the registration desk to dip into their own resources to hire attorneys and cover court costs. Moreover, since some of the challenges involved claims that local registration officials unfairly enforced literacy tests, it might require extensive digging through years of registration records to build a case that the registrar had rejected educated black applicants while allowing illiterate whites to become voters. Another advantage of having the attorney general sue the registrar was that the plaintiff would be the United States and not a local individual who might suffer physically or economically at the hands of outraged whites.

In the immediate aftermath of *Brown v. Board of Education*, the Montgomery bus boycott, and the Emmett Till lynching, southern congressional leaders recognized that the winds of change could no longer be contained. The most they could achieve was to water down the bill. Senator Richard Russell (D-Ga.), who led the southern opposition, felt that he had negotiated the best possible deal on the 1957 legislation. At Russell's urging, the legislation provided that suits filed by the attorney general would be tried by juries in the federal district court in which the offending registrar resided. Russell anticipated that it would be difficult to find a jury—one that would be overwhelmingly if not exclusively white—that would convict a registrar who sought to prevent black registration. Only if a registrar who had been enjoined to stop discriminating against blacks continued the illegal practices would the second suit be tried by a federal judge, not a local jury. The 1957 act also created the U.S. Commission on Civil Rights, which over the next several years conducted extensive studies documenting the inequalities confronted by many African Americans in the South.

Russell convinced all but one of his fellow southern Democratic senators to allow the bill to become law. The Georgia senator recognized that he had too few allies to maintain a filibuster and feared that the effort would prove counterproductive, since angry northerners might insert harsher provisions. The agreement almost came undone, however, when Senator Strom Thurmond (D-S.C.) staged a one-man filibuster.[5] The Thurmond effort proved unavailing but did set a record that still stands for the longest solo filibuster; Thurmond stayed on his feet and spoke on the Senate floor for more than twenty-four hours.

Slow progress in the wake of the 1957 legislation (see next section) led Congress to revisit the problems of black registration in 1960. One problem that illustrated the continued opposition to black voting in the South became apparent when federal attorneys and investigators went about preparing their cases. To demonstrate that local election registrars discriminated against blacks, prosecutors had to show that black and white applicants were treated differently, for example, with black applicants held to higher standards than whites when trying to register. To build these cases required the gathering of extensive data held by registration officials. Efforts to get records from past elections often came up short, as when local officials claimed that the requested documents had been lost or destroyed. In Alabama little-known local judge George Wallace took control of the voting records for two counties in his jurisdiction and refused to make them available to federal officials until he was threatened by his former law school classmate and friend, federal judge Frank Johnson, with contempt. Wallace, seeking to attract the name recognition that would ultimately help him win four terms as Alabama's governor, released the requested documents to the county grand juries, which then gave the material to federal investigators. Even as he complied, Wallace portrayed himself as standing alone against federal officialdom, a role he reprised on national television as governor in an equally futile attempt to prevent desegregation of the University of Alabama. In a self-serving move, Wallace prepared and had the grand jury issue the following statement: "We commend the courageous action of the honorable George C. Wallace who risked his very freedom in the federal courts in carrying out his duties and oath of office as a Circuit Judge. . . . The great need of the South today is for more men of the foresight and determination of Judge George C. Wallace."[6]

The Civil Rights Act of 1960 sought to plug holes in the 1957 act like those encountered in Alabama. The 1960 law required that officials maintain all election documentation for up to twenty-two months after an election and that they make it available to federal officials. The 1960 legislation also authorized the appointment of a federal official to register blacks in a county if, after a trial, a judge found that a pattern or practice of discrimination had characterized the registration process.

In 1964, President Johnson goaded Congress into adopting a sweeping civil rights bill that addressed school desegregation, equal employment opportunities, and access to public accommodations along with further efforts to facilitate black access to the ballot. The main thrust of the 1964 law was not voting rights, but the new legislation did stipulate that any applicant who had completed the sixth grade in an American school was presumed literate. This change meant that, for applicants who had made it to junior high, the local registrar bore the burden of demonstrating the applicant's illiteracy rather than the applicant having to convince the registrar that he or she could read and write. Henceforth literacy tests must be conducted in writing, and anyone who failed had the opportunity to review the basis for the rejection. The legislation also forbade election registrars from rejecting applicants who had minor errors or omissions in their paperwork.

## IMPLEMENTATION OF EARLY VOTING RIGHTS PROTECTIONS

The 1957 legislation got off to a glacial start in part because it autho-rized the hiring of only one additional attorney at the Department of Justice. Over the next three years the attorney general filed just three cases. The first litigation pursuant to the 1957 Civil Rights Act, *U.S. v Raines*, filed on September 4, 1958, challenged voting procedures in Terrell County, Georgia, which had a 55 percent black population. Judge Davis of the Middle District of Georgia dismissed the suit the next spring on the grounds that the legislation under which the suit was brought was not appropriate for enforc-ing the Fifteenth Amendment. The legislation authorized the U.S. attorney general to sue "any person [who] has engaged or there are reasonable grounds to believe that any person is about to engage in any act or practice which would deprive any other person of the right or privilege [to vote]." Davis concluded that the action of the election officials did not involve state action. The Supreme Court reversed that decision in February 1960.[7]

Ultimately the Terrell County court found discrimination in the administration of the literacy test. Blacks had been given more diffi-cult provisions to read and write than whites, and some blacks had to take the test from dictation whereas whites were allowed to copy the materials. Two African Americans holding master's degrees and another two with bachelor's degrees were found to be illiterate by the county's registrar.[8] The registrar turned away four black Terrell County teachers for mispronouncing "equity" and "original."[9] In sharp contrast, more than 95 percent of adult whites had registered to vote in Terrell County. After the court found discrimination in *Raines*, it ordered that four of thirty black applicants have their names added to the registration lists. Another seven had already registered, but that left nineteen who would still have to go through the registration pro-cess, although the court order banned discrimination when process-ing these applications.[10] The *Raines* court denied the attorney general's request to find a "pattern or practice" of discrimination. Had the court found a pattern or practice of discrimination, then a federal referee could have been appointed. A federal referee could temporarily replace the local registrar in order to ensure equal access to registra-tion. Although the attorney general won in *Raines*, the number of black registrants inched up only from forty-eight to ninety-eight, as shown in table 1.1.[11] Even with ninety-eight black registrants, less

TABLE 1.1    Registration in Terrell County, Georgia

| | Black registration | | White registration | |
|---|---|---|---|---|
| | No. | % of VAP | No. | % of VAP |
| 1956 | 48 | 1.8 | NA | NA |
| 1962 | 98 | 2.4 | 2,935 | 96.6 |
| 1967 | 2,188 | 53.9 | 3,374 | 110.1 |
| 1980 | 2,280 | 51.8 | 2,182 | 62.3 |
| 2012 | 3,427 | 84.6 | 2,350 | 82.6 |

*Source*: 1956 data from U.S. Commission on Civil Rights, *Civil Rights '63* (Washington, D.C.: Government Printing Office, 1963), 33; data from 1962 and 1967 from U.S. Commission on Civil Rights, *Political Participation* (Washington, D.C.: Government Printing Office, 1968), 236–237. More recent data calculated from figures with the Georgia Office of the Secretary of State.

*Note:* VAP = voting age population.

than 3 percent of the county's adult African Americans had made it onto the voter rolls. In the wake of the Voting Rights Act, registration shot up white registration so that by 1967 the registration rolls included more whites than the 1960 adult population in the county. Of the 2,188 blacks who were registered in 1967, two-thirds had been signed up by federal registrars appointed under new law. Georgia did not maintain registration data by race during the 1970s but reinstituted the process in 1980. As table 1.1 shows, by 1980 black registration actually exceeded white registration by approximately one hundred people. By 2012, African Americans accounted for more than 57 percent of Terrell's registrants.

The second suit brought under the 1957 legislation, *U.S. v Alabama*, involved the registrar of Macon County.[12] In Macon County, to satisfy the requirement that a prospective registrant demonstrate literacy by copying a portion of the Constitution, black applicants often had to transcribe the entirety of Article II.[13] One voter filled eight and half pages.[14] Having black applicants transcribe lengthy passages from the Constitution was part of an effort to slow the process so that the Macon County registrar handled no more than five applications per day.[15] Macon County had 25,784 adult blacks in the 1950 census. From 1951 through mid-November 1958, 1,585 African Americans tried to register to vote in Macon County, of whom 510 succeeded. This led to an estimate that with blacks registering at that rate it would take 203 years before all black adults currently in the county could register.[16] Some African Americans had sought, unsuccessfully, to register as many as ten times. Frequently they had to wait a full day, since the county would not process more than two black applicants at a time. In addition to the literacy test, Macon County required that a prospective voter be vouched for by a registered voter, and it limited the number of new voters for whom one could vouch to two per year.[17]

## DISCRIMINATORY PRACTICES

Many other southern jurisdictions were as inhospitable to black registrants as Terrell County and Macon County. As of 1958, the modal share of the black voting age population registered to vote in a southern county was less than 10 percent in each of the Deep South states except South Carolina, where the modal category was 10–19 percent of black adults being registered.[18] In 89 percent of Mississippi counties, fewer than 10 percent of the black adults had registered. No county in Mississippi or South Carolina had as many as 40 percent of its adult blacks registered to vote. Across the entire South, in only 19 percent of counties had most adult blacks registered.

Donald Matthews and James Prothro found that in the early 1960s the higher the black percentage in a county, the lower the share of adults who were registered.[19] The relationship increased once the black population exceeded 30 percent, and by the time black percentage in a county reached 60 percent African American registration was near zero. Matthews and Prothro also found that the higher the concentration of blacks, the more opposed whites were to black registration, in keeping with Key's black threat hypothesis.[20]

Once Congress began passing civil rights laws, the Alabama, Louisiana, and Mississippi legislatures reacted by adopting laws designed to make it *harder* for blacks to register to vote. In 1960, Louisiana increased the number of felonies that disqualified a prospective voter to include having two or more illegitimate children or participating in a sit-in. In addition, illiterates could no longer register to vote, and all perspective voters had to sign an affidavit affirming their willingness to abide by all state laws, including various racially discriminating provisions.[21]

The hostile environment had the desired effect; between 1956 and 1959 the number of registered blacks declined in forty-six of

Louisiana's sixty-four parishes. In some parishes black registration, which had not been widespread, dropped dramatically. In Bienville black registration fell from 587 in 1956 to twenty-eight in 1958, and in Red River it plummeted from 1,512 to only fifteen in 1958. White registration also fell in these two parishes, although by only 600 to 4,759 in Bienville and by less than 40 percent among whites in Red River.[22]

The Commission on Civil Rights calculated that in thirty-seven Mississippi counties black registration actually declined from 3,251 in 1955 to only 2,267 seven years later.[23] Across these thirty-seven counties, barely 1 percent of adult blacks had managed to sign up to vote. The registrar on Forrest County, Mississippi, refused to register blacks. One African American tried sixteen times to register, without success. Also in Forrest County, a minister who held two degrees from Columbia University was not allowed to register. Even an order by the 5th Circuit Court of Appeals to stop discriminating had little impact. After two years of litigation in the course of which the trial court held the registrar in contempt, only twenty-two blacks had registered—less than 0.33 percent of the county's black adults.[24]

The Civil Rights Commission uncovered evidence that North Carolina registrars failed black applicants on the literacy test for mispronouncing a word in the state constitution, making spelling errors, and providing unsatisfactory answers to questions such as "Was I born like Queen Elizabeth?" and "When God made you and Eisenhower, did He make both of you the same?" Other applicants failed to qualify because of problems in taking dictation when the local registrar read parts of the Constitution.[25]

At hearings held by the Civil Rights Commission in Alabama, of thirty-three witnesses who had not been allowed to register to vote, six held doctorates and four others had college degrees. All but seven had completed high school. Several were veterans, two of whom had earned Bronze Stars. Some unsuccessful applicants had previously registered in other states.[26]

In two Louisiana parishes, black applicants had difficulty locating the registrar even after multiple visits to the court house. Another prerequisite in Louisiana allowed the registrar to require that an applicant present two registered voters who could identify that individual. This proved especially difficult in counties in which no blacks were registered. Some counties limited the number of times that a person could identify a perspective voter.[27]

The Louisiana Constitution required computation of age down to the exact month and day and applicants could be rejected for failure to do so. In other instances registrars rejected applicants for underlining rather than circling a title such as "Mr." Applicants who indicated they had lived "all my life" in their parish, precinct, or ward were rejected since they needed to indicate the year when they had first lived in that location.[28]

Although many blacks seeking to register to vote in Plaquemines Parish failed the requirement that they interpret a provision of the Constitution, most whites had little problem. One white was asked to interpret the following: "No law shall be passed to curtail or restrain the liberty of speech, or of the press." The successful white applicant simply wrote "I agree."[29] In Tallahatchie County, Mississippi, the sheriff refused to accept poll tax payments from blacks.[30]

For a fifty-year span in Haywood County, Tennessee, no blacks were allowed to register to vote. Blacks in that county also had to observe a curfew, were not allowed to dance or drink beer, and could not come near the courthouse except for official business. Public officials imposed these restrictions despite evidence suggesting that blacks owned more land in the county and paid more taxes than whites.[31] In an effort to turn back the clock and ignore *Smith v. Allwright*, in 1959 the Democratic executive committee of Fayette County, Tennessee, sought to limit participation in the primary to whites.[32]

In a survey conducted shortly before passage of the VRA, one in six African Americans reported an incident of intimidation when local blacks sought to become politically active.[33] Of those recalling a racial incident, 46 percent mentioned economic sanctions being used against the brave African Americans and another 29 percent mentioned violence. Economic intimidation directed at politically active blacks included refusal to gin their cotton or to buy their soybeans. White merchants also refused to deliver fuel oil to black registrants. In Fayette County, Tennessee, a white banker warned, "My secretary's got the names of the 325 [blacks] who registered. I tell them, anybody on that list, no need coming into the bank. He'll get no crop loans here. Every store has got that list."[34] Sharecroppers who sought to register might be driven off the land they farmed, and teachers who became politically active would be let go by the white school board. Only African Americans not dependent on whites for their livelihood could risk political involvement without fear of economic consequences.[35] Of course, even those not dependent on whites for their income might be the victims of violence.

The survey conducted by Matthews and Prothro found that in the mid-1960s only one-third of southern adult blacks had registered to vote, half the rate for whites. That same survey found that 86 percent of adult whites claimed to have voted at least once, compared with 41 percent of blacks. The authors observed that "voter registration seems to be a far more purposive and less routine act for Negroes than for whites." A third of registered blacks indicated that they did so in order "to be a citizen" or "to be a man," a response given by only 13 percent of whites. Except for high school dropouts, at every level of education African Americans expressed greater interest in politics than whites.[36]

In 1963 the Civil Rights Commission issued a pessimistic report despite enactment of two pieces of civil rights legislation. "The evil of arbitrary disfranchisement has not diminished materially." The Commission went on to state that "progress towards achieving equal voting rights is virtually at a standstill in many localities. . . . We have concluded, sadly, but with firm conviction, that without drastic change in the means used to secure suffrage for many of our citizens, disfranchisement will continue to be handed down from father to son."[37]

In 1961 the Civil Rights Commission identified one hundred counties in eight southern states in which serious impediments kept African Americans from voting. A follow-up study in 1963 noted that prior to the enactment of the 1957 Civil Rights Act only 5 percent of the adult black population in these counties had registered. Six years later, the share of the black adult population registered to vote in these counties had crept up to 8.3 percent. In thirteen of the counties, no black had yet registered as of 1962, and in fifteen other counties, all but three in Mississippi, 1962 figures showed fewer than ten blacks registered. The Commission attributed the slow progress to "the high cost of litigation, the slowness of the judicial process on both the trial and appellate level, the inherent complexity of supervising the enforcement of decrees, intimidation and reprisals against Negroes who seek to vote, and the employment of diverse techniques by state and local officials to subvert the Constitution of the United States." The Commission continued: "After five years of Federal litigation, it is fair to conclude that case-by-case proceedings, helpful as they have been in isolated localities, have not provided a prompt or adequate remedy for widespread discriminatory denials of the right to vote."[38] Conditions varied widely among states. "The absence of complaints to the Commission, actions by the Department of Justice, private litigation, or other indications of discrimination, have led the Commission to conclude that, with the possible exception of a deterrent effect of the poll tax which does not appear generally to be discriminatory upon the basis of race or color— Negroes now appear to encounter no significant racially motivated impediments to voting in 4 of the 12 Southern States: Arkansas, Oklahoma, Texas, and Virginia."[39]

The stark difference offered voters in the 1964 presidential election helped spur increased black political mobilization in the South. Voters had a choice between the president who had just pushed through the most comprehensive piece of civil rights legislation in generations and Barry Goldwater, one of the few Republicans who had voted against that legislation. Although black registration in the South increased dramatically between 1962 and 1964, even in that latter year only 43 percent of adult southern blacks had registered. Even with the impetus to vote, black registration varied widely across the South in 1964, ranging from a low of 6.7 percent in Mississippi to a high of 69.5 percent in Tennessee. Only in Tennessee and Florida had most adult blacks signed up to vote.[40] In four southern states, fewer than one in three black adults had registered.

## IMPETUS FOR LEGISLATIVE PROTECTIONS

The March 1965 protests in Selma, Alabama, played a decisive role in the passage of the 1965 Voting Rights Act. For weeks protestors sought to register in this Black Belt county. Long lines of applicants stood for hours outside the courthouse as the registration process moved with glacial speed. Rev. Martin Luther King shifted the focus of his efforts to this majority-black community west of Montgomery after an unsuccessful protest effort in Albany, Georgia. King conducted nightly meetings in local churches and daily marches to the courthouse. Yet these efforts had little impact on registration. Table 1.2 presents figures showing the largely fruitless efforts to register in Dallas County, of which Selma is the county seat. In 1956, prior to enactment of the first modern civil rights act, 275 blacks but more

TABLE 1.2   Registration in Dallas County, Alabama

| | Black registration | | White registration | |
|---|---|---|---|---|
| | No. | % of VAP | No. | % of VAP |
| 1956 | 275 | 1.8 | 7,213 | 50.1 |
| 1960 | 130 | 0.9 | 9,195 | 63.9 |
| 1962 | 242 | 1.7 | 8,953 | 62.2 |
| 1964 | 320 | 2.1 | 9,463 | 65.7 |
| 1967 | 10,644 | 70.4 | 13,134 | 91.2 |

*Source*: Data come from three reports of the U.S. Civil Rights Commission: data for 1956 and 1962 from *Civil Rights '63* (Washington, D.C.: Government Printing Office, 1963); data for 1964 and 1967 from *Political Participation* (Washington, D.C.: Government Printing Office, 1968); data for 1960 from *Voting: 1961 Commission on Civil Rights Report* (Washington, D.C.: Government Printing Office, 1961).

*Note:* VAP = voting age population.

than 7,000 whites had registered. The 1960 census showed the county to have more adult blacks than whites, with 15,115 blacks and 14,400 whites. At the time of the passage of the 1960 Civil Rights Act, black registration had actually dropped, with only 130 remaining on the registration rolls while white registration had increased by almost 2,000. In the next four years, black registration rose slightly to 320 compared to almost 9,500 whites. Black registration remained miniscule while approximately two-thirds of white adults had signed up to vote.

Finally, frustrated applicants and their supporters from around the country proposed to march from Selma to Montgomery on March 7. On that fateful Sunday afternoon, led by the Student Nonviolent Coordinating Committee's John Lewis, as the marchers crossed the humpback Edmund Pettus Bridge and were set upon by members of the Alabama State Highway Patrol, some of whom were mounted on horseback. Other officers waded into the retreating protesters with flailing truncheons. Lewis suffered a concussion, and many of his fellow marchers were injured in the melee. Television news coverage showing patrolmen beating peaceful marchers prompted calls and telegrams from around the country urging enactment of President Johnson's proposals to open the voting booths to southern African Americans. It was the beginning of eighteen days of protest and confrontation in Alabama between blacks seeking voting rights and white political authority, which culminated in a much larger successful trek to Montgomery.

The beatings of the marchers at the Edmund Pettus Bridge were but one in a sorry line of physical intimidations directed at those who challenged voting prohibitions. After the completion of the march to Montgomery, Viola Liuzzo became the only white woman killed as part of the voting rights effort when she was shot while driving marchers back to Selma.

A high-profile lynching occurred in Mississippi during the Freedom Summer of 1964. Two out-of-state, white civil rights workers along with one local African American who were working in freedom schools designed to help blacks prepare for the Mississippi literacy test disappeared. Weeks later their bodies were unearthed from beneath a newly built dam for a farm pond. Violence became so prevalent in Birmingham with Klansmen using dynamite as their preferred weapon that the city became known as Bombingham. In the most famous of criminal acts carried out in that city, three young African American girls died when their church was blown up one Sunday morning. Random acts of violence occurred across the South, as they had for years, when individual local blacks sought to register or vote or encourage others to become politically active.[41]

## 1965 VOTING RIGHTS ACT

The goddamdest, toughest voting rights act that Nicholas Katzenbach and his aides could devise targeted southern jurisdictions that had a tradition of discriminating against African Americans. The key to this legislation appeared in Section 4, which contained a two-part "trigger" that identified the districts destined for special scrutiny. The first element focused on participation in the just-completed 1964 presidential election. If less than half of the adults in a jurisdiction had registered or voted, the jurisdiction might then be subject to preclearance. Note that the focus was on the total adult population and not just on African American adults. If most prospective voters had not voted in the presidential election, then one could anticipate even lower rates of participation in other elections. The second part of the trigger asked whether the jurisdiction employed a test or device as a prerequisite for participation; these were typically literacy tests but could also be tests of understanding or character. Notably, having a poll tax did not serve as a trigger, and by excluding the poll tax President Johnson's Texas did not get singled out for special attention. Jurisdictions identified under Section 4 then became subject to Section 5. The twofold trigger caught Alabama, Georgia, Louisiana, Mississippi, South Carolina, Virginia, and thirty-nine of North Carolina's one hundred counties. In the covered jurisdictions, literacy tests and other tests were banned. In time, three Arizona counties and one county each in Hawaii and Idaho were found to violate the trigger.

The longest-lived and most controversial aspect of Section 5 prohibited covered jurisdictions from implementing any changes relating to registration or turnout without securing federal approval. Approval could come from either of two sources. A jurisdiction could submit its proposal to the attorney general of the United States, who then had sixty days to determine whether the proposal would have the intent or effect of discriminating against African Americans. The second approach involved seeking a declaratory judgment that the proposal would not discriminate against blacks. To avoid "home cooking" by southern judges, judicial approval had to come from the district court of the District of Columbia.

Section 5 froze in place current registration requirements to prevent adoption of new, more demanding standards. Federal officials feared that, with disproportionate numbers of African Americans not on the registration list, southern legislatures might set higher standards that all *new* registrants would have to meet. Such an action would have the effect of perpetuating discrimination already in place, since black applicants would have to meet more demanding requirements than had whites who had already registered.

In addition to needing federal approval before implementing any changes relating to elections, the jurisdictions covered by Section 4 could be subject to other constraints. The attorney general could authorize the designation of federal officers to register voters unfairly turned away by local registrars. If a federal examiner was sent into a county to register voters, it would no longer be necessary to go through the costly and slow process of challenging registration practices in court. The legislation also sought to counter intimidation at the polls. Federal observers could be sent to counties where it was feared that hostile whites might seek to prevent black participation. Although these observers had no authority to intercede, they could report their findings to the attorney general.

South Carolina quickly went to court seeking to block implementation. In the decision upholding the preclearance requirement,

Chief Justice Earl Warren explained: "First: Congress felt itself confronted by an insidious and pervasive evil which had been perpetuated in certain parts of our country through unremitting and ingenious defiance of the Constitution. Second: Congress concluded that the unsuccessful remedies which it had prescribed in the past would have to be replaced by sterner and more elaborate measures in order to satisfy the clear commands of the Fifteenth Amendment." Later in the opinion, the chief justice explained that "Congress had found that case-by-case litigation was inadequate to combat widespread and persistent discrimination in voting, because of the inordinate amount of time and energy required to overcome the obstructionist tactics invariably encountered in these lawsuits. After enduring nearly a century of systematic resistance to the Fifteenth Amendment, Congress might well decide to shift the advantage of time and inertia from the perpetuators of evil to its victims."[42]

The Court acknowledged the extraordinary change in federal relationships prescribed by the Act but found this change acceptable since it would expire in five years. The Court along with the authors of the legislation expected that within half a decade the barriers to black participation could be removed. Thereafter, perhaps relying on the expectations of President Johnson and Reverend King, the enfranchised black electorate would be able to prevent future race-based standards for participating.

## WHY PRECLEARANCE?

Beginning with the post–Civil War Morrill land grant College acts and accelerating with the New Deal, when federal authorities wanted states or localities to behave in certain ways they offered carrots. To encourage the building of sewer systems or highways, the government offered to cover much of the cost. The frequent alternative to the carrot of additional funding has been the threat of litigation. The requirement that certain jurisdictions secure preapproval from federal authorities before implementing practices constituted a third and unique approach to inducing state and local governments to behave as federal authorities thought they should.

With the requirement of preclearance, Congress had moved up the learning curve. The inclusion of this provision stemmed from previous efforts to extend the franchise to southern blacks as well as from observations of how southern whites had reacted to other efforts at promoting equality. In many areas of public policy, if courts strike down certain kinds of behavior, most of those who have practiced those actions will cease and desist. In the South, however, commitment to racial separation and belief in white supremacy was so ingrained that jurisdictions frequently refused to comply with decisions rendered against other jurisdictions that prescribed certain kinds of behaviors. Thus, for example, when the Supreme Court struck down the white primary in *Smith v. Allwright*,[43] states other than Texas against which the suit had been brought, rather than comply, began exploring possible paths for avoidance, none of which succeeded. Separate lawsuits had to be brought against several of these states before they allowed African Americans to vote in the decisive Democratic primary.

Although the effort to avoid compliance with the ban on white primaries is instructive, that occurred in the 1940s. More proximate in time to the 1965 Voting Rights Act were experiences with efforts to desegregate southern schools. In the wake of *Brown v. Board of Education*, southern legislatures, rather than devise means for peacefully dismantling segregated schools, turned their attention to creating additional obstacles to federal challengers of southern educational practices. As Congress went about debating the Act, a generation of students had come of age in most southern school districts never having experienced desegregation. Urban districts had begun to desegregate, but even tokenism had not extended to the numerous rural districts.

The early experience with the 1957 Civil Rights Act suggested that new legislation would confront the same kinds of opposition and consequently produce the same modest changes that had been experienced in school desegregation. Although the incidence of black registration seemed to be increasing by 1964, most black adults in the South still had not registered, and many of these lived in the most resistant districts—rural counties with large black populations.

Without preclearance, the attorney general would have to sue individual counties. The experience with both voting rights and school desegregation indicated how long and arduous that process could be. If hundreds of jurisdictions each used all of the stratagems and delays available in the courtrooms to slow litigation, many years would be required to bring all of the South into compliance with the Fifteenth Amendment.

## IMPACT OF THE 1965 VOTING RIGHTS ACT

The new legislation had an immediate and dramatic impact. The number of blacks registered across the South increased by more than 50 percent from 1964, reaching 3.3 million in 1970. With this increase approximately two-thirds of the black adults in the South had now signed up to vote.[44] The most dramatic improvements came in the states that had been most zealous in blocking black registration. Black registrants in Mississippi rose from fewer than 30,000 at the time of the 1964 presidential election to 181,233 in 1967. Alabama witnessed an increase from 92,737 black registrants in the spring of 1964 to almost a quarter million in 1967. As table 1.3 shows, the numbers of black registrants in Georgia and Louisiana almost doubled during the first two years of the Act. South Carolina and Virginia also experienced substantial increases in black registration. Of the covered states, only North Carolina, where fewer than half the counties were subject to Section 5, experienced modest growth in black registration. By 1967 a majority of the adults in the states subject to Section 5 had registered, thus meeting the first part of the trigger in Section 4. The legislation had already removed the other trigger, use of a test or device.

Even some of the most recalcitrant parts of the South experienced dramatic change after adoption of the Voting Rights Act. Returning to table 1.2, which provides data on registration in Dallas County, Alabama, two years after VRA passage, black registration exceeded 10,000, with more than two-thirds of black adults now eligible to cast ballots. The 1967 black registration figures also reveal the impact of federal registrars who were sent into the county pursuant to the VRA to sign up African Americans who had found it impossible to register with the local office. Of the 10,644 black registrants, federal examiners had signed up 8,972.[45] Despite the progress and even though blacks outnumbered whites, the 1967 figures still show whites with a substantial advantage among registrants. It may be, however, that some white registrants had died or no longer lived in the county but the registrar had yet to purge their names.

Turning to table 1.1 with the registration figures for Terrell County, the 1967 data show a dramatic increase in black registration. Two years after adoption of the new legislation, most black adults had registered. The figures for whites show the stunning result that 110 percent of them had signed up to vote. As with the figures for Dallas

TABLE 1.3    Black voting registration in Section 5 states before and
after the 1965 Voting Rights Act

| | Before (% of VAP) | 1967 (% of VAP) | 1970 (% of VAP) |
|---|---|---|---|
| Alabama | 19.3 | 51.6 | 60.6 |
| Georgia | 27.4 | 52.6 | 57.9 |
| Louisiana | 31.6 | 58.9 | 49.7 |
| Mississippi | 6.7 | 59.8 | 66.0 |
| North Carolina | 46.8 | 51.3 | 45.8 |
| South Carolina | 37.3 | 51.2 | 51.3 |
| Virginia | 38.3 | 55.6 | 52.1 |

*Source*: Figures before and after come from U.S. Commission on Civil Rights, *Political Participation* (Washington, D.C.: Government Printing Office, 1968), 222–223. The post-act figures are all from 1967 and the pre-act figures are all from 1964 except Georgia, which has figures for 1962. The 1970 data were provided by M. V. Hood III and were used in M. V. Hood III, Quentin Kidd, and Irwin Morris, *The Rational Southerner* (New York: Oxford University Press, 2011).

*Note:* VAP = voting age population.

County, the white registration reflects inflation due to a failure to remove whites no longer eligible to vote in the county.

Black registration rates continued to grow from 1967 to 1970 in Alabama, Georgia, and Mississippi, as reported in table 1.3. These states had the lowest levels of black registration prior to passage of the 1965 legislation. South Carolina experienced no growth, and in the other three states the 1970 figures fell below those of 1967. In North Carolina the drop down to 45.8 percent actually indicates a lower percentage of African Americans having registered than in 1964! Again, recall, that most North Carolina counties were not subject to preclearance. The less dramatic declines in Louisiana and Virginia may be due to the purging of nonparticipants coupled with 1970 being a midterm election and thus one less likely to stimulate participation than a presidential election.

New black registrants soon began to make a difference at the ballot box. At the time the Voting Rights Act was adopted, virtually no blacks held elective office in the South. Georgia, for example, had three African American officeholders. The first African Americans to be elected to public office in Alabama since Reconstruction won local posts in 1964, two winning seats on the Tuskegee city council.[46] By 1970 the enumeration done by the Joint Center for Political Studies identified 702 African American officeholders in the South, primarily in states subject to Section 5.

## 1970 VOTING RIGHTS ACT

Despite the substantial increase in black registration and a few blacks winning public office, Section 5 did not expire in 1970. After lengthy hearings, Congress decided to extend preclearance requirements for an additional five years. Congress accepted the argument that, although gains had been registered, the history of discrimination in the covered jurisdictions was so ingrained that to allow preclearance to lapse risked backsliding. In addition to extending preclearance, Congress established a second trigger while leaving the initial one in place. Under the new trigger, jurisdictions that had tests or devices as prerequisites to voting and in which less than half of the adult population had registered or voted in the 1968 presidential election became subject to preclearance. The 1975 trigger extended preclearance to three New York City boroughs, three counties in California, and a few other local jurisdictions.

More consequential than the 1970 trigger was the 1968 decision by the Supreme Court in the *Allen v. State Board* case.[47] In *Allen* the Court interpreted Section 5 broadly so as to encompass all state laws and local ordinances that in any way touched on elections or public office holding. The Court reasoned that Congress intended its definition of laws affecting participation to be interpreted broadly. After *Allen*, jurisdictions had to secure preclearance before moving polling places, changing conditions for the election of public officials, implementing redistricting plans, changing voter identification requirements, or changing early voting dates, and cities had to gain approval prior to annexing territory. After *Allen*, the numbers of submissions for preclearance increased dramatically.

## 1975 VOTING RIGHT ACT

Using arguments similar to those five years earlier, supporters of maintaining Section 5 argued in 1975 that it would be a mistake to not renew them. They warned that, despite the progress that continued to be made in the South, without preclearance on the books some southern jurisdictions would revert to their old discriminatory practices. Proponents of continuing Section 5 succeeded in extending it for another seven years so that redistricting plans drawn after the 1980 census would have to be approved before being put into effect.

The 1975 version of the legislation added a third trigger. At the behest of Hispanics who wished to see political progress for their ethnic group parallel that demonstrated by African Americans, the 1975 legislation expanded to include language minorities. Jurisdictions that had a substantial non-English-speaking population but in which the election materials in the 1972 presidential election did not accommodate those non-English speakers were made subject to preclearance. This had the effect of bringing Texas, Alaska, and Arizona along with counties in a few other states into the orbit of Section 5. The language minorities now protected by the Voting Rights Act included Hispanics, Native Alaskans, and Native Americans.

With the passage of the second renewal of Section 5, the maximum coverage was achieved. Jurisdictions subject to preclearance appear in table 1.4. The end of the table lists the jurisdictions once caught by the triggers in Section 4 but which succeeded in bailing out so that they no longer had to secure federal approval of their voting changes. Jurisdictions that convinced a court that they met the criteria for bailing out include several Virginia local governments along with a scattering of others, so Virginia was largely (but not entirely) covered by the Section 4 trigger.

## 1982 VOTING RIGHTS ACT

As the deadline in the second renewal approached, supporters of Section 5 successfully argued once again that, despite the progress achieved, jurisdictions subject to the triggers could not be trusted. Consequently, the Section 5 preclearance requirement was extended for twenty-five more years. Unlike with the two previous renewals, the 1982 extension did not include a new trigger. It did, however, make a significant change that involved Section 2. Prior to the 1982 legislation, Section 2 had no independent effect. Congress rewrote Section 2 to provide a basis on which minorities could challenge *existing* voting requirements and election arrangements without the need to prove that the offending provision had been adopted or maintained for discriminatory purposes. The motivation to rewrite Section 2 grew out of *City of Mobile v. Bolden*.[48] Mobile, Alabama, had an at-large electoral system, and since it had not proposed changes Section 5 did not provide a method to challenge this arrangement. Plaintiffs who had gone to court noted that, although the city's

TABLE 1.4   Jurisdictions covered by Section 5

| States covered as a whole | Coverage date |
|---|---|
| Alabama | Aug. 7, 1965 |
| Alaska | Oct. 22, 1975 |
| Arizona | Sept. 23, 1975 |
| Georgia | Aug. 7, 1965 |
| Louisiana | Aug. 7, 1965 |
| Mississippi | Aug. 7, 1965 |
| South Carolina | Aug. 7, 1965 |
| Texas | Sept. 23, 1975 |
| Virginia | Aug. 7, 1965 |

**Partial coverage states**

*California*
| | |
|---|---|
| Kings County | Sept. 23. 1975 |
| Monterey County | Mar. 27, 1971 |
| Yuba County | Mar. 27, 1971 |
| Yuba County | Jan. 5, 1976 |

*Florida*
| | |
|---|---|
| Collier County | Aug. 13, 1976 |
| Hardee County | Sept. 23, 1975 |
| Hendry County | Aug. 13, 1976 |
| Hillsborough County | Sept. 23, 1975 |
| Monroe County | Sept. 23, 1975 |

*New York*
| | |
|---|---|
| Bronx County | Mar. 27, 1971 |
| Bronx County | Sept. 23, 1975 |
| Kings County | Mar. 27, 1971 |
| Kings County | Sept. 23, 1975 |
| New York County | Mar. 27, 1971 |

*North Carolina*
| | |
|---|---|
| Anson County | Aug. 7, 1965 |
| Beaufort County | Mar. 29, 1966 |
| Bertie County | Aug. 7, 1965 |
| Bladen County | Mar. 29, 1966 |
| Camden County | Mar. 2, 1966 |
| Caswell County | Aug. 7, 1965 |
| Chowan County | Aug. 7, 1965 |
| Cleveland County | Mar. 29, 1966 |
| Craven County | Aug. 7, 1965 |
| Cumberland County | Aug. 7, 1965 |
| Edgecombe County | Aug. 7, 1965 |
| Franklin County | Aug. 7, 1965 |
| Gaston County | Mar. 29, 1966 |
| Gates County | Aug. 7, 1965 |
| Granville County | Aug. 7, 1965 |
| Greene County | Aug. 7, 1965 |
| Guilford County | Mar. 29, 1966 |
| Halifax County | Aug. 7, 1965 |

TABLE 1.4    Jurisdictions covered by Section 5 (*continued*)

| *North Carolina (continued)* | Coverage date |
|---|---|
| Harnett County | Mar. 29, 1966 |
| Hertford County | Aug. 7, 1965 |
| Hoke County | Aug. 7, 1965 |
| Jackson County | Oct. 22, 1975 |
| Lee County | Mar. 29, 1966 |
| Lenoir County | Aug. 7, 1965 |
| Martin County | Jan. 4, 1966 |
| Nash County | Aug. 7, 1965 |
| Northampton County | Aug. 7, 1965 |
| Onslow County | Aug. 7, 1965 |
| Pasquotank County | Aug. 7, 1965 |
| Perquimans County | Mar. 2, 1966 |
| Person County | Aug. 7, 1965 |
| Pitt County | Aug. 7, 1965 |
| Robeson County | Aug. 7, 1965 |
| Rockingham County | Mar. 29, 1966 |
| Scotland County | Aug. 7, 1965 |
| Union County | Mar. 29, 1966 |
| Vance County | Aug. 7, 1965 |
| Washington County | Jan. 4, 1966 |
| Wayne County | Aug. 7, 1965 |
| Wilson County | Aug. 7, 1965 |
| *South Dakota* | |
| Shannon County | Jan. 5, 1976 |
| Todd County | Jan. 5, 1976 |
| *Michigan* | |
| Clyde Township | Aug. 13, 1976 |
| Buena Vista Township | Aug. 13, 1976 |

**Jurisdictions currently bailed out**

Wake County, North Carolina—Jan. 23, 1976

Curry, McKinely, and Otero Counties, New Mexico—July 30, 1976

Towns of Beddington, Cadwell, Carroll, Charleston, Chelsea, Connor, Cutler, Limestone, Ludlow, Nashville, New Gloucester, Reed, Sommerville, Sullivan, Waldo, Webster, Winter Harbor, and Woodland, Maine—Sept. 17, 1976

Choctaw and McCurtain Counties, Oklahoma—May 12, 1978

Campbell County, Wyoming—Dec. 17, 1982

Towns of Amherst, Ayer, Belchertown, Bourn, Harvard, Sandwich, Shirley, Sunderland, and Wrentham, Massachusetts—Sept, 29, 1983

Towns of Groton, Mansfield, and Southbury, Connecticut—June 21, 1984

El Paso County, Colorado—July 30, 1984

Honolulu County, Hawaii—July 31, 1984

Merced County, California, including some eighty-four other government units— Aug. 31, 2012

Towns of Antrium, Benton, Boscawen, Millsfield, Newington, Pinkham's Grant, Rindge, Stewartstown, Stratford, and Unity, New Hampshire—Mar. 1, 2013

*Source*: U.S. Department of Justice website.

population was approaching 40 percent African American, no black had served on the city commission in recent memory. Plaintiffs prevailed at the trial court but had their victory reversed by the Supreme Court. The high court overturned the decision because plaintiffs had not presented evidence to show that the harm they claimed resulted from an intentional discriminatory act by the city. The plaintiffs and other civil rights groups were outraged and asked whether it was even possible to produce evidence on what had motivated the adoption of the at-large system decades earlier.

In rewriting Section 2, Congress undid the intent standard imposed by the Supreme Court in *Bolden*. Sen. Orrin Hatch (R-Utah) objected, "I do not believe a community ought to be labeled a civil rights violator unless there is some wrongful motivation on its part." In urging rewriting of Section 2 to eliminate the need to prove intent to discriminate, the head of the Department of Justice (DOJ) Voting Rights Section argued the impossibility of demonstrating motive, noting that "[the DOJ] is not dealing with dummies. They're not about to be so blatant that you can trace intent."[49]

Under the new provision, plaintiffs need only demonstrate that they had less opportunity than whites to elect their preferred candidates. By replacing the intent requirement with a results or effects test, the burden on plaintiffs challenging existing electoral systems became much lighter. Opponents of the rewrite were worried that the new provision might result in proportional representation of minorities. Since it would not be necessary for a challenger to demonstrate an intent to discriminate, opponents fretted that all a plaintiff group had to do was show that its share of seats on a collegial body was smaller than its share of the adult population. In reaction to that concern, the legislation specifically stated that it was designed to ensure proportional representation. But the question remained: how would a judge go about resolving a case in which plaintiffs argued that the current system prevented them from choosing their preferred candidates even in the absence of evidence of discrimination?

To give guidance to jurists, the Senate report that accompanied the legislation laid out a totality of the circumstances test for judges to consider. The test elements (see box 1.1) came from previous court decisions. Foremost among these considerations was whether minorities had won elections in the jurisdiction. The second most important element was the level of black participation. Other elements included whether a candidate slating system existed from which minorities were excluded. Did the community have a history of official discrimination? Did enhancing factors such as staggered elections make it harder for minorities to elect their preferences? At a lower level of consideration were whether minorities had succeeded in securing public services and whether the electoral arrangement in question was atypical for the state. Not all elements in the totality of circumstances test would be appropriate in every case. Jurists were directed to do more than simply count up the number of items on which the evidence favored the plaintiffs and the number on which it favored the defendants in deciding the cases. Judges were also told that they need not limit their consideration to the items in the test.

---

Box 1.1
Elements of the totality of the circumstances test for
Section 2 of the Voting Rights Act

MAJOR FACTORS

1. Have members of the minority group won election to public office in the jurisdiction?
2. Are elections in the jurisdictions characterized by racially polarized voting?
3. Have overt or subtle racial appeals been made in local political campaigns?
4. Have members of the minority group been excluded from candidate slating groups?
5. Does the political subdivision being sued have a history of official voting-related discrimination?
6. Do members of the minority group from which plaintiffs come bear the effects of discrimination in areas such as education, employment, and health, which impede their ability to participate in the political process?
7. Does the jurisdiction employ voting practices or procedures that make it more difficult for members of the plaintiff group to elect their preferences? The practices include unusually large election districts, majority-vote requirements, and prohibitions against bullet voting.

MINOR CONSIDERATIONS

A. Has the jurisdiction being sued been unresponsive to the policy concerns of the groups bringing suit?
B. Is the election procedure being challenged tenuous?

Source: Senate Report No. 97–417, 97th Cong., 2d Sess. (1982), 28–29.

---

The first case growing out of the amended Section 2 reached the Supreme Court in 1986. In *Thornburg v. Gingles* the Court gave guidance for future litigation, establishing a three-prong test; plaintiffs had to prevail on each of the three items to win their case.[50] If the plaintiffs prevailed on the three items, then the Court would consider evidence on the totality of circumstances. The first element in the *Gingles* test asked whether the minority community was sufficiently large and compact that it could constitute a majority of the adult population in a district. Subsequently the question became whether the minority population was sufficiently large that it could constitute a majority of the adult *citizen* population. If plaintiffs could not demonstrate sufficient size and compactness, then there was no remedy the Court could provide to a challenge to an at-large electoral system like that in Mobile or to a redistricting plan—two of the most common challenges filed under Section 2; that is, the Court would not be able to draw a district that the minority electorate would dominate. The emphasis on citizenship has become increasingly important as Hispanics have become plaintiffs in a greater number of cases.

The second *Gingles* prong questioned whether the minority group bringing suit was politically cohesive. If minority-preferred candidates lost because of division in the ranks of the minority voters, then again a remedy might not be available. The third prong asked whether a politically cohesive minority electorate usually lost to a white bloc vote. If minority candidates usually won, then the electoral arrangement being challenged did not impede their ability to elect their preferred candidates.

The bulk of the Section 2 litigation has involved at-large electoral systems used by local governments. Plaintiffs argue that, if the seats were apportioned among single-member districts, they would be able to win one or more. Plaintiffs hire demographers to demonstrate the feasibility of drawing a set of districts at least one of which would constitute a majority of the minority adult citizen population. In such a district, if the minority population mobilizes and unites behind a candidate, it should be able to elect its preference. Plaintiffs also introduce evidence from past elections designed to show that typically the candidates preferred by the minority group lose under the present system, which forces those candidates to run citywide or countywide rather than in a district dominated by the minority population.

Unlike Section 5, Section 2 applies nationwide and is permanent, thus not needing periodic extension. In fairly short order, minorities across the nation filed hundreds of suits seeking single-member districts for local governments. Cases originated as far north as Anchorage, Niagara Falls, and Boston. In addition at-large local systems and multimember legislative districts in Section 5 jurisdictions came under attack. Although many of the cases had African American plaintiffs, other Section 2 suits have had Hispanic, Native American, and Asian American plaintiffs. When plaintiffs won, the remedial action involved drawing single-member districts. Invariably in one or more of these single-member districts the plaintiff group constituted a majority; these new districts facilitated the election of scores of African Americans to local collegial bodies such as city councils, county commissions, and school boards.[51]

Although the most common Section 2 litigation challenges at-large electoral systems, this title of the legislation has also been used to challenge redistricting plans. In the early 1990s, DOJ incorporated Section 2 into its reviews of redistricting plans submitted pursuant to Section 5. Prior to this, Section 5 reviews had turned on whether the submitting authority was guilty of retrogression. If the new plan left minorities no worse off than under the status quo, then DOJ would approve the submission. But once DOJ included Section 2 in its preclearance evaluations, it required that jurisdictions draw additional majority-minority districts when possible. Thus, whereas Section 5 had been a negative power that allowed DOJ to block plans that would have reduced the prospects for electing minorities, Section 2 became a positive tool used to force jurisdictions to maximize the opportunities for minorities. In the highest-profile examples, DOJ used Section 2 as a goad to force Georgia, Louisiana, and North Carolina to draw additional congressional districts that in 1992 sent African Americans to Congress. Other states, such as Texas and Florida, did not wait to have their plans rejected by DOJ and instead drew additional majority-minority districts. These efforts to appease DOJ resulted in lawsuits being filed in each of these states.

The Supreme Court stepped in and began undoing some of the changes demanded by DOJ pursuant to Section 2. The Court first expressed its displeasure with North Carolina's state-long, narrow 12th Congressional District, which in some places was no wider than two lanes of Interstate-85. Writing for the Court, Justice Sandra Day O'Connor fretted that the precision with which the state had separated blacks and whites in order to fashion a majority-black district reminded her of South African apartheid. Two years later the Court fleshed out its reasoning in a challenge to the third majority-black congressional district DOJ had demanded in Georgia. In *Miller v. Johnson*, the Court acknowledged that, although race must be considered in drawing districts, if race overshadowed other factors such as compactness, contiguity, and adherence to political boundaries then the plan violated the Equal Protection Clause of the Fourteenth Amendment.[52] Subsequent litigation successfully challenged majority-black congressional districts drawn predominately on the basis of race in Louisiana, Florida, Virginia, Texas, and a New York majority-Hispanic district.[53]

Ultimately the Supreme Court went further than simply overturning some of the actions required by DOJ as a result of its reliance on Section 2. In a school district case from Louisiana, the Court chastised DOJ for incorporating Section 2 into Section 5 reviews. The Court underscored its decision from *Beer v. United States* that retrogression provided the *only* basis for rejecting redistricting plans. In *Reno v. Bossier Parish School Board*, the Court removed Section 2 from the arsenal of instruments available to DOJ when reviewing a districting plan.[54] As part of the 2006 renewal of the Voting Rights Act, Congress reversed the Supreme Court's decision and authorized inclusion of Section 2 considerations in future Section 5 reviews.

Section 2 has also had another use in redistricting cases. By a 5–4 vote the Supreme Court has held open the possibility of winning a case on the grounds of a partisan gerrymander,[55] but no plaintiff has located the path leading to victory. Consequently, political parties that have lost in the legislative arena have turned to courts seeking relief, claiming not that they suffered because of their partisanship but rather that the plan adopted by the legislature mistreated a racial or ethnic group. Both political parties made such claims when challenging plans drawn using the 2010 census. Illinois Republicans sought to undo Democratic plans for the legislature and Congress, contending that the GOP alternative provided additional representation for Hispanics. In New Mexico, Democrats attacked the GOP-drawn plan, claiming that it provided fewer districts for Native Americans than the Democratic alternative.

Even although the legislation specifically denied any intention of having proportional representation, invariably an important part of a Section 2 trial involves a comparison of the presence of the plaintiff group among the community's adult citizen population and its share of seats on the governing body.

# 2    Implementing the Act

The Voting Rights Act of 1965 was an implementation success. Designed to correct systemic denial of access to the ballot on the basis of race, the legislation significantly altered political behavior of southern states. These policy levers included aggressive oversight of local and state government, the use of election monitors, new and powerful litigation tools, and the suspension of the most egregious and obnoxious election practices. These tools succeeded in transforming southern politics.

The implementation of the Voting Rights Act occurred most frequently through Section 5 preclearance reviews, followed by challenges to existing election practices using Section 2. Less frequently used have been the bailout provision of Section 4, through which a jurisdiction can escape Section 5 coverage, and Section 3, through which the Department of Justice can extend Section 5 coverage over a previously uncovered jurisdiction.

## FEDERAL MONITORING UNDER SECTION 5

Section 5 was a proactive effort to discourage discriminatory practices. The provision froze in place all election laws and practices in state or local jurisdictions identified by the Act's coverage trigger. When these cities, counties, or states sought to change their laws or practices, they had to submit the change for approval to the federal district court of the District of Columbia or undergo administrative review through the Department of Justice's Voting Rights Section. This review would allow the jurisdiction to demonstrate that the proposed change had no retrogressive effect that would make minority voters worse off than if the change did not take place. DOJ had to respond to preclearance requests within sixty days, but it could seek more information from the submitting authority before ruling on the proposal.

Most jurisdictions selected the administrative option. There has been substantial variation in the success of different states in their submission of proposed changes, but most changes are routinely accepted. Of 208,047 preclearance review submissions between 2000 and 2012, DOJ rejected just 0.04 percent. Scholars Dan Tokaji and Rick Pildes examined rates of administrative preclearance objection by type of submission since 2000 (see table 2.1).[1] Their analysis finds, as one might expect, very few denials. Justin Levitt's analysis points out that 86 percent of objections involve county and municipal governments, and that many of the statewide objections are to changes that actually affect only one local jurisdiction or local area.[2] Most of the action comes from redistricting, which must occur every ten years following the census.

According to Pildes and Tokaji, redistricting generated "vastly more objections than any other category—more than half of all objections DOJ made since 2000 (39 of 76)." Redistricting was ten times more likely to generate an objection than any other change. Changes that actually governed direct access to the ballot—registration, qualification, changes of voting venue—rarely drew objections from DOJ. Pildes and Tokaji characterize this as a "disjunction between perception and reality when it comes to what the preclearance regime was actually doing before *Shelby County.*" Writing in the immediate wake of the *Shelby County* decision, they argue that Section 5 was less effective in protecting the ballot than was generally believed. The use of Section 5 against voter ID laws in Florida, Texas, and South Carolina did effect some change: South Carolina modified its law, and the Florida and Texas laws were temporarily halted. But those applications are exceptions rather than the rule. Instead, the main impact was in leveraging redistricting change:

> A widespread perception exists that, in the years before the Court's decision in *Shelby County v. Holder,* the Section 5 preclearance regime was a powerful tool in protecting access to the ballot

TABLE 2.1    Section 5 submissions and objections, 2000–2012

| Proposed change | Submissions | Objections | % |
|---|---|---|---|
| Redistricting/reapportionment | 4,132 | 39 | 0.94 |
| Annexation | 46,151 | 3 | 0.01 |
| Polling place/absentee and early voting locations | 37,995 | 1 | 0.00 |
| Precinct | 19,182 | 1 | 0.01 |
| Reregistration/purge | 41 | 0 | 0.00 |
| Incorporation/dissolution | 2,103 | 0 | 0.00 |
| Bilingual procedures | 1,934 | 3 | 0.16 |
| Method of election | 7,653 | 20 | 0.26 |
| Form of government (elective/appointed) | 519 | 0 | 0.00 |
| Consolidation/division of political units | 967 | 0 | 0.00 |
| Special election | 17,330 | 2 | 0.01 |
| Voting methods | 7,395 | 0 | 0.00 |
| Candidate qualifications | 2,205 | 2 | 0.09 |
| Voter registration procedures/voter qualifications | 5,400 | 5 | 0.09 |
| Miscellaneous | 55,040 | 0 | 0.00 |
| **Total** | 208,047 | 76 | 0.04 |

Source: **Rick Pildes and Dan Tokaji,** "What Did VRA Preclearance Actually Do? The Gap between Perception and Reality." *Election Law Blog*, compiled from data at www.justice.gov/crt/about/vot/sec_5/obj_activ.php and www.lawyerscommittee.org/projects/Section_5.

box for minority voters. . . . the reality is that Section 5 was rarely used in this way, at least in its last three decades. Section 5 did not, primarily, function to protect access to the ballot box. Instead, the overwhelming uses of Section 5 were to ensure more majority-majority election districts or to stop at-large election systems and other practices believed to weaken minority voting strength. Some of these uses, especially the compelled creation of majority-minority election districts, are more controversial (even among conventional "liberals") than are robust protections for access to the ballot box. Yet in practice, Section 5 was used primarily for redistricting and other matters of vote dilution rather than protecting the right of eligible citizens to cast a vote.

State-by-state examination of the use of Section 5, as demonstrated below, reveals a pattern in which objections, although frequent during the 1970s and 1980s, have become a rarity.

Mississippi

The remarkable change in African American political activity in Mississippi would not have occurred but for the vigilance of DOJ, which rejected 173 proposed changes in the Magnolia State's electoral environment. This is the third-largest number of objections, ranking behind Texas and Georgia. Those other states, however, have far more counties and municipalities than Mississippi, and thus more jurisdictions that might fail to meet DOJ expectations. Efforts in Mississippi to minimize the impact of the Voting Rights Act and to perpetuate discriminatory practices led to *Allen v. State Board of Elections*, which vastly broadened the scope of the VRA such that it regulated far more than changes directly aimed at voter registration and turnout.[3]

Prior to the implementation of the *Allen* decision, when only changes direly related to registration or casting a ballot were thought to be subject to Section 5, DOJ issued only three objections in Mississippi. As table 2.2 shows, during the next half decade, after the initial renewal of Section 5 in 1970, the state experienced thirty more objections. During the period of the second renewal of Section 5 (1976–1982), twenty-five proposed changes drew objections, and DOJ subsequently withdrew three of these. This history of submission and rejection prompted Mississippi senator Thad Cochran's observation that the Voting Rights Act compelled "local officials [to] have to go to Washington, get on their knees, kiss the ring and tug their forelock to all these third-rate bureaucrats."[4]

The extension of Section 5 for a quarter-century in 1982 was followed by 111 objections, forty-five of which challenged redistricting plans after the 1990 census. It would require a careful review of these to determine the basis for the denials, but this was during the time that DOJ had incorporated Section 2 considerations into Section 5 reviews—a practice successfully challenged at the state level in the *Shaw*, *Miller*, *Vera*, and *Bossier Parish* cases. In all likelihood at least some of these challenges were similarly tainted. During the last decade before the 2006 renewal, Mississippi experienced only five objections. This small number of objections has been interpreted as evidence that Section 5 operated as intended—that is, its presence deterred discriminatory actions.[5] Despite the rarity of recent objections, one played a prominent role in the 2006 congressional debate about extending the life of Section 5. Many members of both houses

TABLE 2.2   DOJ objections and withdrawals by state
and Section 5 renewal period

| | Objections | | | | | Withdrawals | | | | |
|---|---|---|---|---|---|---|---|---|---|---|
| | 1965–70 | 1971–75 | 1976–82 | 1983–2006 | 2006 | 1965–70 | 1971–75 | 1976–82 | 1983–2006 | 2006 |
| Alabama | 10 | 12 | 27 | 32 | 1 | 1 | 3 | 5 | 11 | 1 |
| Georgia | 5 | 49 | 44 | 74 | 5 | 0 | 4 | 6 | 9 | 0 |
| Louisiana | 2 | 40 | 14 | 90 | 2 | 2 | 3 | 5 | 17 | 0 |
| Mississippi | 3 | 30 | 25 | 111 | 4 | 0 | 2 | 3 | 12 | 0 |
| North Carolina | 0 | 8 | 14 | 40 | 3 | 0 | 0 | 4 | 9 | 1 |
| South Carolina | 0 | 22 | 30 | 69 | 2 | 0 | 2 | 3 | 9 | 1 |
| Virginia | 1 | 10 | 8 | 14 | 0 | 0 | 2 | 2 | 2 | 0 |
| California | 0 | 0 | 2 | 4 | 0 | 0 | 0 | 1 | 2 | 0 |
| New York | 0 | 3 | 3 | 7 | 0 | 0 | 0 | 1 | 0 | 0 |
| Alaska | 0 | 0 | 0 | 1 | 0 | 0 | 0 | 0 | 0 | 0 |
| Arizona | 0 | 2 | 3 | 17 | 0 | 0 | 0 | 1 | 0 | 0 |
| Florida | 0 | 0 | 0 | 5 | 0 | 0 | 0 | 0 | 1 | 0 |
| Michigan | 0 | 0 | 0 | 0 | | | | | | |
| New Hampshire | 0 | 0 | 0 | 0 | | | | | | |
| South Dakota | 0 | 0 | 2 | 1 | 1 | 0 | 0 | 0 | 1 | 0 |
| Texas | 0 | 1 | 97 | 98 | 10 | 0 | 0 | 13 | 13 | 0 |

of Congress pointed to the actions of a Mississippi town as evidence that Section 5 needed to be extended for another quarter-century and that the scope of its coverage should not be altered. The action that attracted so much attention was the decision by the town of Kilmichael to cancel a municipal election. The city council acted after candidate filing had ended and it appeared that African Americans, who now constituted a majority among registered voters, were on the verge of winning most of the offices, including that of mayor. Although DOJ was slow to respond, not getting an objection off until more than half a year after cancellation of the election, it demanded an election. Two years later, when the election was finally held, blacks won three council seats and the mayor's office.[6]

Canceling an election was extraordinary. A review of all DOJ objections issued since 1995 turns up only one similar objection, and that involved Grenada, Mississippi. Nevertheless, some members of Congress pointed to the audacity of suspending a regularly scheduled election just as blacks appeared poised to make gains as evidence that jurisdictions subject to Section 5 could not yet be trusted to treat minorities fairly and therefore must continue to be monitored by federal authorities.

In addition to garnering objections, Mississippi has frequently been asked to provide more information for proposed changes submitted to DOJ. From 1990 through 2005, DOJ requested more information 474 times. Approximately a quarter of these involved redistricting plans and another quarter involved voter registration procedures. Approximately one-sixth of these involved polling places or precincts. Once the jurisdiction provided more information, DOJ approved the proposal 60 percent of the time, which accounted for 284 of these submissions. In fifty-five instances, DOJ objected upon receiving fuller information. In forty-four cases, the jurisdiction proposing the change withdrew it.[7]

## Alabama

Table 2.2 shows that during the first five years of the VRA almost half of all objections involved Alabama, with all but one of these questioning a county's poll list signature requirement. Each succeeding renewal period saw the number of objections increase. Between 1983 and 2006, DOJ rejected forty-three proposed changes in election laws and procedures. After the 2006 renewal, only two proposed changes drew objections and one of these involved 177 parcels and a redistricting plan for a town in Shelby County.

Alabama jurisdictions withdrew 181 proposed changes after DOJ asked for further information. The federal government used its authority under the Act to send observers in to monitor elections extensively. From 1965 to 2005, federal officers have observed 176 elections in twenty Alabama counties.[8] Fifteen of those counties have been visited by observers since 1982. Perhaps the national record for having had the greatest number of elections monitored goes to Hale County, which has had monitors on the scene for twenty-two separate elections. In the immediate aftermath of the 1965 VRA, federal officials went to a dozen counties and registered more than 65,000 voters, but that authority has not been used recently in the state.[9]

## Georgia

Despite the political advances made by the black community, DOJ has denied 186 proposed changes in Peach State election laws. During the first decade of Section 5, Georgia had more of its proposed changes in election laws rejected (forty-eight) than any other state.

During the second renewal (1976–1982), only Texas, which has ninety-five more counties and far more municipalities, exceeded Georgia's fifty denials. From 1983 to 2006, 107 Georgia initiatives drew objections, although DOJ withdrew seventeen of these. After 1995 only sixteen submissions from Georgia failed to meet with DOJ approval, with five of these coming after the most recent renewal. Nine of the most recent objections involved redistricting plans, with one of these being directed at the plan adopted by the majority-black Albany city council. To put the incidence of DOJ objection in perspective, from 1990 to 2005 Georgia submitted 34,733 election law changes to DOJ, 139 of which DOJ found to be objectionable, for an approval rate of 99.6 percent.

Georgia's recent experience with Section 5 illustrates the conflicts that began to emerge between DOJ and the federal courts, which share responsibility for administering Section 5. Six objections beginning in 1989 involved the creation of additional judgeships. DOJ objected to these new judgeships because the judges would be elected circuit-wide. DOJ wanted subdistricts created, some of which would have African American majorities in their populations. The state disagreed, and after it prevailed in a judicial challenge DOJ withdrew the objections.[10]

Three other sets of objections involved Georgia's redistricting plans for congressional and state legislative districts in the early 1990s. Ultimately the Supreme Court ruled that DOJ had overstepped its bounds by forcing Georgia to subordinate traditional districting principles to considerations of race in order to meet DOJ demands that the state maximize the number of majority-black districts.[11]

DOJ asked for more information on 1,325 of the more than 34,000 submissions received from Georgia jurisdictions from 1990 to 2005. Almost half of these requests involved annexations, 342 dealt with methods of elections, and 108 related to redistricting. Ultimately forty-four of the 1,325 requests sparked an objection, but in 1,055 instances no objection followed. The submitting authority withdrew ninety proposals, which may indicate another ninety instances in which Section 5 prevented implementation of a change believed to disadvantage minorities.

## Louisiana

During the course of the 1982 renewal, 107 Louisiana changes drew objections, although forty-two of these involved redistricting plans, including that for Bossier Parish, which resulted in the Supreme

Court rapping DOJ's knuckles for having included Section 2 considerations when carrying out Section 5 reviews. It is highly likely that some, perhaps most, of the other redistricting objections were similarly flawed, although the local governments, perhaps because of a lack of resources, did not go to court to question DOJ's actions. From 1995 through 2005, the state had more election proposals rejected by DOJ than any other state (nineteen). Eight of these involved redistricting plans drawn to accommodate shifts in population identified by the 2000 census. Five other objections involved efforts by the City of Shreveport to annex adjoining land. These were all withdrawn in 1997 when the city agreed to change the format of its elections.

Table 2.2 shows that, after the initial renewal, Louisiana tied with Georgia in having the most proposed changes turned back by DOJ. During the second renewal period (1976–1982) Louisiana had relatively few rejections, with only nineteen items drawing objections, five which DOJ withdrew. The previous decade (1985–1994), Louisiana had the third-largest number of objections (sixty-two), following Texas and Mississippi. During that decade, easily the most common basis for DOJ objection was a redistricting plan. Although an examination of each of these objections is far beyond the scope of this chapter, it is likely that DOJ's inclusion of Section 2 as a consideration when making a Section 5 review figured into some of them. DOJ rejected the state's proposal for the Board of Elementary and Secondary Education for failure to increase the number of majority-black districts, and this prompted the state to draw a second majority-black congressional district. The Supreme Court struck down that district on *Shaw* grounds. Another objection ultimately reviewed and overturned by the Court involved the Bossier Parish School District. This objection also rested on the failure of the submitting jurisdiction to increase the number of districts likely to elect African Americans. It would not be surprising if other objections also stemmed not from a retrogressive plan but from a plan that did not maximize the number of black districts.

Fraga and Ocampo identified 17,765 submissions made by Louisiana jurisdictions to DOJ pursuant to the requirements of Section 5 between 1990 and 2005. Across these sixteen years, DOJ objected to 158 submissions, or 0.9 percent of the total. In addition to registering objections 158 times, DOJ asked the submitting authority to provide additional information on 983 of the submissions. The most frequent bases for these requests for additional information were precincts (355), annexations (186), polling places (185), and redistricting (147). Upon receiving additional information, an objection was levied eighty-one times, and in another thirty-eight instances the submitting authority withdrew its request for approval. The relatively large number of requests for additional information on proposals for redistricting conforms with our suspicion that DOJ was often seeking to prompt a jurisdiction to create additional majority-black districts.

As we noted in the previous discussion of Alabama and Mississippi, in the early 1990s DOJ frequently demanded that jurisdictions take steps to maximize black representation in the course of reviewing reapportionment plans. It was a Louisiana case that ended those efforts. Prior to the 1990s the standard under which DOJ had reviewed reapportionment plans had been nonretrogression as established in the *Beer* case.[12] Under *Beer*, so long as a new plan did not reduce the number of majority-minority districts or substantially reduce minority concentrations in majority-minority districts, DOJ would approve the plan. During the early 1990s, however, DOJ incorporated Section 2 into its Section 5 reviews.[13] As a result of this policy, DOJ objected to plans that were not guilty of retrogression but where the department believed the submitting authority had failed to prove the absence of a discriminatory purpose in the plan it submitted. Thus, even a plan that increased the number of districts likely to elect African Americans would fail to secure preclearance if DOJ believed that still greater numbers of majority-minority districts could have been drawn and the jurisdiction failed to provide an acceptable explanation for why it did not adopt such a plan. Years after most of these redistricting plans had been reviewed by DOJ, the Supreme Court held that the only appropriate standard for Section 5 review was retrogression. Whether it would be possible to fashion additional majority-minority districts in a jurisdiction could not be considered during the course of a preclearance review.[14] Had this interpretation of the preclearance process been in effect in the early 1990s, the 4th Congressional District won by Cleo Fields would never have existed.

## Virginia

Despite having relatively low rates of black registration and turnout, Virginia has drawn fewer objections from DOJ than most of its southern neighbors. During the first decade of the Voting Rights Act, Virginia received only eight objections. The only southern state with fewer was North Carolina, and unlike the Tar Heel State, where Section 5 applied to only forty counties, all of Virginia was subject to the preclearance requirement. In each of the next two decades, Virginia had fewer objections than any other southern state that had been covered by Section 5 since its initial passage. From 1975 to 1984, DOJ objected to ten submissions from Virginia, and in the next decade the number of objections fell to seven. In the next decade, DOJ turned back six submissions from the Old Dominion. That number exceeds the figures for Alabama (two) and North Carolina (four). Of the six most recent objections, five came in response to redistricting plans drawn to accommodate the 2000 census, with three of these directed at Northampton County. No Virginia submission has failed since 2003.

From 1990 through 2005, Virginia jurisdictions submitted a total of 16,697 proposed changes to DOJ for approval and experienced twelve objections. On approximately 1 percent of these submissions (176), DOJ requested additional information. Approximately a quarter of these requests involved the location of polling places, a quarter dealt with precincts, and almost a fifth involved redistricting. Upon receiving additional information, DOJ found nothing to object to in 146 of these instances. Only eight items in which more information was requested resulted in an objection.

## South Carolina

In the forty years following passage of the Voting Rights Act, 120 proposed changes in election laws from South Carolina drew objections from DOJ. Eighty-six of these occurred between 1975 and 1994. In the most recent decade DOJ issued only fourteen objections to Palmetto State jurisdictions. Half of these most recent objections involved redistricting plans. Two of the others involved annexations. All were local proposals except an objection to the 1997 redistricting of the state senate. From 1990 through 2005, South Carolina submitted 15,358 proposed changes to DOJ, and DOJ objected to sixty-six. In addition to the objections, there were 579 instances in which DOJ asked the submitting authority for more information. In the vast share of these instances (432), once more information was received DOJ approved the proposed change.

## North Carolina

Of the southern states identified by Section 4 of the 1965 Voting Rights Act, North Carolina had the fewest objections to its proposed changes in election law. Only five of its proposals in the first decade drew objections. This low incidence of problems may reflect the fact that less than half of the state was covered by Section 5. During the next decade, DOJ rejected twenty-three proposed changes, fewer than any other covered southern state except Virginia, which had only ten rejections. During the decade of 1985 to 1994, again, of the states originally covered except Virginia, North Carolina had received fewer objections from DOJ. In the most recent decade, North Carolina had fewer objections than Virginia, with only four, although Alabama did even better with only two objections. DOJ registered only two since 1997, and both of these involved redistricting plans from Harnett County.

An examination of DOJ preclearance activity from 1990 through 2005 identified 8,229 preclearance admissions from North Carolina jurisdictions. Of these, 99.6 percent were precleared. DOJ's initial response to 232 of the 8,229 submissions was to request additional information. Approximately half of these involved a change in the method of election. Another thirty dealt with annexations, and twenty-eight involved redistricting plans. Upon getting further information, DOJ approved 169 of the 232 submissions about which it had raised questions. The submitting authority withdrew twenty-one of the questioned submissions. Five of these withdrawals have come since 2000. Three of the submissions withdrawn during the current decade involved redistricting plans.

## Texas

Since Texas was brought under Section 5 by the 1975 Voting Rights Act, DOJ has rejected 203 proposed changes of law in the state. Over half of these objections (107) came after the 1982 extension of the VRA statute. Only Mississippi has encountered a larger number of objections than Texas, but Texas has far more counties, cities, and school districts than any other southern state. The submitting authority withdrew another 388 proposed changes after DOJ sought additional information.[15] Most of the objections over the past quarter-century (sixty-one) have involved redistricting plans. At least some of the objections came because DOJ was requiring jurisdictions to devise plans that also pass muster under Section 2.

From 1990 through 2005, Texas jurisdictions submitted 112,261 proposed changes to DOJ for preclearance. Ultimately, 120 of these, or 0.1 percent, failed to receive preclearance. For slightly more than 1 percent of the proposed changes, DOJ requested further information before passing upon the proposed changed. The most frequent of these requests involved changes in polling places (394) and methods of election (381). Another 174 involved redistricting, and in 105 a municipality sought to annex property. Upon receiving further information, DOJ approved 897 of the 1,512 proposals for which it sought additional information. Another 140 proposals were withdrawn by the submitting authority, and in forty-three cases the submitting authority never responded to the request for additional information.

In the years immediately preceding *Shelby County*, Section 5 was used to stop the implementation of retrogressive state and congressional redistricting plans in Texas after the 2010 census. Section 5 authority also halted, temporarily, the implementation of a tough voter identification law. In these cases, Texas pursued simultaneous submission to DOJ and to the district court of the District of Columbia (see chap. 6). Subsequent to the overturn of Section 4, Texas moved forward with redistricting and voter identification law changes and immediately encountered new litigation from DOJ under other provisions of the law.

The federal government has infrequently exercised its option of sending observers to the Lone Star State to monitor its elections. From 1988 through 2004, observers monitored only ten elections.

## Florida

Federal monitors have not been sent into any of Florida's five Section 5 counties to watch election practices.[16] Nor has the power of objection been widely used in Florida. Of the five DOJ-registered objections, four involved actions of the state legislature. The 1992 senate redistricting plan drew an objection, as did the state house redistricting plan a decade later. The two other objections emerging from Section 5 coverage and directed at legislative action involved absentee voting. The only objection specifically directed at a county covered by Section 5 involved Hillsborough County and was issued in 1984. It was subsequently withdrawn.

From 1990 through 2005, Florida submitted 2,409 proposed changes to DOJ for preclearance. DOJ objected to only seven of the proposed changes, which included five separate elements in a 1998 objection. In addition to the handful of objections, DOJ requested more information on 176 proposed changes and ultimately approved 170 of these. Three of the items on which more information was requested were withdrawn, and in three instances DOJ did register an objection. The great bulk of the requests for more information, 100 of the 176, involved proposed changes in methods of election.

## Preclearance since 2006

Subsequent to the *Shelby County* decision, the U.S. Senate convened hearings regarding the future direction of the Act and the preclearance regime. Sen. Charles Grassley (R-Iowa) queried Prof. Justin Levitt regarding enforcement efforts under Section 5 since the renewal of the Act. Levitt provided a detailed response in which he documented the preclearance objections.[17] According to his data, of twenty-nine preclearance objections the majority were related to some aspect of redistricting. Some were major, statewide objections, such as those brought against the Texas House of Representatives and U.S. House maps after the 2010 reapportionment. Others were local, often involving sparsely populated counties. Of the remaining thirteen objections, three involved aspects of candidate eligibility (including the case of an incumbent being drawn out of his district), six touched on voting and voting practices, and four were election administration cases. Consistent with the larger body of data examined by Tokaji and Hansen, Levitt affirmed the heavy emphasis on redistricting in preclearance objections.

Levitt also reported on another twenty-five cases in which a jurisdiction withdrew a change subsequent to a DOJ request for more information. Whether these requests detected unintended retrogressions or called a bluff on a change is not known. But this was not the limit of withdrawals: an additional 220 changes were withdrawn during this same period, though Levitt could not determine if the action resulted from DOJ seeking additional information. But, of the twenty-five withdrawals after a request for information, nine involved redistricting changes. One was an annexation, two cases involved the use and availability of bilingual ballot materials, and one dealt with a local change in voter registration and qualification.

## SECTION 2 CASES

Section 2 challenges are rare.[18] A Section 2 challenge can be brought against a state or local jurisdiction by either a private party or DOJ. The burden of proof resides with the plaintiff and requires a demonstration of discriminatory effect that dilutes the ability of minority voters to participate equally in the electoral process.

There are approximate 89,000 political jurisdictions in the United States that conduct elections. Only 330 Section 2 suits resulting in published opinions were brought against state or local governments between 1982 and 2006. Many of these suits (139, 42.1 percent) challenged the use of at-large elections to elect local governments or state lawmakers. Another 108 (32.7 percent) challenged reapportionment and redistricting plans passed by local or state governments. Just thirty-four cases (10.3 percent) questioned changes in elections procedures, and five (1.5 percent) claimed discriminatory behavior in election administration. Of the reported cases, 192 (58 percent) were in the eleven-state South; 227 were in states where all or some part of the state was covered by Section 5 preclearance (see table 2.3). Not all Section 2 cases have generated published opinions. In anticipation of renewal of the Voting Rights Act, the National Commission on Voting Rights staff compiled lists of unpublished opinions.[19] The National Commission provides counts of cases won by plaintiffs but not of those in which the jurisdiction being sued prevailed. In the discussion below, we report on both the results of published opinions gathered by the Katz team and the unpublished decisions identified by the National Commission.

Section 2 challenges are not usually successful. In cases generating published opinions, plaintiffs prevailed in just over a third the 330 suits brought between 1982 and 2006 (table 2.3). Challenges under Section 2 were usually most successful in the South, with eighty-four of 192 challenges (43.8 percent) leading to a finding of violation of the Voting Rights Act. Challenges in the non–Section 5 states were slightly more successful (8 of 17, 47.1 percent) than challenges in the Section 5 states (76 of 175, 43.4 percent). Outside the South there were fewer Section 5 challenges, just 138, and also far fewer successes (39, 28.3 percent). The lowest success rate was in the states covered at least in part by Section 5 (9 of 52, 17.3 percent), and challenges in non–Section 5 states succeeded over a third of the time (30 of 86, 34.9 percent).

TABLE 2.3   Section 2 challenges since 1982

|  | Number | Number successful | % successful |
|---|---|---|---|
| Southern | 192 | 84 | 44 |
| Sec. 5 covered | 175 | 76 | 43 |
| Sec. 5 not covered | 17 | 8 | 47 |
| Non-southern | 138 | 39 | 28 |
| Sec. 5 covered | 52 | 9 | 17 |
| Sec. 5 not covered | 86 | 30 | 35 |

Of the ten states that most frequently had Section 2 challenges, seven are in the South (see table 2.4). Of the southern seven, Texas ranked first with thirty-four challenges, followed by Mississippi, Alabama, Florida, Louisiana, North Carolina, and Georgia. New York ranked above Alabama but below Mississippi, with twenty-seven challenges. Illinois (twenty) ranked between Florida and Louisiana. California, with fifteen challenges, ranked below North Carolina but ahead of Georgia. The remaining southern states—Virginia, Arkansas, Tennessee, and South Carolina—had only one more challenge combined than Texas did on its own. Of the other non-southern states with Section 2 challenges, only ten challenges were in states covered in whole or part by Section 5 at the time.

Success in Section 2 cases has varied from state to state in the South. Every southern state has had at least three successful Section 2 challenges brought against some jurisdiction. The largest number of successes has been in Mississippi, and the highest success rate in North Carolina. Section 2 challenges have had a winning record in just four southern states—North Carolina, Mississippi, Louisiana, and Tennessee. The most challenges have been brought in Texas, but the success rate in Texas is low, ranking it as the state where Section 2 challenges have the lowest success rate of any southern state except Georgia from 1982 to 2006. Focusing on the states wholly subject to Section 5 plus North Carolina, the National Commission identified another 587 cases in which the minority plaintiffs prevailed.

## Texas

The Lone Star State has more local government jurisdictions than any other state in the South, with 254 counties and thousands of

TABLE 2.4    Southern Section 2 challenges, by state, 1982–2006

|  | Number | Number successful | % successful |
|---|---|---|---|
| Texas | 34 | 9 | 26.5 |
| Mississippi | 29 | 18 | 62.1 |
| Alabama | 25 | 12 | 48.0 |
| Florida | 23 | 7 | 30.4 |
| Louisiana | 17 | 10 | 58.8 |
| North Carolina | 16 | 10 | 62.5 |
| Georgia | 14 | 3 | 21.4 |
| Virginia | 11 | 4 | 36.4 |
| Arkansas | 10 | 4 | 40.0 |
| Tennessee | 7 | 4 | 57.1 |
| South Carolina | 7 | 3 | 42.9 |

cities, towns, school districts, and special districts. It also had the highest number of Section 2 challenges between 1982 and 2006 of any state. Texas and its jurisdictions have, however, been successful in defending themselves in Section 2 cases. Of thirty-four challenges, just nine (26.5 percent) were successful. Of these, twenty challenged at-large elections used to elect local commissioners, board members, or judges; seven of these cases were successful, and two included a finding of intent to discriminate on the part of the jurisdiction. The other two successful cases were redistricting cases. One involved the drawing of the Jefferson County commission districts in the 1980s. In the second success, the League of United Latin American Citizens convinced the Court that the 2003 congressional districting map diluted Hispanic influence in District 23 and packed Hispanics into District 9. Four other local and three other state legislative redistricting challenges failed during this period. Far outstripping the nine successful suits in reported cases, the National Commission identified another 199 suits that did not result in published opinions in which minorities prevailed.

## Mississippi

The Magnolia State has had the second-highest number of published Section 2 challenges (twenty-nine) in the country. But unlike the successful defendants in Texas, Mississippi has had the largest number of plaintiff victories (eighteen) and the second-highest rate of victories (62.1 percent), behind only North Carolina. Unlike North Carolina, where the Section 2 challenges were almost entirely about at-large voting systems that followed the *Gingles* case (discussed below), just six of thirty-four cases involved challenges to at-large voting (four of which plaintiffs won). Another five cases dealt with issues of election administration such as the use of absentee ballots (two won by plaintiffs), and one challenged a supermajority bond issue vote (loss for plaintiffs).

The majority of the reported Mississippi Section 2 cases have been redistricting and reapportionment challenges. Fourteen cases were challenges to county and municipal government, of which ten were won by plaintiffs. The remaining three cases include a failed challenge to the apportionment of seats to the state transportation board and a failed challenge to the method of electing judges to the Mississippi Supreme Court.[20] The remaining case is one of the more significant early applications of Section 2, the 1984 challenge to the apportionment of congressional districts in Mississippi in *Jordan v. Winter*.[21] In this case, the federal court found that the minority concentration in the majority-black, Delta-based 2nd Congressional District was insufficient to enable African Americans to elect a candidate of choice.

In addition to prevailing in eighteen reported decisions, minorities won another forty-nine cases that did not result in a published opinion. The total of seventy-four plaintiff victories ranks Mississippi fourth among Section 5 states.

## Alabama

From 1982 to 2006, twenty-five Alabama Section 2 cases led to published opinions, with the plaintiffs prevailing in twelve. Of those wins, six included a finding of intent to discriminate by the jurisdiction, meaning that the case would have satisfied the standard from *Mobile v. Bolden* that was in place before 1982. Fourteen challenges involved at-large voting systems, eight of which plaintiffs won. In three of those cases, intent was found to be present. Eight cases targeted election administration, procedures, or the use of appointive power to fill vacancies, two of which plaintiffs won. The remaining three cases were redistricting and reapportionment cases. In two of these cases, plaintiffs prevailed.

In 1983, plaintiffs successfully challenged the crafting of city council districts in the city of Montgomery, with the court finding both discriminatory effect and intent present.[22] Nine years later, a suit against the state's congressional districts in *Wesch v. Hunt* resulted in the court implementing a congressional map, after the legislature failed to act.[23] The court determined sufficient discriminatory effect in violation of Section 2 that it adopted a map that included a new majority-African American congressional district.

The National Commission identified 180 Section 2 suits in which minorities prevailed. With a total of 192 cases won by plaintiffs, Alabama is second only to much larger Texas in terms of the number of successful challenges brought under Section 2.

## Florida

Of the twenty-three Section 2 cases brought in Florida between 1982 and 2006, just seven were successful. Much like in North Carolina, most of the challenges (18 of 23) were to local at-large voting systems, and of these seven were successful. In just one case, in the rural Panhandle county of Gadsden, did a court make a finding of discriminatory intent.[24] The remaining five challenges in Florida included three election procedure or administration challenges—one a failed effort to challenge felon voter disfranchisement, plus failed challenges to the state's legislative seats in 1994 and to the congressional district boundaries in 2002.[25]

Only one successful Section 2 case came from a county subject to Section 5.[26] In addition to the six wins by plaintiffs in reported Section 2 cases from counties not required to seek preclearance, an additional eleven cases from these counties won by minorities went unreported.

## Louisiana

Section 2 plaintiffs enjoyed more success than failure in Louisiana between 1982 and 2006: ten of seventeen reported suits succeeded. Nearly all of the cases dealt with either at-large elections (six) or reapportionment (ten), and one unsuccessful case challenged a method of judicial appointment. Of the at-large election cases, four were won by plaintiffs, as were six of nine challenges to parish police jury or local school board reapportionment plans. In the one case involving a statewide reapportionment, plaintiffs prevailed in the 1983 challenge to the apportionment of the state legislature.[27] Minority successes in unreported cases were rare, with only seven victories.

## North Carolina

The Tar Heel State had the worst record in court in the period under study when challenged under Section 2, with ten plaintiff victories in sixteen reported suits. All but two of the suits brought in North Carolina challenged local at-large election systems. Of the remaining suits, one was a challenge to a reapportionment plan in Durham County; the other was *Thornburg v. Gingles*, which challenged the use of multimember and countywide at-large legislative districts for the North Carolina legislature.[28] This case lends its name to the three-pronged statistical and legal test described in chapter 1, the *Gingles* test, which established the three factors that plaintiffs must prove in order to succeed in a Section 2 case. Intent was not found in any of the North Carolina cases.

Six of the successful reported Section 2 cases came from counties covered by Section 5.[29] These forty covered North Carolina counties generated an additional thirty victories by minority plaintiffs that did not generate a published opinion. The sixty counties not subject to Section 5 had fifteen minorities wins in unreported cases.

## Georgia

From 1982 through 2006, plaintiffs in Section 2 cases had the lowest rate of success in the Empire State of the South. Out of fourteen reported challenges brought in Georgia, just three (21.4 percent) succeeded. The overall success rate in Georgia was less than the success rate of plaintiffs in non-southern jurisdictions not covered by Section 5. Eight of the cases challenged at-large election systems, including all three of the successful Section 2 cases brought in the state. One of the unsuccessful challenges, in the case *Holder v. Hall*, sought to overturn the use of sole commissioner government in Bleckley County, a case decided by the Supreme Court, which allowed the county to keep its one-man governing body.[30] The remaining six challenges failed. Of these, four were challenges to election administration or procedures in the state; one challenged the reapportionment of the Sumter County school board; and another attempted to overturn the state's majority vote requirements for local and state elections.[31]

Although plaintiffs scored only three victories in published opinions, they prevailed in an additional sixty-six cases that did not make it into print. The total number of minority wins in Section 2 cases in Georgia trailed the number in Texas and Mississippi, although constituting only about one-third as many successes as in those other two states.

## Virginia

There were just eleven Section 2 suits reported in Virginia from 1982 to 2006; four succeeded. Of these, two questioned the use of at-large elections in Nottoway County and in the City of Norfolk; one other at-large challenge failed. The other two successful challenges were redistricting and reapportionment challenges for the boards of supervisors of Henrico and Richmond Counties, respectively. Three other challenges to local and state legislative reapportionment failed. Three other unsuccessful challenges sought to challenge felon disfranchisement, compelling a candidate to be placed on the ballot, and the appointment to a vacancy on a school board.

The few plaintiff victories in reported cases have not been augmented by frequent wins in unreported litigation. Plaintiffs succeeded in only eleven unreported cases.

## South Carolina

Of the southern states subject to Section 5, the Palmetto State had the fewest Section 2 reported decisions (seven) and tied with Georgia for the fewest successful challenges brought (three). Four challenges were to at-large election systems for county commissions, including the three successful prosecutions. The one failed challenge to a commission, in Richland County, failed in an effort to challenge a modified reapportionment plan that mixed single-member and at-large representation. The other three cases dealt with election administration, annexation, and procedural matters in a county council.

Relatively few unreported successful Section 2 cases originated in South Carolina, with plaintiffs winning thirty such cases.

## Arkansas

Of the ten Section 2 suits brought in Arkansas between 1982 and 2006, four succeeded. One, *Jeffers v. Clinton*, challenged the 1981 state legislative redistricting plan. The court also found an intent to discriminate and bailed in Arkansas via Section 3 of the Voting Rights Act (discussed further below).[32] Bail-in, however, applied only to proposals relating to runoff elections. Five reported challenges sought single-member districts. Three of these succeeded, including two challenges to the use of multimember districts to elect state lawmakers.[33] A subsequent 1990 challenge to the state Democratic Party's use of the majority vote requirement in legislative primaries did not succeed.[34]

In addition to four successful reported cases, plaintiffs won twenty-four suits that did not result in published opinions.

## Tennessee

The Volunteer State is one of two southern states that was not covered by Section 5 of the Voting Rights Act and, unlike Arkansas, has not been bailed to preclearance coverage via Section 3. Only seven Section 2 cases were reported in Tennessee. Plaintiffs won four of these along with two unreported cases between 1982 and 2006. Three reported cases challenged local at-large election plans, including one in Tennessee's only majority-black rural county, Haywood, and the other sought to undo the apportionment of the state house (a companion suit challenging the senate failed in 1995).[35]

## Alaska

One of two non-southern states wholly subject to Section 5, Alaska did not see a plaintiff win a Section 2 suit.

## Arizona

The National Commission study shows two plaintiff victories in Arizona, although neither of these came with a reported opinion.

Effect versus Intent

Findings of intent were rare in Section 2 redistricting cases in the period. There were just eighteen cases, and six of them were in Alabama; only one other state had more than one (Texas). Of the eighteen intent findings, eleven were in the South, and of those two were in states not covered by Section 5. Of the seven cases where discriminatory intent was found in the use of at-large elections, three were in Alabama and two in Texas; the others were in Florida (Gadsden County) and Tennessee (Haywood County). Of the five local reapportionment plans found to be tainted by intentional discrimination, two were in the South (Alabama and Arkansas) and the others in Ohio, New York, and California. The California case, which involved reapportionment of the Los Angeles County Commission, led DOJ to bail in the county (make it subject to Section 5 preclearance) using Section 3. The remaining cases in which discriminatory intent was found dealt with voting procedures. Two were in the Alabama; the others covered diverse behaviors, including a problem with polling station location in Providence, Rhode Island; absentee ballot issues in eastern Pennsylvania; and candidacy requirements in Illinois and Hawaii.[36]

## BAILOUT

Coverage by Section 5 of the Voting Rights Act was determined by formulae in Section 4 (see chap. 1). In addition to determining coverage, this provision of the law provided a mechanism for a jurisdiction to appeal its coverage or to seek to exit the requirement to preclear election law changes. This provision, termed *bailout*, appeared in the original 1965 Act as a remedy for over-inclusiveness when applying the trigger. For example, in the 1960s and 1970s local jurisdictions in Alaska, Colorado, Connecticut, Hawaii, Idaho, Maine, Massachusetts, New Mexico, Oklahoma, North Carolina, and Wyoming were bailed out from Section 5 coverage after the trigger picked them up.

Amendments to the Act in 1982 allowed jurisdictions to seek bailout despite previously meeting the statutory standard for coverage. To bail out, a jurisdiction petitioned a three-judge panel in the district court of the District of Columbia seeking a declaratory judgment allowing the termination of Section 5 preclearance. To qualify for bailout, the jurisdiction had to make an affirmative demonstration that, over the previous ten years

- No test or device had been used within the jurisdiction for the purpose or with the effect of voting discrimination.
- All changes affecting voting had been reviewed under Section 5 prior to their implementation.
- No change affecting voting had been the subject of an objection by the attorney general or the denial of a Section 5 declaratory judgment from the District of Columbia district court.
- There had been no adverse judgments in lawsuits alleging voting discrimination.
- There had been no consent decrees or agreements that resulted in the abandonment of a discriminatory voting practice.
- There were no pending lawsuits that alleged voting discrimination.
- Federal examiners had not been assigned to monitor elections in the jurisdiction.
- There had been no violations of the Constitution or federal, state, or local laws with respect to voting discrimination unless the jurisdiction established that any such violations were trivial, were promptly corrected, and were not repeated.

In addition, the jurisdiction must have eliminated voting procedures and methods of elections that inhibited or diluted equal access to minority voters; demonstrated constructive efforts to eliminate intimidation and harassment of persons seeking to register and vote; and expanded opportunities for voter participation. The jurisdiction also had to present affirmative evidence of minority electoral participation. These facts had to be demonstrated not just for the jurisdiction seeking bailout but also for any inferior jurisdiction within its boundaries, such as a town, school board, or special district. Once bailed out, a jurisdiction had to keep clean for ten years, during which DOJ could reopen proceedings and petition to have Section 5 coverage reinstated based on evidence of discriminatory activity.

Between 1984, when the revised bailout provision took effect, and 2006, thirteen jurisdictions and the smaller political entities included in the county or independent city bailed out from preclearance coverage. All were in Virginia, mainly in northern Virginia near Washington, D.C., or in the mountainous western part of the state where minority populations are sparse.[37] Subsequent to the renewal of the Act but prior to the arrival at the Supreme Court of the bailout challenge brought in the *NAMUDNO* case (see chap. 6), five more jurisdictions exited Section 5 preclearance. As with the previous thirteen bailouts, all were in Virginia.[38]

After the successful *NAMUDNO* challenge, another twenty-three jurisdictions bailed out from Section 5 preclearance review. And for the first time since the 1982 renewal of the Act, bailouts occurred for jurisdictions outside of Virginia. In addition to the utility district in Texas that brought litigation challenging the denial of bailout by the D.C. district court, jurisdictions in Georgia (City of Sandy Springs), Texas (Jefferson County Drainage District No. 7), North Carolina (City of Kings Mountain), California (Alta Irrigation District, City of Wheatland, Browns Valley Irrigation District, and Merced County), Alabama (City of Pinson), and all of the covered townships in New Hampshire[39] had the preclearance requirement dismissed. Another fifteen jurisdictions in Virginia also successfully bailed out.[40]

Other jurisdictions such as those in the mountainous portions of southern states—areas with few if any minority residents—could bail out. But the judicial process needed to escape Section 5 did not appear to be so costly. When Sandy Springs, Georgia, sought to bail out from under Section 5 subsequent to the *NAMUDNO* case, the cost of bailout was less than $14,000 according to city sources. But the costs associated with *NAMUDNO* had been far higher, as it was the test case that opened the door for Sandy Springs to bail out. And Sandy Springs is one of the most affluent cities in the South, with ample capacity to pursue this course of action. For smaller and less prosperous cities and counties, even five-figure litigation might seem daunting compared to the habit of complying with federal oversight.

## THE POCKET TRIGGER

It is possible to extend the preclearance requirement to jurisdiction that did not trip the Section 4 trigger. A little used component of the Act, Section 3, is often referred to as the *bail-in* or *pocket trigger*.

Under this portion of the law, if DOJ successfully prosecutes a case against a jurisdiction under the permanent section of the law (Section 2) and can demonstrate an intent to discriminate, then it can bail in the jurisdiction so that it must seek preclearance for future changes. This authority exists absent a coverage trigger for Section 5, and it has been a component of the law since 1965.

Section 3 is a potentially powerful tool. If DOJ wins a case against a state and proves intentional discrimination, then the state and all of the inferior jurisdictions within the state become subject to Section 5. In Section 3 cases, terms of preclearance and length of coverage can be set in a consent decree. It is possible to limit the scope of practices subject to preclearance review. Consider Arkansas as an example. After that state lost a voting rights case in 1989, the preclearance requirement was imposed on the majority vote requirements in elections, but not on redistricting or other activities. As a strategic matter, should DOJ seek to reassert its preclearance authority, Section 3 is the best available tool. And challenging state redistricting plans is the most effective means to use that tool, because the one-person, one-vote decisions necessitate that states change district boundaries every ten years, thus providing targets of opportunity for DOJ. If DOJ succeeds in proving intent, then a statewide bail-in results.[41]

The pocket trigger is potentially powerful. But the use of Section 3 authority is far more demanding than either Section 2 or Section 5. Unlike Section 5, Section 3 requires greater proactive action on the part of DOJ. The department must first win litigation against a state or jurisdiction, thereby placing the burden of proof on it as the plaintiff. A DOJ win on a Section 2 claim showing a discriminatory effect does not trigger Section 3. DOJ must meet the much higher intent standard, which generally impeded success when applying the Act before 1982. DOJ has placed only seven jurisdictions under preclearance authority using the pocket trigger, including the state of New Mexico for ten years, the state of Arkansas for issues of majority vote requirements, and six counties and one city.[42]

Cost is also a factor that mitigates against the widespread use of the pocket trigger. Litigating any one of these cases causes both the defending jurisdiction and the national government to incur several million dollars in legal costs. And, as we noted previously, Section 2 cases are typically not successful, and far fewer result in an actual intent finding. Only about a third of reported Section 2 cases brought from 1982 to 2006 succeeded, and of those just eighteen included a finding of intent. Of the successful prosecutions between 1982 and 2006 where intent was found, none challenged statewide redistricting or other statewide voting practices.

## CONCLUSION

The Voting Rights Act is an example of an old-school implementation success. In such an implementation, clear directives are issued and authority is exercised by passionate and dedicated actors in order to modify behavior surrounding a clearly defined problem. The Voting Rights Act targeted with increased scrutiny states and local governments that were most likely to engage in racially discriminatory behavior in the conduct of elections. It compelled these egregious offenders to submit to a rigorous preclearance regime, which effected real change in minority voter access. The Act provided different tools to allow the Department of Justice to engage discrimination nationwide and then to impose powerful remedies on jurisdictions as needed, depending of the scale of violation successfully prosecuted.

Section 5 of the Act was the most powerful tool available to DOJ. Hundreds of thousands of major and minor changes in election practice were subjected to scrutiny. By contrast, the next-most-powerful tool, Section 2, has been implemented only a few hundred times and, when used, has most often not been successful.

# 3 A Comparative Analysis of the Impact of the Voting Rights Act in the South

The consensus is that the Voting Rights Act has been inordinately successful. Virtually no one denies that African Americans have dramatically more influence today than before the first version of the legislation became law in 1965. In chapter 2 we discussed the scope of implementation of the Act. In this chapter we consider the impact of the Act's implementation with two questions in mind: How has progress compared across the South? Which states have come farthest?[1]

To answer these questions, we compare the progress of the southern states on several dimensions of voter participation and electoral outcomes. We aggregate data on voter registration, voter turnout, and office holding from the local to the national level for each state across time and compare them to determine progress in assuring minority voter access and influence. Because African Americans were the predominant minority of interest to the original Voting Rights Act and the most substantial minority group across all but two southern states, this chapter focuses on black voting rights progress.

We report the raw numbers of political participants and public officials, but in social science there is always more than raw numbers, because raw numbers without context mask important information. In this instance, raw numbers can be deceptive because of differences in the size of the black population and of collegial bodies across states. To develop a metric that facilitates comparison across states, we create index numbers by dividing the percentage of African Americans in the category of interest by the black share of the state's voting

59

age population. For example, an index of 1.0 means that African Americans' share of offices equals their share of the state's voting age population (VAP). Scores in excess of 1.0 indicate that African American officeholders exceed their share of the adult population, and scores below 1.0 indicate a smaller percentage of blacks in office than in the adult population.

It must be noted that states have no obligation to have minorities represented in public office at levels equal to their share of the potential electorate. Indeed, Section 2 of the Voting Rights Act as amended in 1982 includes an explicit proviso disclaiming any obligation to achieve racially proportional representation. As the statute states, "Nothing in this section establishes a right to have members of a protected class elected in numbers equal to their proportion of the population." Therefore, although we calculate index numbers based on the concept of proportionality, this does not indicate an expectation that states will achieve proportionality. The degree to which a state approaches proportionality provides a baseline against which to compare performance. Students of electoral systems have long recognized that in single-member district electoral formats, as are widely used in the United States, it is unlikely that a minority will achieve proportionality; the majority usually achieves a larger share of seats than their portion of the electorate.[2] Indeed, the definition of electoral bias used to assess the fairness of a districting arrangement accepts that the majority party will get a share of the seats that exceeds its share of the votes. A system is judged to be free of bias if the bonus that goes to the majority party is roughly equal for either party should it achieve majority status.[3]

Readers may be troubled by inconsistency in the years from which the data used in this chapter come. Where possible, data reflect the most recent elections. Census Bureau estimates of registration and turnout are for 2012.[4] Figures for local office holding come from the most recent survey done by the Joint Center for Political and Economic Studies, and that enumeration occurred in 2001. Data on African American presence in other offices come from 2011 and 2013, the point at which individuals elected in 2010 or 2012 took office. These represent the latest data available at the time of writing.

Persons interested in examining longitudinal data on these variables for each state should consult our *Triumph of Voting Rights in the South*.[5] The individual state chapters in that volume present longitudinal figures on registration and turnout. Since the focus here is on relative rates of participation for blacks and whites, calculations are made using voting age citizens within the group. The white figures are for non-Hispanics.

## PROGRESS IN VOTER PARTICIPATION

Throughout this volume we direct readers to important data created by the voting rights legislation, such as the estimates of participation the Bureau of the Census is required to collect through post-election surveys. These surveys estimate the share of the VAP that registered or turned out to vote. As of 2012, at least 65 percent of the adult population in each southern state had registered to vote. Although the trigger mechanism did not specify that a majority of the African American adults should be registered, by 2012, according to Census Bureau estimates, most black adults had registered.

Some southern states have substantial numbers of recent immigrants, not all of whom are citizens, and therefore a share of their adult population is ineligible to register. If the registration rates are adjusted to exclude noncitizens, then the Census Bureau estimates for adult black registration range from 65.3 percent in Arkansas to 84.2 percent in Mississippi. When the self-reported registration figures for 2012 are compared with the estimates for the early 1960s, prior to the adoption of the Voting Rights Act, it becomes clear that the relative standing of states has changed dramatically. Mississippi, which had the lowest incidence of black registration in the early 1960s, with fewer than a tenth of the adults signed up to vote, had the highest percentage by 2012. Alabama, which had the second-lowest registration among blacks in 1962, gained the fourth-highest incidence of black registration ranking behind Mississippi, North Carolina, and Virginia at the other end of the scale. In contrast, Florida, which had the second-highest rate of black registration in the early 1960s, ranked ninth in 2012. Tennessee, which had the highest percentage of black registrants prior to the Voting Rights Act, ranked tenth half a century later.[6]

The median figures at the bottom of table 3.1 provide a measure of change for the eleven-state South. Prior to the adoption of the Voting Rights Act, the median proportion of blacks who had registered stood at 39.4 percent. Just a couple of years after adoption of the legislation, the median figure had increased to 58.9 percent. In the 2012 Census Bureau survey, the median was 70.7 percent (Georgia).

TABLE 3.1  Voter registration

| | African Americans | | | | | | White | | |
|---|---|---|---|---|---|---|---|---|---|
| | Pre-VRA % | Pre-VRA rank | Post-VRA % | Post-1965 VRA rank | 2012 % | 2012 Rank | White 2012 % | White 2012 rank | Black-white ratio |
| Alabama | 19.3 | 9 | 51.6 | 9 | 68.7 | 9 | 75.5 | 5 | 0.910 |
| Arkansas | 40.4 | 4 | 62.8 | 3 | 61.3 | 11 | 67.7 | 11 | 0.905 |
| Florida | 51.2 | 2 | 63.6 | 2 | 65.8 | 10 | 68.9 | 9 | 0.955 |
| Georgia | 27.4 | 8 | 52.6 | 8 | 72.3 | 7 | 72.0 | 8 | 1.004 |
| Louisiana | 31.6 | 7 | 58.9 | 6 | 77.1 | 3 | 77.3 | 3 | 0.997 |
| Mississippi | 6.7 | 10 | 59.8 | 5 | 90.6 | 1 | 82.4 | 1 | 1.100 |
| North Carolina | 46.8 | 3 | 51.3 | 10 | 85.3 | 2 | 77.9 | 2 | 1.095 |
| South Carolina | 37.3 | 6 | 51.2 | 11 | 75.8 | 4 | 72.0 | 7 | 1.053 |
| Tennessee | 69.5 | 1 | 71.7 | 1 | 71.1 | 8 | 68.3 | 10 | 1.041 |
| Texas | NA | | 61.6 | 4 | 73.2 | 5 | 73.0 | 6 | 1.003 |
| Virginia | 38.3 | 5 | 55.6 | 7 | 72.6 | 6 | 75.8 | 4 | 0.958 |
| Median | 39.4 | | 58.9 | | 72.6 | | 73.0 | | 1.004 |

*Source:* Pre– and post–Voting Rights Act figures from U.S. Commission on Civil Rights, *Political Participation* (Washington, D.C.: U.S. Government Printing Office, 1968), 222–223.

*Note:* The 2012 figures are the percentage of the "black alone or in combination" citizen voting age population who reported in the Census Bureau survey that they had registered. The white figure is for white non-Hispanic citizens.

Table 3.1 also provides figures on the proportion of the white non-Hispanic citizen VAP registered to vote in 2012. The range here is from a low of 53.3 percent in Arkansas up to 74.5 percent in Mississippi. The rank ordering suggests that some states generally have larger shares than others of their voting age citizens registered, regardless of race. For example, Mississippi has the highest percentage of its African Americans registered and also ranks first for white registrants. North Carolina and Louisiana also do well for both races in terms of registration. On the other hand, Arkansas and Tennessee, the two states not subject to Section 5 of the Voting Rights Act, have relatively small shares of their adult citizens registered regardless of race.[7] Florida also ranks poorly. Thus the rate of registration may be partially influenced by the ease of registering within a state, outreach efforts, or some other phenomenon beyond the scope of this book.

One way to control for differences in registration at the state level is to compare the black rate to the white rate within an individual state by calculating the black-white registration ratio. The figures for that calculation in 2004 appear in the rightmost column of table 3.1. If blacks register at higher rates than whites, then the figure exceeds 1.0, as reported for Mississippi, North Carolina, South Carolina, Tennessee, Georgia, and Texas. At the other extreme, in Arkansas the ratio is 0.90:1.00 and in Florida it is 0.96:1.00. The median for the South is 1.004, indicating a slightly higher proportion of black than white registrants. Mississippi has the highest score, further evidence that the state once most resistant to black registration has become one of the most open.

Table 3.2 reports on Census Bureau estimates of black and white turnout in the 2012 general election and the total population of the states. Since in addition to blacks and whites states have Hispanic and Asian citizens, the total figure for all voters can actually reside at a number greater or less than the turnout figures for blacks and whites. As with registration, the state that most vigorously opposed black participation before enactment of the 1965 Voting Rights Act (Mississippi) scored very well in 2012 in the share of its black VAP that reported casting ballots. Mississippi ranked first (82.4 percent), followed by two other original Section 5 states, North Carolina and Louisiana. The two states that have never been subject to the preclearance requirement, Arkansas and Tennessee, ranked eleventh and ninth, respectively, in black turnout. Black turnout exceeded 60

TABLE 3.2    Estimates of voter turnout among citizens, 2012

|  | Black % | Rank | *White % | Rank | Total % | Rank | Black-white ratio | Rank |
|---|---|---|---|---|---|---|---|---|
| Alabama | 63.1 | 7 | 62.0 | 7 | 61.9 | 6 | 1.018 | 8 |
| Arkansas | 49.4 | 11 | 55.7 | 10 | 53.3 | 11 | 0.887 | 11 |
| Florida | 57.6 | 10 | 61.9 | 8 | 60.8 | 8 | 0.931 | 10 |
| Georgia | 65.0 | 6 | 62.0 | 6 | 61.9 | 7 | 1.048 | 6 |
| Louisiana | 69.5 | 3 | 65.2 | 4 | 66.3 | 4 | 1.066 | 5 |
| Mississippi | 82.4 | 1 | 71.8 | 1 | 74.5 | 1 | 1.148 | 2 |
| North Carolina | 80.2 | 2 | 66.3 | 3 | 68.9 | 2 | 1.210 | 1 |
| South Carolina | 69.3 | 4 | 63.5 | 5 | 64.7 | 5 | 1.091 | 4 |
| Tennessee | 61.1 | 9 | 54.8 | 11 | 55.7 | 9 | 1.115 | 3 |
| Texas | 63.1 | 8 | 60.9 | 9 | 53.8 | 10 | 1.036 | 7 |
| Virginia | 67.2 | 5 | 67.5 | 2 | 66.9 | 3 | 0.996 | 9 |

*Source:* Computed from Census Bureau estimates reported in "Voting and Registration of the Total Voting-Age Population, by Sex, Race and Hispanic Origin for States," November 2012.

*The white figure is for white non-Hispanics alone.

percent in nine states, of which eight were covered by Section 5. A majority of the black adult citizens voted in every state except Arkansas, where only 49.4 percent went to the polls.

As with registration, turnout may vary by state, since both blacks and whites are more likely to vote in some states than others. In just three states the proportion of white voting age citizens who went to the polls exceeded the proportion of blacks; in the other eight states black turnout exceeded white turnout. In Mississippi turnout was almost 14 percentage points higher among black citizens. The range for white turnout as reported in table 3.2 is from 54.8 percent in Tennessee to a high of 71.8 percent in Mississippi. There are few stark differences in the rankings of states in terms of their black and white participation rates. Only one state, Virginia, ranked more than one position apart on black and white turnout.

To assess black turnout in relation to white turnout, we computed a ratio and ranking (table 3.2, two rightmost columns). As noted earlier, black turnout exceeded white turnout in Mississippi, North Carolina, Tennessee, South Carolina, Louisiana, Georgia, Texas, and Alabama; the two races voted at roughly equal rates in Alabama. The lowest ratio was in Arkansas, the only state in which black turnout was less than 90 percent of white turnout. The median turnout ratio for these eleven states is 1.048. The self-reported results in table 3.2 indicate that socioeconomic disparities that have long been thought to produce lower participation rates among blacks than whites do not affect all states in the same manner.[8] Perhaps the differences revealed in table 3.2 stem from variations in get-out-the-vote efforts or local black civic organizations, as suggested by Tate and Wielhouwer.[9]

One component of the trigger mechanism in the 1965 and 1970 Voting Rights Act was whether most of the voting age population in a state had voted. As reported in table 3.2, a majority of the adult citizens in every southern state voted in 2012. The lowest turnout rate occurred in Arkansas (53.3 percent), a state not subject to pre-clearance. Eight states had turnout rates above 60 percent, led by Mississippi at 74.5 percent.

These most recent voting statistics represent a modern high-water mark for African American voting, in both relative and absolute terms. Compared to our previous analysis of data from 2004, African American turnout rates in 2012 equaled or exceeded white non-Hispanic participation in most southern states, and among states covered by Section 5 beginning in 1965 only in Virginia did black turnout not exceed white turnout.[10]

## PROGRESS IN OFFICE HOLDING

Since passage of the initial Voting Rights Act, the numbers of African American elected officials in the South grew from a few dozen to almost six thousand as of 2001. At the time of the last of what were once annual enumerations of black officeholders conducted by the Joint Center for Political and Economic Studies, Mississippi led the nation with 892 black officeholders, followed by Alabama and Louisiana, each with more than seven hundred. Florida had the fewest African American officeholders, with only 243. As table 3.3 shows, in terms of the share of all offices filled by African Americans, Mississippi and Alabama led with approximately 18 percent of their posts filled by blacks. In Louisiana and South Carolina, 14 percent of the officials were black. At the low end are the two states with the most substantial Hispanic populations. In Florida, blacks filled 4.6 percent of the offices; in Texas, only 1.7 percent.

TABLE 3.3   African American elected officials, 2001

| | Number | % | Index |
|---|---|---|---|
| Alabama | 756 | 17.5 | **0.709** |
| Arkansas | 502 | 6.0 | 0.394 |
| Florida | 243 | 4.6 | 0.348 |
| Georgia | 611 | 9.3 | 0.339 |
| Louisiana | 705 | 14.2 | 0.469 |
| Mississippi | 892 | 18.0 | 0.528 |
| North Carolina | 491 | 8.9 | 0.427 |
| South Carolina | 534 | 14.5 | 0.517 |
| Tennessee | 540 | 7.9 | 0.526 |
| Texas | 460 | 1.7 | 0.143 |
| Virginia | 246 | 7.9 | 0.425 |

*Source:* Joint Center for Political and Economic Studies. First published in *The Triumph of Voting Rights in the South,* by Charles S. Bullock III and Ronald Keith Gaddie; © 2009, University of Oklahoma Press.

*Note:* **Bold** entry ranks highest on black representativeness.

When the percentage of black officeholders in the state is divided by the black VAP as of 2000, Alabama has the highest index number, with the proportion of black officeholders just over 70 percent of the black portion of the VAP. In Mississippi, Tennessee, and South Carolina, the index number exceeds .5. In Louisiana, North Carolina, and Virginia, the index is greater than .4. Three other states have index numbers between .339 and .394. Texas has the lowest index number at .143. In no state do African Americans hold a share of public offices commensurate with their share of the VAP.

### State and Legislative Elected Officials

Except in Georgia, few African Americans currently hold statewide office in the South. Even in Georgia, as the state shifted from being predominantly Democratic to a GOP stronghold the number of statewide black elected officials declined. In the middle of the first decade of the century, Georgia far outstripped any other state, with African Americans holding two constitutional offices, attorney general and commissioner of labor. In 2005 a third African American held one of the five seats on the Public Service Commission. The state's supreme court had three black members, and another three served on the court of appeals, which is also elected statewide. Since then, several either retired or in one case lost reelection, leaving just four statewide officeholders. Far behind Georgia comes Texas, where the supreme court has two African Americans. Six other states each have one African American in a statewide position; Alabama, Arkansas, and South Carolina have none. The presence of African Americans in statewide offices has varied over time. For a dozen years, the auditor of North Carolina was an African American, but he lost reelection in 2004. Florida once had a black commissioner of education, but he too lost a reelection bid. South Carolina is represented in the U.S. Senate by an African American, Republican Tim Scott, who was appointed to a vacant seat in 2013.

All southern states except Arkansas and Tennessee sent at least one African American to Congress in 2012, as shown in table 3.4. Alabama, Louisiana, Mississippi, South Carolina, and Virginia, among the states initially subject to Section 5 of the Voting Rights Act, each had one African American member of Congress. North Carolina had two and Georgia had four. Texas, which became subject to Section 5 in 1975, had three black representatives, as did Florida, the other southern state impacted by the 1975 Voting Rights Act. Tennessee, which has never had to comply with Section 5, had a black member of Congress for thirty-two years. In 2006, when Harold Ford, Jr., gave up the seat to run for the Senate, a white, Stephen Cohen, won the seat as a result of getting a plurality in a Democratic primary field that featured fifteen contenders and resulted in the black vote splitting multiple ways.

Georgia, with four African-American members of Congress in its fourteen-seat delegation, has the highest index score (0.93); blacks have achieved essentially proportional representation in the Peach State. In Florida, North Carolina, and Mississippi, African Americans' proportion of the congressional delegation is approximately three-fourths their share of the adult population. Of the states with blacks in their congressional delegations, Virginia is at the bottom, with a score just under .50.

As of 2013, African Americans hold more than 20 percent of the state legislative seats in four states. Their highest proportion, 38 percent, comes in Mississippi. The other states having more than 20 percent black legislators are Alabama at 24 percent, South Carolina at 22 percent, and Georgia at 24 percent. Just below the 20 percent threshold is Louisiana at 19 percent. North Carolina and

TABLE 3.4 African Americans in congressional, state, and local office

| | Members of Congress* | | State senators* | | State house* | | Supreme courts** | |
|---|---|---|---|---|---|---|---|---|
| | % | Index | % | Index | % | Index | % | Index |
| Alabama | 14.3 | 0.560 | 20 | 0.784 | 24.8 | 0.971 | 0.0 | 0.0 |
| Arkansas | 0.0 | 0.0 | 11.4 | 0.777 | 9 | 0.612 | 0.0 | 0.0 |
| Florida | 11.1 | 0.771 | 15 | **1.103** | 15 | **1.103** | 14.3 | **0.993** |
| Georgia | 28.6 | **0.93** | 23.2 | 0.771 | 23.8 | 0.794 | 28.6 | 0.935 |
| Louisiana | 16.7 | 0.542 | 21.6 | 0.718 | 18.2 | 0.601 | 14.3 | 0.475 |
| Mississippi | 25 | 0.716 | 23.1 | 0.661 | 30.3 | 0.869 | 11.1 | 0.318 |
| North Carolina | 15.4 | .722 | 14 | 0.657 | 15 | 0.704 | 14.3 | 0.671 |
| South Carolina | 14.3 | **0.528** | 19.6 | 0.714 | 22.6 | 0.824 | 20.0 | 0.742 |
| Tennessee | 0.0 | 0. 0 | 9.1 | 0.579 | 15.2 | 0.965 | 0.0 | 0.0 |
| Texas | 8.3 | 0.624 | 6.5 | 0.508 | 11.3 | 0.892 | 11.1 | 0.834 |
| Virginia | 9.1 | 0.471 | 12.5 | 0.648 | 13 | 0.674 | 28.6 | **1.49** |

| | County commissioners*** | | Mayors*** | | City councilors*** | | School boards*** | |
|---|---|---|---|---|---|---|---|---|
| | % | Index | % | Index | % | Index | % | Index |
| Alabama | 24.2 | **0.979** | 10.6 | 0.427 | 19.9 | **0.807** | 23.3 | **0.942** |
| Arkansas | 0.0 | 0.0 | 6.6 | 0.434 | 8.9 | 0.579 | 6.5 | 0.424 |
| Florida | 6.7 | 0.503 | 3.6 | 0.269 | 6.0 | 0.451 | 4.6 | 0.344 |
| Georgia | 14.1 | 0.512 | 5.4 | 0.196 | 9.4 | 0.341 | 10.6 | 0.387 |
| Louisiana | 20.0 | 0.661 | 11.0 | 0.362 | 11.9 | 0.394 | 23.6 | 0.778 |
| Mississippi | 25.6 | 0.749 | 18.4 | **0.539** | 25.9 | 0.756 | 21.2 | 0.620 |
| North Carolina | 19.0 | 0.913 | 6.0 | 0.288 | 11.2 | 0.539 | 8.9 | 0.430 |
| South Carolina | 23.4 | 0.836 | 10.6 | 0.377 | 16.8 | 0.602 | 23.2 | 0.828 |
| Tennessee | 2.3 | 0.155 | 0.9 | 0.06 | 3.6 | 0.242 | 2.8 | 0.189 |
| Texas | 1.3 | 0.112 | 3.0 | 0.248 | <1 | — | 1.2 | 0.097 |
| Virginia | 9.4 | 0.505 | 2.2 | 0.117 | 5.3 | 0.285 | 9.3 | 0.501 |

*Source:* Data compiled by the authors and are for 2005 unless otherwise noted.

*As of Jan. 20, 2011.

**As of Jan. 2013, data collected by authors.

***Joint Center for Political and Economic Studies; data are from 2001.

*Note:* **Bold** entry ranks highest on black representativeness.

Florida have about 15 percent black legislators. Among other states subject to Section 5 are Virginia at 13 percent and Texas at just below 11 percent. The two states not subject to Section 5, Arkansas and Tennessee, have approximately 10 percent and 14 percent black lawmakers, respectively.

Focusing on the individual chambers, African Americans do better at winning seats in lower chambers where district populations are smaller. The smaller the population, the easier it is to design a district with a black concentration likely to elect an African American, all other things being equal. Across the eleven southern states, the median index for state houses is 0.824 and the median senate figure is 0.714. As reported in table 3.4, Florida and Alabama have the highest house scores. Tennessee, a non–Section 5 state, has an index of 0.965, which is a notable increase from a half-decade before. The other Section 5 states, except Virginia and Louisiana, have scores between 0.7 and 0.9. Louisiana trails Section 5 states with an index of only 0.601. Arkansas, the other state not subject to Section 5, also scores better in black representation in the state house with an index of 0.612.

Florida and Alabama also have the highest senate scores. Florida ranks much higher than any other state, at 1.103, making it the only state in which the black share of senate seats exceeds the black share in the VAP. Alabama ranks second, and Louisiana, South Carolina, and Georgia are other states with index scores above 0.7. Four of the remaining Section 5 states have scores between 0.5 and 0.7. Texas and its tiny senate of thirty-one members, which makes the drawing of heavily black districts difficult, has the lowest score. The scores for the two non–Section 5 states are 0.58 for Tennessee and 0.787 for Arkansas.

Southern states use various methods for selecting the justices on their highest courts. In Alabama, Arkansas, Georgia, Louisiana, Mississippi, North Carolina, and Texas justices are elected. Louisiana justices are elected from districts; in the other states they are elected at large. Florida and Tennessee use a Missouri Plan under which the governor appoints justices, who periodically must win a referendum to retain their seats. Virginia justices are also appointed by the governor when the legislature is not in session; if the legislature is in session when a vacancy occurs, then the lawmakers make the selection. In several other states, such as Georgia, Arkansas, and North Carolina, the governor can make interim appointments to the state supreme court when vacancies occur; in these states the newly appointed justice must run in the next general election. South Carolina justices are selected by the legislature.

In two Section 5 states that elect judges, African Americans once held a larger share of the seats than their proportion of the VAP, with

Texas at 1.866 and Georgia at 1.56 in 2005.[11] More recently the two have dipped below 1.0 but still rank in the top half of all Section 5 states. One Missouri Plan state, Florida, does well; Tennessee, on the other hand, has an index of 0. In the four other states that have black justices, the index scores range from a high of 1.48 in Virginia to a low of 0.32 in Mississippi.[12] Alabama and Arkansas have no African Americans serving on their courts of last resort as of 2013. Alabama justices compete in partisan elections, and currently only Republicans serve on the state's highest tribunal.

It has been suggested that minorities are more likely to achieve powerful positions when the selection is made via an appointment rather than a popular election. Moreover, studies of municipal politics have often concluded that blacks are more likely to be elected from districts than at large.[13] The high scores for the states that employ a Missouri Plan where the governor appoints all justices support the appointment hypothesis. Also in line with that hypothesis is Georgia's score. Although justices are elected in Georgia, the current African Americans serving on the two statewide courts—and most of their white and Asian Pacific colleagues—were initially tapped by governors to fill interim vacancies. Contrary evidence comes from the states in which the legislature is most likely to name justices, with Virginia, which has two African Americans on the seven-member court, ranking first while South Carolina ranks fifth. After the rewrite of Section 2 in 1982, minorities seeking to have a districting plan implemented sued several states that elect judges statewide. Unlike at the municipal level where district elections often produce more black council members than at-large elections, Louisiana, with its district elections of justices, does worse than Texas, Georgia, and North Carolina, where justices run statewide.

## Local Elected Officials

County governments have traditionally been the most important local government unit in the South. Southern states have large numbers of counties, with Texas (254) and Georgia (159) having more than any other state. Most southern states have between sixty and 120 counties, with South Carolina an outlier at the lower end with only forty-six.

Traditionally, many counties elected their commission members at large. However, Section 2 was rewritten in the 1982 Voting Rights

Act to encourage challenges to at-large elections if they resulted in minorities having less opportunity to elect their candidates of choice than Anglo voters. As a result, many counties with substantial minority populations incorporated at least some single-member districts. In the wake of those changes, the numbers of African American councilors increased as plaintiffs challenged jurisdictions where they believed a district could be created that would be heavily minority in voting age population.[14]

According to the most recent enumeration (2001) conducted by the Joint Center for Political and Economic Studies, the South had 678 African American commissioners (see table 3.4). At the upper end, Louisiana had 131 such officials, which in that state are called police jurors, and Mississippi came in second with 105. At the other extreme, Arkansas had no black county commissioners, and in Texas there were only seventeen. The proportion of all commission seats held by African Americans approached one in four in Mississippi and Alabama. In North Carolina and Louisiana, approximately one-fifth of the commissioners were African Americans, and in Georgia the ratio was one in seven. In the other states, fewer than one in ten commissioners was an African American.

In Alabama and North Carolina, African Americans came close to holding a share of commission seats equal to their share of the VAP.[15] In South Carolina, the index exceeds 0.8, and in Mississippi it approaches 0.75. At the lower end, in Texas where seventeen black county commissioners are spread across 254 counties, the index is a lowly 0.112. The two states never subject to Section 5 rank last and ninth in their indices for county commissioners.

In 2001 the Joint Center for Political and Economic Studies identified 309 African American mayors serving in the South. The largest numbers came in Mississippi (fifty-four) and Alabama (forty-six). Virginia had only five black mayors and Tennessee just three. Table 3.4 shows that, in terms of the share of all municipal mayoral positions filled by African Americans, Mississippi led with 18.4 percent. The other states in which blacks filled at least a tenth of the mayorships in 2001 were Louisiana, Alabama, and South Carolina. In Tennessee, black mayors led fewer than 1 percent of all cities, and in Virginia it was only 2.2. percent. The index numbers show that blacks came closest to holding a proportional share of mayoral offices in Mississippi, but even there the proportion of black mayors is barely equal to half the black percentage in the VAP. Alabama and Arkansas were the only other states in which the index exceeds 0.4. In two other states the index is greater than 0.3. The median index is 0.288. In Georgia, Virginia, and Tennessee, the index is less than 0.2.

The relative representation of black mayors is substantially below that for county commissioners except in the two states with the lowest scores for county commissioners. Overall the index numbers for mayors are the lowest of any office considered. This may be at least partly attributable to the mayor being a single office within a community whereas the other positions considered here are collegial offices. Since the mayor's position is a single office filled citywide, it is impossible to create a majority-minority district that would elect a black. The majority in the electorate may be more reluctant to choose a minority for a single office than when the minority member will be part of a board that contains some members of the majority.

In 2001 almost 2,500 southern African Americans served on city councils. The greatest number of black council members, 421, served in Alabama, followed by Mississippi with 362. Most other states had between two hundred and three hundred black councilors, with only Tennessee and Virginia having fewer than seventy-five. African Americans held more than a quarter of all city council positions in Mississippi and almost a fifth of the council seats in Alabama (see table 3.4). In South Carolina, African Americans composed roughly one-sixth of all city councils, and in Louisiana and North Carolina just over 11 percent of the council members were African American. Alabama has the highest index at 0.807, followed by Mississippi at 0.756. Three other states have indices above 0.5, and the median value is Florida's 0.451. Virginia and Tennessee have indices below 0.3.

African Americans held more than 1,000 seats on local boards of education in 2001. The greatest number served in Louisiana, which had 161 and was closely followed by South Carolina with 157. Mississippi, Arkansas, and Georgia each had more than one hundred African American school board members. The fewest blacks served in Tennessee and Florida, which had twenty-seven and sixteen, respectively. Table 3.4 indicates that in four states more than a fifth of all school board members were African Americans. Next are Georgia and Virginia, where approximately one-tenth of the board members were black. At the low end, blacks held fewer than 3 percent of the school board seats in Tennessee and Texas.

In Alabama, African Americans held a share of school board seats almost equal to their percentage of the VAP. In South Carolina the index is greater than 0.8, and in Louisiana it is above 0.75. The only other states with indices above 0.5 are Mississippi and Virginia. The median value, 0.430, comes from North Carolina. The lowest index numbers, which fall below 0.2, are in Tennessee and Texas. Of states that typically make use of countywide school systems (Florida, Georgia, and Louisiana), two have relatively low index numbers and only Louisiana comes close to having blacks proportionally represented. However, having large numbers of school districts does not necessarily facilitate the election of blacks, since Texas, which has the largest number of school districts, ranks last.

## AN OVERALL RANKING ON
## VOTING AND OFFICE HOLDING

Almost half a century after passage of the Voting Rights Act, southern African Americans have made dramatic gains at both the mass and the elite levels. Census Bureau estimates of registration and turnout in the 2012 presidential election show African Americans frequently participating at or above the rates for whites. In six states blacks registered at higher rates than whites, and in Louisiana the rates for the two groups were essentially equal. Even in the state where white registration exceeded black registration by the largest margin, Arkansas, the black figures was 90.5 percent of the white figure. The turnout figures are more impressive than the registration data, with blacks voting at higher rates than whites in eight states and almost achieving parity in Virginia. Again, Arkansas had the worst record on this dimension, but even there the black turnout rate was almost 90 percent of the white figure. The initial objective of the Voting Rights Act, to remove the barriers to African American participation, has unquestionably been achieved. Undoubtedly the presence of Barack Obama atop the Democratic ticket spurred African American interest in the election and encouraged participation. But even if the pattern of black participation outpacing that of whites does not persist in 2016 and beyond, it will not be because the way to the ballot box is blocked on the basis of race.

If, however, the focus shifts to proportional representation in elective office—the primary concern at least since the rewrite of

Section 2 in 1982—the goal remains elusive more often than not. The difficulty confronted in electing a minority group, whether it be a racial or a partisan minority, in numbers proportionate to its share of the electorate is well understood and expected in the absence of an electoral system designed to achieve proportional representation. Of 110 measures of office holding considered (eleven states across ten dimensions of political participation and office holding), African Americans achieved proportional representation on only fifteen, and on another twenty-one they garnered index scores between 0.8 and 0.99.

Table 3.5 presents the rankings from the dozen criteria that have been reviewed in this chapter. The rankings are summed across categories to yield a total score, and the rightmost column presents a composite ranking. The lower the composite score for a state, the better its overall performance. The differences in indices between states on some dimensions are at times small, so one should be careful not to make too much of a state's precise ranking. Therefore, it may make sense to focus on the clustering of states. Mississippi emerges as a state in which African Americans have been most successful politically, with Alabama a close second. South and North Carolina cluster together behind the leaders. Georgia, Florida, and Louisiana clump together. Virginia, Tennessee, and Texas constitute another set, and Arkansas brings up the rear.

A review of mass and elite participation indicates that the two states least hospitable to African American participation prior to passage of the Voting Rights Act in 1965 have become the very ones in which blacks face the fewest obstacles to equality. Across the twelve categories, Mississippi ranks first in black registration and on the index for black mayors. Alabama ranks first in terms of African American elected officials and three local collegial bodies—county commissions, city councils, and school boards. Mississippi ranks second on turnout, the sum of elected officials, and city council members. On none of the dimensions does Mississippi place worse than eighth. Alabama scored second in terms of state house members and senators.

Four other states have a first-place ranking on at least one dimension. Florida scores best in terms of black representation in both chambers of its legislature, and Georgia performs best in terms of African American representation in its congressional delegation and in statewide offices. Virginia has the best score in African American

TABLE 3.5   Summary of state rankings

| | Registration | Turnout | Elected officials | Statewide | Members of Congress | State senators | State representatives |
|---|---|---|---|---|---|---|---|
| Alabama | 10 | 8 | 1 | 10 | 6 | 2 | 2 |
| Arkansas | 11 | 11 | 8 | 10 | 10.5 | 3 | 10 |
| Florida | 9 | 10 | 9 | 6 | 2 | 1 | 1 |
| Georgia | 5 | 6 | 10 | 1 | 1 | 4 | 7 |
| Louisiana | 7 | 5 | 5 | 6 | 7 | 5 | 11 |
| Mississippi | 1 | 2 | 2 | 6 | 4 | 7 | 5 |
| N. Carolina | 2 | 1 | 6 | 6 | 3 | 8 | 8 |
| S. Carolina | 3 | 4 | 4 | 10 | 8 | 6 | 6 |
| Tennessee | 4 | 3 | 3 | 6 | 10.5 | 10 | 3 |
| Texas | 6 | 7 | 11 | 2 | 5 | 11 | 4 |
| Virginia | 8 | 9 | 7 | 6 | 9 | 9 | 9 |

| | Supreme court | County commission | Mayors | City council | School board | Total score | Composite rankings |
|---|---|---|---|---|---|---|---|
| Alabama | 9 | 1 | 3 | 1 | 1 | 54 | 2 |
| Arkansas | 9 | 11 | 2 | 4 | 7 | 96.5 | 11 |
| Florida | 2 | 8 | 7 | 6 | 9 | 70 | 6 |
| Georgia | 3 | 6 | 9 | 8 | 8 | 68 | 5 |
| Louisiana | 7 | 5 | 5 | 7 | 3 | 73 | 7 |
| Mississippi | 8 | 4 | 1 | 2 | 4 | 46 | 1 |
| N. Carolina | 6 | 2 | 6 | 5 | 6 | 59 | 4 |
| S. Carolina | 5 | 3 | 4 | 3 | 2 | 58 | 3 |
| Tennessee | 9 | 9 | 11 | 10 | 10 | 89.5 | 9 |
| Texas | 4 | 10 | 8 | 11 | 11 | 92 | 10 |
| Virginia | 1 | 7 | 10 | 9 | 5 | 89 | 8 |

representation on its high court, and North Carolina scores first in turnout.

At the other end of the scale, Arkansas has the lowest composite ranking. It rates last or next to last in terms of registration, turnout, and black representation among members of Congress, state representatives, its high court, county commissioners, and statewide offices. The state that most closely rivals Arkansas for last place, Texas, ranks last or next to last in city councils, school boards, senators, county commissioners, and total elected officials.

On the composite ranking, states covered by Section 5 throughout its life tend to score best. The top five states are ones caught by the trigger mechanism in the initial Voting Rights Act. Louisiana, another state identified by the 1965 trigger, places seventh as part of the cluster that includes Georgia and Florida (picked up by the 1975 amendments). Virginia, the other state required to seek pre-clearance beginning in 1965, places eighth and is much closer to the last three states than to the cluster that includes Louisiana. Florida and Texas, which had at least partial clearance after 1975, place sixth and tenth, respectively, on the composite scale. Arkansas and Tennessee, the states never required to comply with Section 5, rank last and ninth, respectively.

There are, of course, many factors that may explain the ranking of the states in terms of openness to African American participation early in the twenty-first century. If one were to focus exclusively on the impact of the Voting Rights Act, one could make the case from these data that, not only did the legislation have a tremendous impact, but the earlier a state became subject to Section 5 the greater that impact. An even stronger case for the length of Section 5 coverage could be made in 2004, when the top six slots went to states covered by Section 5 from the outset.[16]

Although we took into consideration the size of the black population in each state when computing index numbers, African Americans remain more likely to make headway politically when their numbers are larger. There is certainly not a strong one-to-one relationship, since Alabama, the state that ranks second in the composite ranking, places only fifth in terms of the black percentage in its population. Meanwhile, North Carolina ranks fourth on the composite ranking but sixth in terms of its black percentage. Although the relationship is not perfect, the Spearman's rho between the ranking of the states by their black percentage in the population in 2010 and the composite score is .700.[17] Thus it appears that African Americans tend to win a larger share of offices and to be most likely to participate politically in states in which their presence is greatest.

The rankings here do not indicate that having a substantial Latino population contributes to African American political success. Florida and Texas, the two states with the largest Latino concentrations and the only southern states with more Hispanics than African Americans, rank in the lower half of the southern states. It has been suggested that having substantial Latino concentrations may contribute to the election of African Americans to the U.S. House of Representatives,[18] but that does not seem to be a factor across the wide range of other offices. It may be a factor in Texas's ranking second on the congressional index, since none of its three districts that currently send an African American to the House has a black majority, whereas each is more than one-third Latino. But for several other frequently districted offices, such as state senators, county commissioners, and school board members, Texas ranks at or near the bottom of the southern states. Thus it does not appear that black-Latino coalitions are uniting to elect African Americans to these collegial bodies. Since Florida's Cuban Americans in Miami tend to be Republicans, they are unlikely to elect African Americans. Although members of the Latino population in other parts of the state such as Tampa and Osceola County are generally Democrats, the impact of a coalition with blacks, if it exists, is not picked up in our data.

There may, of course, be a multitude of other factors that help account for the rankings displayed in individual tables and the composite ranking. Factors such as mobilization efforts, relative strength of the Democratic and Republican parties, leadership within the black community, fund-raising, and other elements may all help explain why some states scored better than others.

Undoubtedly there is more that can be done to account for the patterns displayed, but it is striking that Ross Barnett's Mississippi, Strom Thurmond's South Carolina, and George Wallace's Alabama, less than two generations after those noted opponents of racial progress sought to block the force of history, had the best composite scores. Indeed, the Deep South states, where lack of racial progress resulted in the imposition of the Section 5 preclearance requirement, fill four of the top five ranks on the composite index.

# 4    The VRA, Mr. Obama, and the 2008 and 2012 Presidential Elections in the South

If the polls are right, if it don't rain and the creek don't rise, the winner of the presidential election is sure to be Lyndon Baines Johnson.

*Richard Cohen, November 4, 2008*

I ain't got time to die 'cause I've got to see a black president.

*Ann Nixon Cooper, age 106, to the*
*Cable News Network, November 6, 2008*

In chapter 3 we described the variable progress across the South in the election of African Americans to state office. Progress was associated with the longevity of enforcement of Section 5 in the state, with states under Section 5 longer showing greater progress. In this chapter we examine the most high-profile case of African American political success ever—the election and reelection of Barack Obama as president of the United States—and show the role of the Voting Rights Act in creating an electoral environment in the South that contributed to securing his nomination and election.

African American electoral success reached the highest office in the United States in 2008. The election cycle ended with the victory by the first African American to become president of the United States. Barack H. Obama, a forty-seven-year-old first-term U.S. senator from Illinois, won 53 percent of the national popular vote and 365 votes in the Electoral College. It is impossible to overstate the historical significance of his election, and also impossible to advance a volume on voting rights in the South without addressing this event. In 2012 incumbent President Obama was reelected with 51.1 percent of the popular vote and 332 electoral votes. In these two elections, he picked the Republican electoral "lock" on the eleven-state South, winning Virginia, Florida, and North Carolina in 2008 and Virginia and Florida in 2012. Although the South was not critical to either Obama victory in the general elections, it did play a central role in his defeat of Hillary Clinton for the nomination in 2008.

We cannot measure descriptive black success for president in the same fashion as other elective offices. There is only one president elected at a time. And President Obama is a unique case. No black man has ever been the major party nominee for president. Assessing the interplay of the Voting Rights Act with the success of black candidates for president is therefore confined to a case study.

The success of the Obama-Biden ticket was pointed to by some critics of continuing the Voting Rights Act's Section 5 authority as proof of the advancement of American politics. If a black man could win the presidency, and do so winning southern states, surely there was no glass ceiling left in the politics of race? Proponents of the law noted that Obama's success, though proof of the effectiveness of the law, was also accompanied by increased racial rhetoric and continued racially polarized voting. They also argued that it did not offset the variable success of other African American candidates and voters across covered jurisdictions.

Regardless of questions about the relevance of the Obama elections on the continued need for the Voting Rights Act, it is a certainty that the Act contributed to Obama's nomination and, ultimately, his election as president.

## 2008: THE PATH TO NOMINATION

The Voting Rights Act was critical to the election of President Barack Obama. Since the 1971 McGovern-Frasier reforms brought primaries to the fore in choosing the Democratic Party's presidential nominee, the South has played a significant role in the primary process, and the Obama campaign owes a substantial portion of its delegate margin in 2008 to impressive wins in the Section 5 states.

South Carolina was the first southern state to hold a (sanctioned) presidential primary in 2008.[1] Entering that event, both the presumptive establishment frontrunner, Hillary Rodham Clinton, and the upstart insurgent, Barack Obama, had garnered highly visible delegate wins. Senator Obama had won the first-in-the-nation Iowa caucus. But Clinton's 3-percentage-point victory in New Hampshire raised questions about the viability of the Obama effort. His upset victory in Iowa had come in a caucus state that requires organization among the politically active but may not necessarily be representative of the preferences of a broader electorate. South Carolina offered the first opportunity to test the candidates' appeal among African Americans. Clinton and especially her husband had enjoyed excellent relations with black leaders and voters during the Bill Clinton presidency. Indeed, Nobel laureate Toni Morrison had christened Bill Clinton as America's first black president.[2] Several black leaders including civil rights icon Representative John Lewis (D-Ga.) were backing Hillary Clinton's bid. A victory in South Carolina would go a long way toward confirming the dominant belief that she was unstoppable and would be the Democratic nominee. Another question that the South Carolina primary might settle was the viability of John Edwards, who had been born in the state, although his adult career had come in North Carolina; he had won the South Carolina presidential primary convincingly in 2004. Edwards had edged out Clinton for second place in Iowa but stumbled badly in New Hampshire.

The Obama campaign connected with the Palmetto State's black voters, who accounted for 56 percent of the turnout in the Democratic primary. Obama trounced Clinton, taking 55 percent of the vote to her 26 percent. The Obama victory rested upon 78 percent support from African Americans along with about a quarter of the white vote. Clinton won only a single county. Edwards, who finished a poor third with 18 percent of the vote, was effectively eliminated from contention.

In subsequent primaries in states covered by Section 5 since 1965, Obama racked up similarly dominant victories: he took 66 percent in Georgia, 64 percent in Virginia (including a majority of white votes), 61 percent in Mississippi, 57 percent in Louisiana, and 56 percent in Alabama and North Carolina. Black voters constituted majorities of Democratic voters in all of these primaries except Virginia. As in South Carolina, Obama's victory in these other Section 5 states relied heavily upon cohesive black support. In Mississippi, North Carolina, and Virginia, exit polls showed Obama winning more than 90 percent of the black vote.[3] In each of the other three states

Obama's performance eclipsed that in South Carolina; his weakest performance came in Alabama, where he took 84 percent of the African American vote. After Obama demonstrated his viability in South Carolina, black support united behind the Illinois senator, and black leaders—such as John Lewis—who had previously been reluctant to sign on switched their allegiance to him from Clinton.[4] Only in Virginia did Obama take a majority of the white vote, although he did manage 43 percent in Georgia, the state in which he had his strongest performance overall.

Clinton won the Texas primary vote by 100,000. However, the Lone Star State had a two-step process for choosing delegates, and in the critical caucuses at which delegates were chosen the better-organized Obama outdid his rival with ninety-nine delegates to Clinton's ninety-four. Obama's clear southern primary setbacks came in Florida (where he did not campaign in the renegade primary), in Tennessee (where he lost by 14 points but took 77 percent of the black vote), and in Clinton's adopted state of Arkansas (where he lost 70–26 percent). Nevertheless, even in Arkansas, where Obama attracted only a sixth of the white vote, he took about three-fourths of the black vote.

Obama's sweep of the South went a long way toward securing the nomination. By uniting the African American vote he positioned himself to do well in northern states with substantial black populations. Across the South, Obama won eighty-five more delegates than did Clinton. That came as a result of his winning eight of the ten primaries. Outside of the South, Clinton won fifteen of twenty-four binding state primaries, but her lead among pledged delegates was only sixty-six. Clinton's last hope was that she might win enough of the superdelegates who went to the convention unpledged. Had Obama not demonstrated such broad support among African Americans in the South, Clinton might have prevailed among the super-delegates by arguing that the Illinois senator was unelectable. Helping the Obama cause was his demonstrated ability to mobilize unprecedented numbers of black voters; their support would be essential in several critical swing states.[5]

## 2008 GENERAL ELECTION SUCCESS

Obama's 2008 victory was stunning in its scope and magnitude. The Democratic nominee secured the largest percentage of the vote by a Democratic presidential candidate since 1964 and had the second-highest vote percentage ever for a Democratic nonincumbent, behind Franklin Delano Roosevelt's 57.4 percent in 1932. Senator Obama won Electoral College votes in every region and became the first Democrat ever to sweep New England, the industrial Midwest, and the Pacific Coast. He was also the first non-southern Democrat to win any southern state since John Kennedy. The Obama-Biden ticket ran stronger among white voters nationwide than any Democratic presidential ticket in forty years.

In the South, Barack Obama commanded 46.7 percent of the two-party presidential vote, or about eighteen million of thirty-eight million ballots cast. Even more impressive, however, was that the Obama-Biden ticket won fifty-five Electoral College votes by taking Florida, North Carolina, and Virginia. These three states, all covered at least in part by Section 5 of the Voting Rights Act, delivered on behalf of the Democratic nominee. For Virginia it was a monumental event; the state had not supported a Democratic presidential candidate since 1964. North Carolina had last voted for a Democratic nominee in 1976 when it narrowly backed Jimmy Carter. Florida had sided with the Democrats in 1964, in 1976, and again in 1996 before shifting narrowly back to Republicans in 2000 and 2004.

These three southern victories can be ascribed to unified bloc voting by black voters combined with some crossover support by a minority of whites and, in Florida, Latino support. As indicated in table 4.1, the Obama-Biden ticket received almost unanimous support from black voters. According to Voter News Service exit polls, between 92 percent and 98 percent of African American voters supported the Democratic ticket. These percentages reflect levels of support seen for other black candidates running in the South but rank at the high end of support for white Democrats. Among white voters, the Democratic ticket posted its strongest support in Florida, Virginia, and North Carolina, with support weakest among whites in the Deep South states of Mississippi, Alabama, and Louisiana. All of the Rim South states except Texas offered at least 30 percent support to Obama, whereas no Deep South state showed more than 26 percent white support for the Democratic candidate. In Florida and North Carolina, Obama ran about 10 percentage points better than John Kerry had four years earlier among black voters.[6] In Virginia, Obama improved on Kerry's black showing by 5 points. Contributing to the Obama victory was his improvement among white

TABLE 4.1    Vote share and racial support for southern
Democratic candidates, 2008

|  | Obama support | | | |
|---|---|---|---|---|
|  | Obama voter % | Black % | White % | Latino % |
| *Obama-Biden* | | | | |
| Alabama | 39.1 | 98 | 12 | |
| Arkansas | 39.8 | 94 | 30 | |
| Florida | 51.2 | 96 | 42 | 57 |
| Georgia | 46.7 | 98 | 23 | |
| Louisiana | 42.1 | 94 | 14 | |
| Mississippi | 43.1 | 98 | 11 | |
| N. Carolina | 50.1 | 97 | 35 | |
| S. Carolina | 45.3 | 96 | 26 | |
| Tennessee | 42.1 | 94 | 34 | |
| Texas | 44.1 | 98 | 26 | 63 |
| Virginia | 53.2 | 92 | 39 | |
| *U.S. Senate* | | | | |
| Alabama (R-I) | 37 | 90 | 11 | |
| Arkansas (D-I) | 100 | -- | -- | |
| Florida | No Senate contest | | | |
| Georgia (R-I) | 47 | 93 | 26 | |
| Louisiana (D-I) | 52 | 96 | 33 | |
| Mississippi Regular (R-I) | 38 | 94 | 8 | |
| Mississippi Special (R-I) | 45 | 92 | 18 | |
| N. Carolina (R-I) | 53 | 96 | 39 | |
| S. Carolina (R-I) | 42 | 87 | 26 | |
| Tennessee (R-I) | 32 | 72 | 26 | |
| Texas (R-I) | 43 | 89 | 27 | 61 |
| Virginia (Open) | 64 | 93 | 56 | |
| *Governor* | | | | |
| N. Carolina (Open) | 50 | 95 | 36 | |

*Source:* Voter News Service exit polls and election returns compiled by the authors. First published in *The Triumph of Voting Rights in the South,* by Charles S. Bullock III and Ronald Keith Gaddie; © 2009, University of Oklahoma Press.

*Note:* R-I indicates Republican incumbent; D-I indicates Democratic incumbent.

voters in North Carolina (by 8 percentage points) and Virginia (by 7 points) over Kerry's showing. In Florida, however, Obama matched Kerry's 42 percent of the vote, meaning that the success among Hispanic voters proved critical since Kerry had lost Florida when he took 44 percent of the Latino vote.

Comparing the Obama-Biden ticket to major statewide races on the ballot in the South indicates some minor penalty for Obama compared to other Democrats, though the differences are highly contextual. The Section 5 states of Alabama, Georgia, Mississippi, South Carolina, Texas, and North Carolina had incumbent Republican U.S. senators on the ballot. In those six states, Obama ran, on average, 6 points ahead of the Democratic challengers among black voters and roughly even with the Democratic challengers among white voters. One Republican incumbent (Elizabeth Dole, N.C.) lost, and Georgia's Saxby Chambliss was thrown into a runoff after failing to attain the majority required by Georgia law. Chambliss's challenger benefitted from the heightened black turnout mobilized by Obama.

In Louisiana, Democratic incumbent Mary Landrieu ran 2 points ahead of Obama among blacks and 19 points ahead among whites in winning reelection to the U.S. Senate. In Virginia's open seat, former governor Mark Warner ran a point ahead of Obama among blacks and 17 points ahead among whites to win, and in Mississippi's special election former Democratic governor Ronnie Musgrave ran 6 points behind Obama among blacks but 7 points ahead among whites in a losing effort. Democratic lieutenant governor Beverly Perdue won North Carolina's open gubernatorial election, closely matching Obama's performance among blacks and whites. In Texas, Obama did slightly better than Democratic U.S. Senate nominee Rick Noriega among Hispanics.

The Obama candidacy in 2008 promoted black voter mobilization. Table 4.2 reports estimates made by the Census Bureau based on surveys conducted immediately after the 2004 and 2008 elections. The denominator for the percentages reported is the number of adult citizens in a racial group rather than the number of registered voters in the group. As the table shows, in each of the Section 5 states except Alabama and in nine of the eleven southern states black turnout increased from 2004 to 2008. The largest increases in black participation came in states covered by Section 5 since 1965. In Virginia the increase was 16.2 percentage points, followed by a 12.9 point increase in South Carolina and a 10.4 point increase in Georgia. Further, at least 62.5 percent of adult blacks voted in each of the original Section 5 states. In contrast, Florida and Texas (two other states touched by the 1975 Voting Rights Act) experienced 3.8 and 7.2 percentage point increases, respectively, in black turnout. In the non–Section 5 southern states, black turnout increased by 7.1 points in Tennessee but fell by 5.3 points in Arkansas. As a result of the increased black participation, African American turnout equaled or exceeded the non-Hispanic white figure in 2008 in Alabama, Georgia, Mississippi, North Carolina, and South Carolina. In 2004 black participation rates had equaled or exceeded those for whites in only three states. The strongest black participation vis-à-vis white participation came in states covered by Section 5 since 1965 except Tennessee, where black turnout was almost 3 points higher than the white figure in 2008. Except in Louisiana, generally black turnout compared most favorably with white turnout in the states with the longest experience with Section 5.

Exit polls provide another perspective from which to assess turnout by race. The exit poll data in table 4.3 show the share of all votes cast in a state coming from blacks and whites. The data involve sampling, so necessarily some error attaches to those estimates. But three southern states provide figures based upon actual turnout, because in these states when a voter registers the information collected includes an indication of the voter's ethnicity. For those states for which actual turnout figures by race are available, we substitute those figures for the exit poll data. In each of the three states that tabulate turnout by race (all of which were covered by Section 5 in 1965), blacks cast a larger share of the vote in 2008 than four years earlier, with the gains ranging from 3 points in Louisiana to 5 points in Georgia. In five of the remaining states, the black share of the vote in 2008 was within a percentage point of the 2004 figure. Alabama experienced a 4-point increase in the share of the vote coming from African Americans, and North Carolina experienced a 3-point drop. In seven states the share of the vote coming from whites declined from 2004 to 2008, with the largest drop occurring in Alabama, where it fell by 8 points. In the other four states whites cast approximately the same share of the vote in the two presidential years. Table 4.3 indicates that in the original Section 5 states, except North Carolina, the black vote became much more important in 2008.

When one uses linear regression to test the relationship between white vote shares of down-ticket candidates for U.S. Senate and governor and the Obama performance among whites, while controlling for incumbency in the contest, the following patterns emerge.[7] First, the fit is good (table 4.3, adjusted $R^2$ = .73).[8] In the absence of incumbency

TABLE 4.2   Estimated adult citizen turnout by race, 2004 and 2008

| | 2004 | | | 2008 | | |
| --- | --- | --- | --- | --- | --- | --- |
| | Black (%) | Non-Hispanic white (%) | Back-white difference | Black (%) | Non-Hispanic white (%) | Black-white difference |
| Alabama | 63.9 | 63.6 | 0.3 | 62.5 | 62.5 | 0 |
| Georgia | 57.5 | 58.3 | -0.8 | 67.9 | 64.1 | 3.8 |
| Louisiana | 62.7 | 65.6 | -2.9 | 66.2 | 72.4 | -6.2 |
| Mississippi | 66.8 | 60.2 | 6.6 | 72.9 | 68.4 | 4.5 |
| North Carolina | 64.6 | 62.3 | 2.3 | 68.3 | 68.3 | 0 |
| South Carolina | 59.7 | 65.0 | -5.3 | 72.6 | 63.5 | 9.1 |
| Virginia | 52.1 | 67.5 | -15.4 | 68.3 | 69.4 | -1.1 |
| Section 5 as of 1975 | | | | | | |
| Florida | 54.7 | 67.4 | -12.7 | 58.5 | 65.2 | -6.7 |
| Texas | 57.7 | 64.5 | -6.8 | 64.9 | 64.7 | 0.2 |
| Non–Section 5 States | | | | | | |
| Arkansas | 49.4 | 61.1 | -16.7 | 44.1 | 55.9 | -11.8 |
| Tennessee | 52.4 | 55.4 | -3.0 | 59.3 | 55.8 | 3.5 |

*Source:* U.S. Census Bureau post-election surveys of registration and turnout.

TABLE 4.3   Black and white turnout percentage in the
2004 and 2008 electorates

|  | 2004 | | 2008 | |
|---|---|---|---|---|
|  | Black | White | Black | White |
| Alabama | 25 | 73 | 29 | 65 |
| Arkansas | 15 | 83 | 12 | 83 |
| Florida | 12 | 70 | 13 | 71 |
| Georgia | 25* | 71* | 30* | 64* |
| Louisiana | 27* | 70* | 30* | 67* |
| Mississippi | 34 | 65 | 33 | 62 |
| N. Carolina | 26 | 71 | 23 | 72 |
| S. Carolina | 27* | 72* | 31* | 69* |
| Tennessee | 13 | 84 | 12 | 84 |
| Texas | 12 | 66 | 13 | 63 |
| Virginia | 21 | 72 | 20 | 70 |

*Source*: Charles S. Bullock III, "Barack Obama and the South," *American Review of Politics* 31 (Spring 2010), 17.

*Figures from official state turnout computations; all others from Voter News Service exit polls.

and assuming no support among whites for Obama, white Democrats got 1.82 percent of the white vote, as indicated by the constant. Second, each percentage point gain for Obama among whites translated into a 1.16 point gain for the down-ticket Democrats (all of whom except the challengers to Jeff Sessions, R-Ala., and Thad Cochran, R-Miss., were white). Put another way, a white electorate that voted 50 percent for Obama voted 59.8 percent for a down-ticket white Democrat. Third, the presence of an incumbent Republican diminished Democratic vote share among whites by 5.66 points, whereas a Republican incumbent enhanced the white vote share by 5.66 points. A one-point gain in black vote share for Obama translated into a 1.18 point gain for down-ticket whites, but the substantial negative intercept (-21.41) indicates that, in a black electorate where everyone voted for Obama, white down-ticket candidates still ran about 3.4 points behind.

There is an indication at a very high level of aggregation that Obama's white vote share is structured by the presence of large, active black voting populations. Regressing the Obama white vote share in the South onto the percentage of the voter turnout that is African American and Latino, respectively, indicates that Obama receives 52.4 percent of the vote when there are no minority voters (the intercept).[9] Every one-point increase in the share of the electorate that is black results in a 1.12 point decrease in the white vote for Barack Obama. A 0.29 point decrease is indicated for every point increase in the Latino share of the electorate, though the relationship is not statistically significant.

Exit poll data from 2004 and 2008 indicate that Barack Obama ran behind John Kerry among white voters in five southern states: Alabama (-12.1 percent), Arkansas (-6.1 percent), Florida (-4.3 percentage points), Louisiana (-9.8 percentage points), and Mississippi (-4.9 percentage points). Obama ran ahead of the 2004 ticket among whites in North Carolina (+8.2 percentage points), South Carolina (+5 percentage points), Virginia (+7.4 percentage points), and Texas (+0.8 percentage points). He ran even with Kerry among whites in Tennessee and Georgia.

Regardless of the gains among blacks in cohesion and turnout or the decline of support among whites, Obama outperformed Kerry in all of the Section 5 states except Louisiana (-0.1 percentage point). The gains in the total vote in the Deep South states are from Alabama (+2.2 percentage points), Mississippi (+3.3 points), South Carolina (+4.4 points), and Georgia (+5.3 points). In the longest-covered Section 5 states of the Rim South the gains are larger, with +6.5 percentage points in North Carolina and +6.8 percentage points in Virginia. The experiences of Texas and Florida, states brought under Section 5 in 1975, fall closer to the Deep South than Rim South members of the class of 1965, with +4.1 percentage points in Florida and +5.9 percentage points in Texas.

The Obama-Biden ticket continued the sorting of the parties' presidential vote in the South on rural-urban and black-white dimensions (see map 4.1). The pattern of counties carried by the Obama campaign will seem familiar to any casual observer of southern political geography: Obama, like Kerry and Gore before him, won the South Florida urban centers; the urban core counties of the Deep South, North Carolina, and Texas; the south Rio Grande Valley; suburban Virginia; urban Memphis; and a nearly contiguous arc of old Black Belt counties from Tidewater Virginia to the Mississippi Delta.

## 2012 REELECTION SUCCESS

The presidential election of 2012 was even more racially divisive than the 2008 contests, both for the South and the nation. When initially

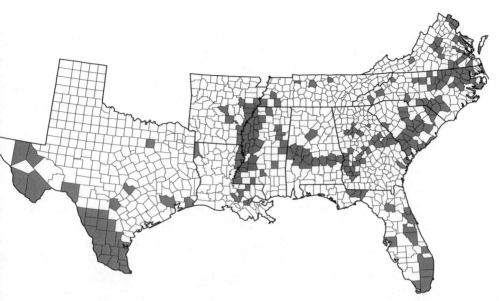

MAP 4.1 Counties won by Obama-Biden (shaded) in 2008. First published in *The Triumph of Voting Rights in the South*, by Charles S. Bullock III and Ronald Keith Gaddie; © 2009, University of Oklahoma Press.

elected, exit polls showed Obama with 43 percent of the white vote; that figure dropped to 39 percent in his reelection bid. Obama's vote share among southern whites declined, but minority voter support and enthusiasm was more than sufficiently strong to allow him to again break the solid South.

Obama's renomination was never in doubt; the president faced no significant challengers. He carried every Democratic primary in the South and won all of the delegates, losing only twenty-seven counties in the Section 5 states, to marginal candidates such as anti-abortion activist Randall Terry and gadfly Tennessee politician John Wolfe, Jr. Strong protest votes against Obama in the primary were most frequent in the upper South, in the non–Section 5 states Arkansas and Tennessee, and in border South states such as Oklahoma, Kentucky, and West Virginia.

In the South, Obama commanded 45.7 percent of the two-party presidential vote, which was slightly less than his share in 2008. The Obama-Biden ticket won forty-two Electoral College votes by taking Florida and Virginia while seeing North Carolina narrowly slip back to the GOP. It was the first time either Virginia or Florida had gone Democratic in consecutive elections since 1944 and 1948. As in 2008, the southern victories can be ascribed to unified bloc voting by blacks combined with some crossover support by a minority of whites. As in 2008, the Obama-Biden ticket received almost unanimous support from black voters. The Voter News Service cut back on exit polling in 2012, conducting surveys in just five southern states.[10] In those states (Alabama, Florida, Mississippi, North Carolina, and Virginia), exit polls found that between 93 percent and 96 percent of African American voters supported the Democratic ticket. Among white voters, the Democratic ticket posted its strongest support in Florida (37 percent, down from 42 percent in 2008), Virginia (38 percent, compared to 39 percent in 2008), and North Carolina (31 percent, compared to 35 percent in 2008), with support weakest among whites in Mississippi (10 percent, compared to 11 percent in 2008) and Alabama (15 percent, up from 12 percent in 2008). In Florida, Obama ran strong with Latinos, taking 60 percent of their votes.

Nationwide, Obama saw his share of the vote decline by 2 percentage points from 2008 to 2012, dropping from 53 to 51 percent, a pattern similar to what occurred in the South. In the Section 5 states, Obama's vote share dropped in all except Louisiana and Mississippi, where it increased by a single percentage point. In four of the other Section 5 states, as shown in table 4.4, Obama's performance declined by a single percentage point. The biggest losses came in Texas, with a 3-point decline, and Virginia, where, even though he managed to win the state, Obama's vote share fell by 2 points. In the two states not covered by Section 5, Obama lost 2 points in Arkansas and 3 points in Tennessee. Overall, Obama's performance in 2012 when compared with his initial election is about the same in the South as nationwide—slightly weaker.

Another basis for comparison of Obama's 2012 performance is other statewide contests. Five southern states elected senators in 2012, and in North Carolina a new governor was selected. Two southern states—Florida and Virginia—elected Democrats to the Senate in 2012, and in both elections Obama ran behind the successful Senate candidate (see table 4.4). In Texas, where Tea Party favorite Ted Cruz cruised to victory, his Democratic opponent matched Obama's 41 percent of the vote. In Mississippi, the Democrat trailed Obama by 3 percentage points. President Obama's strongest performance vis-à-vis a statewide Democratic nominee came in Tennessee,

TABLE 4.4   President Obama's 2012 vote in perspective

| | Obama | | |
| --- | --- | --- | --- |
| | 2008 (%) | 2012 (%) | Democratic senator (%) |
| Alabama | 39 | 38 | |
| Florida | 51 | 50 | 55 |
| Georgia | 47 | 46 | |
| Louisiana | 40 | 41 | |
| Mississippi | 43 | 44 | 41 |
| N. Carolina | 50 | 48 | 43* |
| S. Carolina | 45 | 44 | |
| Texas | 44 | 41 | 41 |
| Virginia | 53 | 51 | 53 |
| | Non–Section 5 States | | |
| Arkansas | 39 | 37 | |
| Tennessee | 42 | 39 | 30 |
| United States | 53 | 51 | |

*The North Carolina vote is for the Democratic gubernatorial and not the senatorial candidate.

where he drew 9 percentage points more of the vote than did the unsuccessful Democratic Senate candidate.

Table 4.5 shows that the impact of the Obama candidacy on black turnout observed in 2008 persisted into 2012. The impact is not necessarily in terms of increasing black turnout rates over those scored in Obama's initial election. Rather, the effect is most pronounced when the black turnout rate is compared to the rate for whites. As the third data column in table 4.5 demonstrates, in all of the initial Section 5 states except Virginia blacks participated at higher rates than did whites. Four years earlier that statement could be made only for three states, Georgia, Mississippi, and South Carolina (see table 4.2). The pattern for states not covered by Section 5 from its initiation is similar to those found four years earlier, although black deficit vis-à-vis whites is less in Florida and Arkansas in 2012 than in 2008, and the black advantage over whites increases from 2008 to 2012 in Tennessee and Texas.

Some have wondered whether the advantage of black over white turnout is nothing more than the phenomenon of having Barack Obama at the top of the Democratic ticket. The thought is that come

TABLE 4.5   Estimated adult citizen turnout by race, 2012

| | Black (%) | Non-Hispanic White (%) | Black-white difference |
|---|---|---|---|
| Alabama | 63.1 | 62.0 | 1.1 |
| Georgia | 65.0 | 62.0 | 3.0 |
| Louisiana | 69.5 | 65.2 | 4.3 |
| Mississippi | 82.4 | 71.8 | 10.6 |
| N. Carolina | 80.2 | 66.3 | 13.9 |
| S. Carolina | 69.3 | 63.5 | 5.8 |
| Virginia | 66.9 | 67.6 | -0.7 |
| | | Section 5 as of 1975 | |
| Florida | 57.6 | 61.9 | -0.7 |
| Texas | 63.1 | 60.9 | 2.2 |
| | | Non–Section 5 States | |
| Arkansas | 49.4 | 55.7 | -6.3 |
| Tennessee | 61.1 | 54.8 | 6.3 |

*Source*: U.S. Census Bureau post-election surveys of registration and turnout.

2016, when Obama will not be on the ballot, earlier patterns of black turnout being weaker than that of whites will reappear. Obviously we cannot know what participation rates in 2016 will look like, but we can perhaps get some idea by examining data from 2010. Since 2010 is a midterm election, we would expect lower participation rates for both blacks and whites. If the mobilization of blacks from 2008 had a continuing effect, then the comparison of black to white turnout in 2010 may indicate relatively higher levels of black participation than four years earlier in the previous midterm election. To see what the relative levels of participation were before and after Obama, we compare 2006 with 2010 (table 4.6). In 2006, white turnout exceeded black turnout in every state except Mississippi and South Carolina. In 2010, black turnout exceeded that for whites in Alabama, Georgia, Mississippi, and South Carolina. In each of the remaining states, although whites continued to participate at higher rates than blacks, the disparity shrank in 2010. Based on this comparison of a before- and an after-Obama election, we suggest that some African Americans mobilized by the Obama candidacy will continue to participate even after he passes from the political scene.

In other words, the Obama candidacy may have a lasting positive impact on black participation.

## CONCLUSION

Two generations removed from the attack at the Edmund Pettus Bridge, a black Democratic candidate won more southern electors than any non-southern Democrat since Kennedy, and more than any Democrat since Jimmy Carter. The pattern of success is consistent with the analysis offered in this volume. Mobilized black voters combined with a sufficient minority of white voters can prevail in southern elections, even in support of black candidates. Black and white candidates are largely indistinguishable in the nature of the coalitions they fashion, though sometimes the lack of distinction is to the decided disadvantage of Democratic candidates. The politics of the South are still the most polarized, and the prospects for major office success for blacks most constrained, in Mississippi, Louisiana, and Alabama. The degree of racial polarization in the 2008 and 2012 presidential campaigns is on par with that present in statewide contests in the South. Obama had done somewhat better than other Democrats with black voters but often done slightly worse than incumbents with whites. In Virginia, Florida, North Carolina, and Georgia, success or near-success came because Obama increased black participation and cohesion while running even or marginally ahead of average for Democrats among white voters.

In 2008, the Obama-Biden ticket got more Electoral College votes from the South than any Democratic Party ticket since Jimmy Carter in 1976. As in Bill Clinton's victories 1992 and 1996, the success in the South was not critical to the election outcome. Subtract the fifty-five southern electoral votes won by Obama or the thirty-nine and fifty-one electoral votes for the two Clinton tickets from their national totals and the Democrats still prevail. Nevertheless, these southern successes indicate an enhancement of tremendous value, because the competitiveness of the Democratic ticket carried the fight to a region off limits to Democrats in the 1980s. Moreover, sweeping the South was essential to George W. Bush's two victories.

The 2012 Obama campaign was weaker in the South than the 2008 edition, but it nonetheless provided a symbolic victory. Southern

TABLE 4.6   Estimated adult citizen turnout by race, 2006 and 2010

| | 2006 | | | 2010 | | |
|---|---|---|---|---|---|---|
| | Black (%) | Non-Hispanic white (%) | Back-white difference | Black (%) | Non-Hispanic white (%) | Black-white difference |
| Alabama | 47.8 | 50.9 | -3.1 | 46.4 | 44.0 | 2.4 |
| Georgia | 40.7 | 46.9 | -6.2 | 46.8 | 43.7 | 3.1 |
| Louisiana | 36.3 | 41.9 | -5.6 | 48.9 | 51.4 | -2.5 |
| Mississippi | 50.5 | 39.9 | 10.6 | 48.7 | 47.7 | 1.0 |
| N. Carolina | 32.2 | 44.1 | -11.9 | 41.0 | 47.0 | -6.0 |
| S. Carolina | 50.6 | 43.7 | 6.9 | 53.7 | 51.0 | 2.7 |
| Virginia | 35.9 | 51.9 | -16.0 | 35.6 | 44.9 | -9.3 |
| **Section 5 as of 1975** | | | | | | |
| Florida | 38.7 | 48.1 | -9.4 | 41.5 | 45.7 | -4.2 |
| Texas | 36.7 | 45.2 | -8.5 | 38.7 | 43.8 | -5.1 |
| **Non–Section 5 of States** | | | | | | |
| Arkansas | 34.0 | 46.7 | -19.8 | 32.5 | 42.6 | -10.3 |
| Tennessee | 39.3 | 47.5 | -8.2 | 36.4 | 38.4 | -2.0 |

*Source:* U.S. Census Bureau post-election surveys of registration and turnout.

electoral votes were not determinative of the election outcome. But forecasts of minority voter demobilization due to presumed disillusionment with Obama or new voter identification laws proved unfounded. Black and Hispanic voter cohesion for Obama remained high. In the three Rim South states that had exit poll data, Obama did suffer a fall-off of white support, but that was consistent with what happened nationwide. This loss of support was critical in just one state—North Carolina.

The most significant long-term effect of the Obama campaigns may be that it brought previously disengaged minorities, especially blacks, to the polls. It is subsequent to the Obama mobilization that African American voter participation rates in the South approximate or eclipse Anglo white voter turnout. If these voters have thrown off apathy, their participation will accelerate the political realignment already under way in the three states Obama carried in 2008 and perhaps not too far away in Georgia and Texas. As the Southern electorate becomes increasingly diverse, the GOP will have to develop an appeal that reaches beyond white voters or begin to see Democrats make headway in statewide contests in places that have been of the deepest red.

But most important for our purposes is the impact of the Voting Rights Act in shaping this historically improbable result. Barack Obama ran strongest in primaries where Section 5 had been in force the longest. In so doing, he largely replicated a pattern observed in Jesse Jackson's 1988 presidential bid, when Rev. Jackson carried all of the original Section 5 states except North Carolina and also split the Texas result. But Obama goes beyond Jackson's accomplishment in securing the nomination. And, in the general election, the presence of a large, activated, and eligible black electorate that was cultivated in part by Section 5 worked to Obama's advantage. He ran better than the two previous Democratic nominees both nationally and in the South because an intensified, unobstructed black electorate combined with white crossover voting to make him competitive in several southern states and even victorious in two Section 5 states twice and another once.

# 5    The 2006 Debate and Renewal of the Act

The Voting Rights Act, renewed three times since its initial passage in 1965, was set to expire in 2007. Rather than wait until 2007, the Republican leadership, fearful that it might lose control of one or both chambers in the upcoming election, opted to act immediately. Republican leaders hoped that by renewing Section 5 and claiming credit for doing so they might begin to chip away at the overwhelming levels of minority group support voters were giving Democrats. President Bush and the GOP leadership of both the House and Senate announced their intention of pushing the renewal through before the end of the 109th Congress. Republicans achieved their objectives, as we see in this chapter, but not without overcoming some unanticipated opposition.

## EDWARD BLUM

The spark for much of the unanticipated opposition to a speedy renewal of Section 5 came from outside of Congress. One of the critics, Edward Blum, had been opposing the impact of Section 5 for more than a decade. Blum's opposition took multiple forms and did not end with the renewal of the VRA. To understand Blum's motivations, some background information is helpful.

In 1972, Texas's 18th District, along with Georgia's 5th District, became the first in the South to send African Americans to Congress in the twentieth century. From Houston came state senator Barbara

Jordan with a resonant voice some described as the voice of God. Although only a first-termer, Jordan played an active role in the House hearings that led the Judiciary Committee to return charges impeaching Richard Nixon. Atlanta elected Andrew Young, one of Martin Luther King's chief lieutenants, who served two terms in the House before becoming U.S. ambassador to the United Nations during the Carter presidency and later served two terms as mayor of Atlanta. Both of these urban districts have now had black representatives in Congress for more than four decades.

The redistricting following the 1990 census gave the Texas 18th District a narrow 51 percent black majority. Adding to the diversity, the population included 15 percent Hispanic origin and 3 percent Asian Americans. The 1988 presidential election in the precincts drawn into the 18th District showed it to be solidly Democratic; Michael Dukakis won 70 percent of the vote. The 1992 version of the district was drawn at a time when the Department of Justice had incorporated Section 2 considerations into its Section 5 reviews. DOJ, operating under what became known as a Max Black strategy, demanded that jurisdictions maximize the number of majority-minority districts in order to secure preclearance.

Districts as lopsidedly one-party as the Texas 18th often go uncontested by the minority party. The incumbent, Craig Washington, had avoided a challenge in 1990. But in 1992 a Republican, Edward Blum, came forward to contest the seat. Washington had won a special election to Congress in 1989, capping a career that included seventeen years in the state legislature. In contrast, Blum was a political novice. "I didn't grow up in a political household. I didn't grow up following electoral politics. I didn't understand the districting process," Blum acknowledged.[1] "I had no idea about campaigning. I had never even seen a map or a photo of the district." Although not deeply engaged in politics, Blum had followed Washington's career sufficiently to believe that he could be a more effective representative of the district's interests than the incumbent.

Had Blum studied a map of the new 18th District, he might have never left his comfortable office at Paine Webber. As the Democratically controlled Texas legislature went about redrawing the boundaries of congressional districts in the Houston area, it sought to create a majority Hispanic district adjacent to Washington's African American district. But since the two minority populations lived in close proximity, creating the two districts required a precision akin to that needed to separate Siamese twins. In the new plan, the 18th District almost completely encircled parts of the 60 percent Hispanic 29th District. Separating the two groups while ensuring that each minority constituted a majority of the population in the district drawn for it, the mapmakers went block by block. Majority-black blocks went into the 18th, majority Hispanic blocks went into the 29th, and majority Anglo blocks ended up in the 25th, a majority-white district represented by Michael Andrews (D). The mapping resulted in precincts being split multiple times, and since Texas law prohibits the use of split precincts in elections the number of precincts in Houston had to be increased dramatically.

Armed with a door-to-door walk list, Blum and his wife Lark conducted a shoe leather campaign and knocked on an estimated 20,000 doors.[2] As he sought votes in the brutal Houston sun and humidity, Blum discovered that many of the individuals he hoped to represent did not know that redistricting had placed them in the 18th District. After hearing Blum's introduction, the listener often responded that he or she lived in the 7th District represented by Bill Archer (R)—an accurate statement before the implementation of the new plan. Blum himself struggled to limit his efforts to the 18th District since "it was hopeless to try to follow maps when campaigning in the district." As Blum quickly discovered, one side of the street would be in the 18th but the other side in another district. In the next block both sides of the street might be in the 18th; one block further on and neither side of the street was in the 18th.

Going into the campaign, the incumbent had some weighty baggage. The year before Washington had filed for bankruptcy and owed more than $250,000 in unpaid taxes.[3] He had angered the business community by opposing dollar-rich federal projects slated for Texas and even seemed unpatriotic when he voted against a resolution honoring the troops that had expelled Saddam Hussein from Kuwait in Operation Desert Storm. These factors resulted in Blum securing the endorsement of Houston's two daily newspapers. Despite his lack of experience, Blum managed to tap his wealthy friends for contributions and outraised Washington by $25,000 in a contest in which the combined expenditures for the two campaigns totaled less than $400,000.[4]

The door-to-door campaigning, aggressive fundraising, and endorsements all proved insufficient; Blum lost by a margin of almost two to one. He returned to his career in the Houston investment community.

In the summer of 1993 when the Supreme Court questioned the constitutionality of North Carolina's 12th Congressional District—the long, narrow district that extended from Charlotte northeast to Durham, the often lampooned "I-85 district"—Blum remembered the convoluted shape of the district in which he had campaigned. "I thought the 18th looked at least as bad as North Carolina 12," said the former candidate. Before testing the constitutionality of the Texas district, Blum first had to find an attorney to represent himself and four other plaintiffs. Local attorneys looked at Blum as if he were Don Quixote. An experienced Republican Washington litigator agreed to take the case but wanted a $1 million retainer. Finally Blum came across Paul Hurd, a Mississippi real estate attorney who was challenging Louisiana's "Zorro district" (2nd Congressional), which extended from Shreveport along the state border with Arkansas, then down the entire border with Mississippi before coming through Baton Rouge and on west to Lafayette.[5] Louisiana's Zorro district like North Carolina's I-85 district and three Texas districts took their extraordinary shapes as states sought to secure preclearance from DOJ.

Hurd agreed to take on the case if Blum would pay him $7,000 a month for six months. In addition to paying Hurd, Blum also covered the expenses of the experts who worked in the Texas case that became *Vera v. Richards*, which challenged the constitutionality of three majority-minority districts—the 18th and 29th Districts in Houston and the 30th District in Dallas.[6] He and his wife literally fed the litigation team, bringing them meals as they prepared to do battle with the legions of attorneys and support staff of the Texas attorney general's office and DOJ, which had intervened in the case. Blum had to continue funding the challenge all the way through the Supreme Court. He estimates that he ultimately spent $100,000 on the *Vera* case.[7] After success there, Blum and the attorneys who represented him recovered the bulk of their expenses.

The trial court concluded that the districts in question violated the Equal Protection Clause since they had been drawn primarily on the basis of race. Although the districts certainly were not unconstitutional because of their convoluted shapes, witnesses for the defense failed to convince the court that the design was not the product of an effort to separate voters on the basis of race. By one common measure of compactness, the Polsby-Popper perimeter ratio, the Texas 18th

TABLE 5.1    Majority-minority Texas congressional
districts at the heart of *Bush v. Vera*

| District | | Racial composition (%) | |
|---|---|---|---|
| | | Before *Vera* | After *Vera* |
| 18 | Black | 51 | 45 |
| | Hispanic | 15 | 23 |
| 29 | Black | 10 | 15 |
| | Hispanic | 60 | 45 |
| 30 | Black | 50 | 45 |
| | Hispanic | 17 | 18 |

*Source*: 1990 Census data as reported in the 1994 and 2000 editions
of Michael Barone and Grant Ujifua, *The Almanac of American Politics*
(Washington, D.C.: National Journal).

District was the 433rd least compact and the neighboring 29th District was less compact than any other district in the nation.[8]

The state appealed the decision of the three-judge trial court and the Supreme Court upheld the lower court. The Supreme Court victory resulted in almost half of Texas's thirty congressional districts getting redrawn prior to the 1998 election cycle. As shown in table 5.1, the minority concentrations in each of three districts at the heart of the litigation declined. As initially drawn, two had narrow black majorities and District 29 was 60 percent Hispanic. When redrawn to comply with the Equal Protection Clause, each of the three emerged with 45 percent of its population belonging to the district's predominant ethnic group. Reducing the minority concentrations had no impact on the incumbent members, each of whom continued to represent the district to which she or he was initially elected before *Vera*.[9]

Blum used some of the funds he recovered in *Bush v. Vera* to challenge other districts drawn primarily on the basis of race. He asked political science professor Ronald Weber, who had been the plaintiff's chief expert in *Vera*, to identify other suspect districts. Blum then rounded up the legal talent and covered the tab for challenges to other racial gerrymanders. The Blum team succeeded in forcing new boundaries for Virginia's 3rd District and New York's 12th District, and in South Carolina the state agreed to redraw the 6th District to bring it into compliance with the Supreme Court holdings in *Vera, Shaw v. Reno*, and *Miller v. Johnson*.[10] Blum described his meagerly funded efforts to eliminate racially gerrymandered districts as "much like a junior achievement project."

Blum did not limit efforts to eliminate what he considered to be violations of the Equal Protection Clause to racially gerrymandered legislative districts. The affirmative action hiring policy of the City of Houston also troubled him. After an unsuccessful effort to pass a ballot initiative banning Houston's affirmative action hiring program, which Blum largely funded, he left Paine Webber. He may have been urged to resign by a firm that feared his efforts against affirmative action would alienate some clients.[11] Yet another Blum-initiated effort challenged the admission policy for the Gifted and Talented program run by the Houston Independent School District.

Having ended his career as an investment broker, Blum moved to Washington, D.C., where he became an unpaid visiting fellow at the American Enterprise Institute (AEI). With Section 5 of the Voting Rights Act sunsetted for 2007, Blum launched multiple efforts intended to either bring an end to Section 5 or, failing that, make it applicable nationwide. He created the not-for-profit Project on Fair Representation, began writing a monograph, and secured funding for an academic assessment of the impact of the Act. He hoped that his monograph would be pivotal, that it would persuade Congress to end the coverage of Section 5 or at least seriously reevaluate the trigger mechanism in Section 4.

Blum used his position at AEI to fund a study of the results of VRA enforcement. This study concentrated on the states subject to Section 5 but also compared change and current conditions in Section 5 states with southern states not covered by the preclearance requirement. The study documented the extensive gains in terms of black registration and office holding in southern states covered by Section 5. Moreover, the Section 5 states had demonstrated greater progress than in other southern states not subject to preclearance. Keith Gaddie relied on this research in his testimony before the judiciary committees in both houses of Congress. Much of this research, which AEI released as single-state case studies, ultimately became incorporated into *The Triumph of Voting Rights in the South*.[12]

The Project on Fair Representation, whose only employee is Blum, has become a means of funding recent judicial challenges. Raising contributions from individuals and foundations through Donors' Trust has allowed Blum to put his checkbook away. Even though he has a more reliable source of funding, and the Project has paid out millions of dollars in legal fees,[13] Blum remains a solo performer. Blum, who is not an attorney, identifies likely plaintiffs—just as he did in *Vera*—lines up legal talent, and closely monitors the progress through the labyrinthine legal process.

## 2006 VOTING RIGHTS ACT RENEWAL IN THE HOUSE

Blum hoped that Congress would not simply extend Section 5 coverage or, as some supporters urged, make it permanent. He expressed his dissatisfaction with the Act in his monograph.[14] He expressed some of the concerns that had troubled Abigail Thernstrom when she had reviewed the 1982 extension of the law.[15] Blum charged that "what began in 1965 as a shield to protect the right to vote for blacks in the Deep South, by 1982 had become a sword to create favorable election outcomes for minority office-holders. . . . Simply put: The quest to achieve racially proportional representation resulted in racially gerrymandered voting districts." Continuing his critique, Blum charged, "It is less a law to protect individuals' right to vote and more of a gerrymandering tool to further the electoral prospects of incumbent politicians of all races." Blum summed up his criticism: "Lyndon Johnson's proudest legislative achievement had degenerated into an unworkable, unfair and unconstitutional mandate that is bad for our two political parties, bad for race relations, and bad for our body politic."

Blum demonstrated how both parties used the VRA to challenge districting plans drawn by their opponents with his discussion of Arizona and Texas redistricting battles. This led him to conclude, "The act has been so distorted that it frequently protects, not minority voters in the Deep South, but incumbent officeholders far afield."[16] Richard Pildes agrees with Blum's perspective on what has become of Section 4: "Section 4 long ago in practice became more about racial redistricting than access to the ballot box."[17] Pildes goes on to point out that DOJ has, in recent years, been far more likely to object to new districting plans than to evidence that the minorities have difficulty casting ballots.

Blum's search for political allies proved almost as futile as his quest for Houston voters in 1992. He had two hour-long meetings with President Bush's chief strategist, Karl Rove, in the hopes that the White House might endorse amendments to refocus and update the trigger mechanisms, but President Bush announced his support for renewal. He met with several Republicans on the House Judiciary Committee, although not with Judiciary chair James Sensenbrenner (R-Wis.). He concentrated his efforts on Republicans from Section 5 states. He also met with staffers of Republicans from Georgia and Texas. Blum reported that, although GOP members and staff received him politely, he suspected that they viewed him as a crackpot, and few showed any eagerness in enlisting in his effort to terminate Section 5 coverage. The most positive responses he got came from a pair of Georgia representatives, Lynn Westmoreland and Charlie Norwood.

Leaders of both parties in both chambers had joined hands in early May pledging to renew the VRA quickly. Republicans, who controlled both chambers, opted to take up renewal a year before the 1982 extension would expire, hoping to win over some minority voters. As a step toward expeditious enactment, the House leadership planned to pass the 2006 Voting Rights Act under suspension of the rules, an approach used for noncontroversial legislation. The GOP House leadership, including majority leader Eric Cantor (Va.), who came from a Section 5 state, wanted to avoid anything that threatened the renewal. The leadership threw its support behind a bill worked out by Sensenbrenner and Mel Watt (D-N.C.). For Sensenbrenner renewal of the VRA took on something of a moral crusade. The Wisconsin representative was proud of his role in the 1982 renewal, and on the wall of his office he has framed what he describes as one of his most cherished keepsakes: one of the pens that President Reagan had used in signing that legislation.

During the 2006 congressional debate on the renewal of Section 5, all sides praised the success of this legislation. Democrats and Republican, liberals and conservatives, those who wanted to see the provision extended without change as well as those who backed amendments—all pointed with pride to the advances in African American political strength since the mid-1960s. One of the most powerful statements came from Rep. Melvin Watt (D-N.C.), one of the first two African American members of Congress from the Tar Heel State since 1901. Watt's district, the 12th Congressional District, had been the source of significant litigation in *Shaw v. Reno* and in three subsequent cases heard by the Supreme Court. Both the district and Watt endured, although the district underwent two changes in efforts to meet constitutional requirements. Speaking in support of the renewal of the Act, Watt observed:

> There are those who argue that the Voting Rights Act has out-lived its usefulness, that it is outdated, and that it unfairly punishes covered jurisdictions for past sins. Yet I stand here as living proof of both the effectiveness of and continuing need for the Voting Rights Act. . . . When George White said his temporary farewell [in 1901], he likely did not think it would be so long. . . . Although the successes of the Voting Rights Act have been substantial, they have not been fast and furious. Rather, the successes have been gradual and of recent origin.[18]

House Judiciary Committee chair Sensenbrenner echoed Watt's conclusion that, black progress notwithstanding, preclearance needed to be maintained in the renewed VRA. The Wisconsin Republican summed up the findings of the Judiciary Committee in an address to the House:

> The extensive record of continued abuse compiled by the Com-mittee over the last year echoes that which preceded congres-sional reauthorization of the VRA in 1982, and which led me to make the following observation during the Committee's consideration of VRA reauthorization legislation then: "Testimony is quite clear that this Act . . . has been the most successful civil rights act that has ever been passed by the Congress of the United States. . . . The overwhelming preponderance of the testimony was that the Voting Rights Act has worked. It has provided the franchise to numerous people who were denied the right to vote for one reason or another. It has provided a dra-matic increase in the number of minority elected officials in covered jurisdictions. I think that very clearly demonstrates the need for an extension. . . . The hearings also very clearly showed that the creativity of the human mind is unlimited when it comes to proposing election law changes that are designed to prevent people from voting.[19]

The effectiveness of Section 5 was praised on all sides. But the meaning of the success was subject to different interpretations. After noting the numbers of minorities who had been elected to Congress,

Rep. Nancy Pelosi (D-Calif.) warned against efforts to limit the length of the extension of Section 5 to a decade: "Make no mistake, the ten-year limitation on key VRA provisions seriously undermines its effectiveness." Pelosi, soon to become Speaker of the House, observed that, "within months of the Voting Rights Act's passage, a quarter of a million new African American voters had been registered. A quarter of a million new voices that had been silenced could finally be heard. They, along with millions to follow, changed the world with a vision of justice, equality, and opportunity for all."[20] Democrats and civil rights leaders pointed to past accomplishments as a basis for arguing that Congress dare not modify the current requirements. Speakers in this camp warned that modification of Section 5 would open the door to backsliding on the part of the covered jurisdictions.

In contrast, legislators who wished to shorten the proposed renewal period from twenty-five years down to a decade or to update the triggers that relied on electoral data from the 1960s and 1970s used the success already achieved as a launching pad for arguing that modifications were appropriate to reward those jurisdictions that had fully complied with the statue. For example, Rep. Lynn Westmoreland (R-Ga.) said on the House floor:

> It is true when the Voting Rights Act was first passed in 1965 Georgia needed Federal intervention to correct decades of discrimination. Now, 41 years later, Georgia's record on voter equality can stand up against any other State in the Union. Today black Georgians are registered to vote at higher percentages than white Georgians, and black Georgians go to the polls in higher percentages than white Georgians. One-third of our state-wide elected officials are African Americans, including our Attorney General and the Chief Justice of our Supreme Court. Plus, African American representation in the State legislature closely mirrors their representation in Georgia's population.[21]

Many congressional Republicans supported renewing preclearance because of anticipated benefits for their party. They believed that the obligations imposed on most of the South by the nonretrogression standard, which requires that minority concentrations in already safely Democratic districts be maintained and even ratcheted up during the course of redistricting, played a key role in enabling

the GOP to retain its overwhelming share of the region's congressional seats.[22] The creation of majority-minority districts usually
requires the bleaching of neighboring districts, which enhances
GOP prospects in those districts; thus, Republicans had no quarrel
with maximizing the numbers of minority districts.

Republicans see few downsides in a world in which Democratic districts elect African Americans while majority-white districts
elect Republicans. Seeking to ensure the maintenance of minority
concentrations, Republicans supported one of the few changes made
to the VRA in 2006. Congress overturned *Georgia v. Ashcroft*, in
which the Supreme Court had ruled that jurisdictions could secure
preclearance of redistricting plans that violated the *Beer* decision,
which had established nonretrogression as the basis for approval.[23]
In *Ashcroft* the Court had accepted a strategy embraced by black
and white Georgia Democrats that reduced African American concentrations in several majority-black Senate districts in order to
bolster Democratic prospects in adjoining districts. By allowing
redistribution of black voters and thereby reducing their concentrations in selected districts, *Ashcroft* might permit white Democrats to win districts that if more thoroughly bleached would have
elected Republicans.

Republican leaders and many rank-and-file members offered
reasons other than selfish, partisan gain for reenacting Sections 4
and 5 with no changes. Some of those who opposed updating the
triggers warned that modifying the legislation might result in dis-
franchising some minorities. Because of the historical significance
of the VRA and the heavy symbolism of the 2006 proposal—the
official title of the legislation is the Fannie Lou Hamer, Rosa Parks, and
Coretta Scott King Voting Rights Act—supporting renewal gave
Republicans a free vote to demonstrate that they were not racists.
Opponents of changing the law pointed out that the existing triggers
had been upheld multiple times by the courts. Supporters of renewal
without change warned that modifications might make the statute
vulnerable to a finding of unconstitutionality.

Although Tea Party rambunctiousness was still a half-decade in
the future, a rebellion worthy of the Tea Party erupted, much to the
consternation of the GOP House leadership. In keeping with the
problems that Speaker Newt Gingrich had encountered in the mid-
1990s and would plague Speaker John Boehner in the 2010s, refusal
to go along with the leadership playbook on VRA renewal came

from junior members. The most visible "rebel," Georgia freshman Lynn Westmoreland, offered one of the amendments. Sponsors of other amendments included Louie Gohmert, a freshman who owed his seat to the mid-decade redistricting of Texas engineered by Tom DeLay. The most popular amendment came from Iowa sophomore Steve King. The most senior of the amendment authors was Georgia's Charlie Norwood, who was in his sixth term. Gohmert was the least senior Republican on the Judiciary Committee, and King was only fourth from the bottom on the committee's seniority list. Neither Norwood nor Westmoreland had a law degree or served on the Judiciary Committee.[24]

Although new to Congress, the fifty-six-year-old Westmoreland had spent a dozen years in the Georgia House, where he had risen to become his party's leader. In that capacity, he had extensive experience working on redistricting plans. During the most recent redistricting he had watched helplessly as Georgia Democrats devised a fiendishly partisan gerrymander that resulted in Republicans losing seats even as they took 52 percent of the statewide vote for state house members in 2002. And though Westmoreland did not get to the Georgia house until 1993, he remembered the congressional district that DOJ had forced Georgia to draw that extended from metro Atlanta through Augusta all the way to Savannah. The Supreme Court invalidated this district in *Miller v. Georgia*. These concerns coupled with a belief that the requirement to secure federal approval was "insulting to Georgia" prompted Westmorland to meet with Speaker Dennis Hastert and Sensenbrenner in an effort to have the VRA scheduled for debate rather than considered under suspension of the rules. Unlike Blum, Westmoreland had no expectations of winning in Congress. He played out what he knew to be a losing hand in order to make a record that contained the kind of information that could be drawn upon in a judicial challenge to Section 5.[25] In public, however, Westmoreland explained his actions using a different rationale: "A lot of it looks as if these are some old boys from the South who are trying to do away with it [the VRA]. But these old boys are trying to make it constitutional enough that it will withstand the scrutiny of the Supreme Court."[26]

In an effort to get his fellow Republicans involved in modifying extensions of Sections 4 and 5, Westmoreland sent out multiple "dear colleague" letters outlining what he saw as potential constitutional issues. Among the concerns he raised was the *City of Boerne v. Flores* decision which, in a different substantive context, had noted that remedies under the Fourteenth Amendment must be proportional to the injury.[27] A seminar for interested legislators and staff focused on the implications of *Boerne* for the VRA, with two seasoned litigators who usually represented Republican interests in voting rights cases present to lead the discussion.

Politics, as has long been recognized, can make for strange bedfellows, and so it was with Westmoreland. One of his allies was Loyola University law professor Richard Hasen, who opposed most everything that Westmoreland stood for. Nonetheless Hasen shared Westmoreland's concern about extending the triggers without modification. Whereas Westmoreland wanted to kill the Act, Hasen wanted to protect it, and toward that end he predicted that if Congress made no changes in the generations-old triggers the Supreme Court would invalidate the legislation. In testimony before the Senate Judiciary Committee, Professor Hasen warned that "Congress has limited power to enact civil rights laws regulating the states."[28] Citing the *City of Boerne* decision, Hasen pointed out that "Congress must produce a strong evidentiary record of intentional state discrimination to justify laws that burden the states. In addition, whatever burden is placed on the states must be congruent and proportional to the extent of the violations." To build his case that a trigger mechanism geared more toward contemporary voting problems needed to be developed, Hasen presented data on the infrequency with which DOJ had denied preclearance. By his count, only 0.05 percent of the submissions received between 1998 and 2002 had failed to secure DOJ approval.

Not only did Hasen join Westmoreland's band in advocating new triggers, the professor also supported the amendment calling for proactive bailout. Because so few districts had availed themselves of the bailout as designed in the 1982 legislation, Hasen reasoned that Congress had set the bar too high and the process was too expensive. Returning to the congruent and proportional argument, Hasen proposed extending Section 5 for seven to ten years rather than the quarter-century that Congress approved. He also warned that reversing *Ashcroft* could contribute to making the renewal suspect, since the alternative to nonretrogression offered Georgia made it easier for jurisdictions to secure preclearance.

Samuel Issacharoff, coauthor of a leading text on voting rights law and a litigator who brought suits under Section 2 before entering academia, also voiced concerns about renewing Section 4 without modification. He stressed that the objective of his testimony before the Senate Judiciary Committee was to make the VRA "more effective in addressing the voting issues that are within its scope, but also [to make it] more likely to withstand constitutional challenge."[29] The voting rights scholar cited *City of Boerne* and speculated that "it is far from clear that the injustices that justified Section 5 in 1965 can justify its unqualified reenactment today." He reminded the committee that in the initial challenge to the VRA, in 1966, the Supreme Court had acknowledged the unprecedented nature of the preclearance provision but had upheld it in light of the extraordinary conditions that it sought to correct. Chief Justice Warren wrote, "This may have been an uncommon exercise of congressional power, as South Carolina contends, but the Court has recognized that exceptional conditions can justify legislative measures not otherwise appropriate."[30] Continuing to require preclearance through 2032 based on election data from 1964 "risks appearing constitutionally antiquated," warned the professor. Though accepting that backsliding might occur, Issacharoff pointed out that current concerns often focused on felon disfranchisement and intimidation and that Section 5 did not address these abuses. He calculated that only six of forty-six DOJ objections since 1997 had dealt with minority ballot access. Increasingly, Issacharoff noted, the VRA was being used by those who lost redistricting tilts in the legislature to challenge plans that favored the other political party. As a corrective he recommended exempting redistricting plans from preclearance.

Issacharoff joined Hasen in calling for an easier path for jurisdictions with unblemished records to bail out. He proposed allowing jurisdictions that had not had a Section 5 objection or lost a Section 2 challenge in more than five years to move to what he termed "an intermediate regulatory status" in which they would post the same material required to secure preclearance on a website. He also suggested modernizing the Section 4 trigger to require preclearance by jurisdictions that had lost a Section 2 challenge or had harassed minority voters during the previous five years.

The deck of testimony was decidedly stacked toward a blanket renewal in the House. Nathaniel Persily of the University of Pennsylvania observed that, of forty-six witnesses called before the House Judiciary Committee Subcommittee on the Constitution, only three advocated revising the Act.[31] On the Senate side, however, Persily noted a more balanced evidentiary record, though the Senate accepted the blanket renewal of the Act approved by the House of Representatives in July.

The leadership removed the legislation from the suspension calendar, put it back on that calendar, but ultimately, after a month of negotiations, agreed to bring the bill to the floor and allow a debate. Westmoreland and his allies wanted more than the opportunity for a full debate on renewal, which suspension of the rules would have precluded. They wanted an open rule that would allow unlimited amendments. Opponents of extending Section 5 failed to get an open rule, and only after a prolonged struggle did the Rules Committee, which is controlled by the majority party leadership, grant a structured rule under which Westmoreland's team could offer four specific amendments.

## AMENDMENT ACTIVITY IN THE HOUSE

As in 1982, the 2006 statute did not introduce a new trigger mechanism. During the House debate, Rep. Charlie Norwood (R-Ga.) offered House Amendment 1183, which would have updated the triggers. Norwood's amendment followed the path blazed by witnesses before the Senate Judiciary Committee such as Hasen and Issacharoff. He argued that election data from 1964, 1968, or 1972 did not accurately reflect the participation opportunities for African Americans in the twenty-first century and would be even less reflective of race relations in 2031, at the end of the 2006 renewal. Norwood and his supporters noted that the election returns of jurisdictions caught by the Section 4 triggers of the 1965 Voting Rights Act would be sixty-six years old in 2030, when very few people who had voted at the time of the initial statute would be alive.

The frustration felt by political leaders from jurisdictions long subject to Section 5 who believed that the sins of the past had been overcome is captured in a bit of hyperbole from Lynn Westmoreland. In a piece published in *The Hill*, Westmoreland speculated, "If Georgia's sins can never be forgiven, shouldn't there be an Accused Witch Protection Act that applies only to Massachusetts? Shouldn't our foreign policy treat South Africa as if it's still governed by a racist apartheid regime?"[32] Rather than continue relying on aging election data, Norwood proposed a dynamic trigger that would cover any jurisdiction in which less than half of the voting age citizens had voted in any of the three most recent presidential elections.

Legislators from states not subject to Section 5 had no dog in the fight, showed little interest in the arguments offered by the worried law professors or representatives from covered states, and saw no reason to take a stand against the civil rights community that carried the risk of being labeled racist. Although legislators from states having no obligation to secure preclearance saw the requirement as imposing only a minimal burden, they opposed the Norwood amendment since it might extended coverage to some jurisdictions in their state. Under the Norwood amendment, Hawaii would have been the only state in 2006 wholly subject to preclearance. Both members of Hawaii's House delegation were quick to register objections to the proposed change.[33]

The Norwood amendment failed on a roll call vote, 96–318 with 18 abstentions. With one exception, only Republicans voted for the amendment. Supporters of Norwood's effort to update the trigger came disproportionately from jurisdictions required to seek preclearance. We examine three measures of the extent to which preclearance impacted the legislators' constituency (table 5.2). Potentially least intrusive is the situation in which some or all of the *state* from which the representative came was caught by one of the triggers in Section 4. A second and more intrusive level includes legislators who represented *districts* at least portions of which had to secure Section 5 preclearance as of 2006. The third level is limited to Republicans from districts that experienced preclearance since the adoption the initial trigger in 1965. As shown in the table, Republicans from Level 1 districts split on the Norwood amendment, with 55 percent approving of the effort at modernization. Republicans from Level 2 districts displayed greater unity, with 69 percent supporting its adoption. Legislators from districts that had experienced preclearance for four decades were the most likely to back Norwood (73 percent support); they were joined by one Democrat, Gene Taylor from Mississippi. In contrast with legislators whose districts had to deal with preclearance, only 28 percent of Republicans from states in which no district had ever had to seek preclearance backed the amendment. The hesitancy of these legislators to support Norwood's efforts undoubtedly had something to do with a fear that one or more of the counties they represented might at some point in the future have to seek preclearance for a twelve-year stretch.

TABLE 5.2     Republican vote on the Norwood amendment,
by degree of Section 5 coverage

**Level 1:**
State at least partially covered by Section 5

| Vote | Yes | No | |
|------|-----|-----|---|
| Aye | 66 | 29 | |
| Nay | 54 | 75 | Chi square = 16.77; Gamma = .519 |

**Level 2:**
Legislator's district at least partially covered by Section 5

| Vote | Yes | No | |
|------|-----|-----|---|
| Aye | 54 | 41 | |
| Nay | 24 | 105 | Chi square = 35.25; Gamma = .704 |

**Level 3:**
Legislator's district subject to Section 5 since 1965

| Vote | Yes | No | |
|------|-----|-----|---|
| Aye | 27 | 68 | |
| Nay | 10 | 117 | Chi Square = 16.52; Gamma = .646 |

House Amendment 1184, proposed by Rep. Louie Gohmert, would have shortened the reauthorization period of the Act to ten years as Richard Hasen had suggested, instead of the twenty-five-year renewal in Sensenbrenner's bill. The amendment failed by a vote of 134–288, with 132 Republicans voting "Aye." Unlike the Norwood amendment, which failed to attract most Republicans, 58.7 percent of the Republicans who participated supported the Gohmert amendment. Republicans from Section 5 states (Level 1) favored Gohmert by more than two to one; other Republicans narrowly opposed the amendment. Table 5.3 reports that legislators from Level 2 districts in which preclearance was required voted for the amendment by more than four to one. Of the thirty-seven legislators from states initially covered by Section 5, all but eight supported the amendment; they were joined by one Democrat each from Georgia and Mississippi. The share of Republicans from Level 3 districts was no more likely to vote for it than were legislators in Level 2. As with Norwood's amendment, Gohmert's received the least enthusiastic reaction from legislators whose states had never been covered by Section 5. A slight majority of these legislators opposed the amendment.

TABLE 5.3     Republican vote on the Gohmert amendment,
by degree of Section 5 coverage

**Level 1:**
State at least partially covered by Section 5

| Vote | Yes | No | |
|------|-----|-----|---|
| Aye | 82 | 50 | |
| Nay | 39 | 54 | Chi square = 8.94; Gamma = .389 |

**Level 2:**
Legislator's district at least partially covered by Section 5

| Vote | Yes | No | |
|------|-----|-----|---|
| Aye | 63 | 69 | |
| Nay | 15 | 78 | Chi square = 24.05; Gamma = ..652 |

**Level 3:**
Legislator's district subject to Section 5 since 1965

| Vote | Yes | No | |
|------|-----|-----|---|
| Aye | 29 | 103 | |
| Nay | 8 | 85 | Chi Square = 7.10; Gamma = .499 |

House Amendment 1185, proposed by Rep. Steve King, would have stricken the minority ballot language provisions of Section 203c from the VRA. The 1975 amendments to the Act created Section 203, which provided that in jurisdictions where at least 5 percent of the voting age population or 10,000 persons of voting age spoke one of several languages other than English (including Spanish, Native American tongues, and a variety of East Asian and Pacific Island languages), voting materials and assistance had to be provided in those languages. The King amendment proved the most popular, but it failed on a vote of 185–238, with support from 181 Republicans and four Democrats. King's amendment was the only one to receive majority support from Republicans whose states had never been covered by Section 5, with almost three-fourths of these individuals voting for the amendment. Supporters included 78 percent of Republican lawmakers from Section 5 states. With 80 percent of all Republicans voting for the amendment, there is less variation depending on the Level of Section 5 coverage. Level 1 legislators gave 87 percent support, as did 90 percent of the Republicans from Level 2 districts. All thirty-seven Republicans from the original

Section 5 states backed the amendment except Tom Davis (R-Va.); they were joined by two Democrats from these states.

House Amendment 1186, offered by Rep. Lynn Westmoreland, called for an expedited bailout from coverage under the preclearance portions of the VRA. The amendment would have produced a great deal of work for DOJ, since it would provide for an expedited, pro-active procedure to bail out from coverage under the preclearance portions of the Act by requiring DOJ to assemble a list of all juris-dictions eligible for bailout and to notify the jurisdictions. DOJ would then be required to consent to the entry of a declaratory judgment allowing bailout if a jurisdiction appeared on the list. It would also set a three-year initial time period (and annually thereafter) for assembly of the bailout list by DOJ.

The amendment failed on a 118–302 vote, with 117 Republi-cans supporting it—52 percent of Republican lawmakers who parti-cipated on the roll call. As reported in table 5.4, thirty of the thirty-seven Republicans from the states originally covered by Section 5 (30 percent) supported Westmoreland's amendment. They were joined by Mississippi's Democrat Gene Taylor, the only Democrat who voted for all four amendments. Support increased along with Section 5 experience. Only 43 percent of Republicans whose districts had never been subject to Section 5 supported the amendment. Of legislators from Level 1 districts, 60 percent backed the Westmore-land amendment, as did 77 percent of Republicans in Level 2 districts.

Overall, 195 lawmakers voted for at least one of these amend-ments. Data for all four roll call votes appear in table 5.5. Only five Democrats voted for even one amendment. In addition to Taylor, two were from Georgia and one each from Minnesota and Pennsylvania. The lack of Democratic support is hardly surprising since that party's leadership had vowed to defeat renewal if any of the proposed amend-ments were attached.[34] Table 5.6 shows the number of amendments supported by Republicans depending on the extent of Section 5 coverage they experienced. The 104 Republicans with no experience with preclearance generally did not support the amendments, with 23 percent of these legislators opposing all of them and another 28 percent supporting only one, usually the King amendment. Only a quarter of the legislators not from Section 5 backed all four amend-ments. Fewer than one in ten legislators representing areas that had some experience with preclearance opposed all the amendments.

TABLE 5.4     Republican vote on the Westmoreland amendment,
by degree of Section 5 coverage

**Level 1:**
State at least partially covered by Section 5

| Vote | Yes | No | |
|------|-----|-----|------|
| Aye | 73 | 44 | |
| Nay | 48 | 59 | Chi square = 6.92; Gamma = .342 |

**Level 2:**
Legislator's district at least partially covered by Section 5

| Vote | Yes | No | |
|------|-----|-----|------|
| Aye | 60 | 57 | |
| Nay | 18 | 89 | Chi square = 29.24; Gamma = .678 |

**Level 3:**
Legislator's district subject to Section 5 since 1965

| Vote | Yes | No | |
|------|-----|-----|------|
| Aye | 30 | 87 | |
| Nay | 7 | 100 | Chi Square = 14.78; Gamma = .663 |

The proportion of legislators voting for all the amendments increased with the degree of Section 5 impact, with almost three quarters of the representatives whose districts had dealt with DOJ preclearance since 1965 favoring all amendments. With two Georgians taking the lead in seeking to modify the legislative proposal, it may not be surprising that the Georgia Republican delegation voted for all of the amendments. At the other end of the scale, Virginia's Tom Davis was the only Republican from a Level 3 state who opposed all of the amendments, although the Virginia Republican delegation generally was less supportive of the amendments than the delegations of the other Level 3 states. More than 60 percent of legislators representing districts from states covered in whole or in part by Section 5 (Level 2) backed all amendments. Legislators from states subject to Section 5 but whose districts did not include areas that had to seek preclearance had voting records much like those of Republicans whose states did not need preclearance. As the third column in table 5.6 shows, 56 percent of Republicans representing districts not covered by Section 5, although part of their state was,

TABLE 5.5   Who voted to amend the Voting Rights Act in 2006?

| Lawmaker | State | Amd. 1183 | Amd. 1184 | Amd. 1185 | Amd. 1186 | Amendments supported | Vote on final passage |
|---|---|---|---|---|---|---|---|
| Aderholt | AL | Aye | Aye | Aye | Aye | 4 | |
| Akin | MO | Aye | Aye | Aye | Aye | 4 | |
| Alexander | LA | Aye | Aye | Aye | Aye | 4 | |
| Bachus | AL | | Aye | Aye | Aye | 3 | |
| Baker | LA | Aye | Aye | Aye | Aye | 4 | Nay |
| Barrett | SC | Aye | Aye | Aye | Aye | 4 | Nay |
| *Barrow* | GA | | | Aye | | 1 | |
| Bartlett | MD | Aye | Aye | Aye | Aye | 4 | Nay |
| Barton | TX | Aye | Aye | Aye | Aye | 4 | Nay |
| Bass | NH | Aye | Aye | Aye | | 3 | |
| Beauprez | CO | | Aye | Aye | Aye | 3 | |
| Bilbray | CA | | | Aye | Aye | 2 | |
| Bilirakis | FL | | Aye | Aye | Aye | 3 | |
| Bishop | UT | Aye | Aye | Aye | Aye | 4 | |
| Blackburn | TN | | Aye | Aye | Aye | 3 | |
| Blunt | MO | Aye | Aye | Aye | Aye | 4 | |
| Bonilla | TX | Aye | Aye | Aye | Aye | 4 | |
| Bonner | AL | Aye | Aye | Aye | Aye | 4 | Nay |
| Boozman | AR | | Aye | Aye | | 2 | |
| Boustany | LA | | | Aye | | 1 | |
| Bradley | NH | Aye | Aye | Aye | | 3 | |
| Brady | TX | Aye | Aye | Aye | Aye | 4 | |
| Brown | SC | Aye | Aye | Aye | Aye | 4 | |
| Brown-Waite | FL | Aye | Aye | Aye | Aye | 4 | |
| Burgess | TX | | Aye | Aye | | 2 | |
| Burton | IN | Aye | Aye | Aye | Aye | 4 | Nay |
| Buyer | IN | | | Aye | | 1 | |
| Calvert | CA | | Aye | Aye | | 2 | |
| Camp | MI | | | Aye | | 1 | |
| Campbell | CA | Aye | Aye | Aye | Aye | 4 | Nay |
| Cannon | UT | | | | Aye | 1 | |
| Cantor | VA | Aye | Aye | Aye | Aye | 4 | |
| Capito | WV | | | Aye | | 1 | |
| Carter | TX | | Aye | Aye | Aye | 3 | |
| Chocola | IN | | Aye | Aye | Aye | 3 | |
| Coble | NC | Aye | Aye | Aye | Aye | 4 | |
| Cole | OK | Aye | Aye | Aye | Aye | 4 | |
| Conaway | TX | Aye | Aye | Aye | Aye | 4 | Nay |
| Crenshaw | FL | Aye | Aye | Aye | | 3 | |
| Cubin | WY | | Aye | Aye | Aye | 3 | |
| Culberson | TX | Aye | Aye | Aye | Aye | 4 | |
| Davis | KY | | | Aye | | 1 | |
| Deal | GA | Aye | Aye | Aye | Aye | 4 | Nay |

TABLE 5.5   Who voted to amend the Voting Rights Act in 2006? (*continued*)

| Lawmaker | State | Amd. 1183 | Amd. 1184 | Amd. 1185 | Amd. 1186 | Amendments supported | Vote on final passage |
|----------|-------|-----------|-----------|-----------|-----------|----------------------|-----------------------|
| Doolittle | CA | Aye | Aye | Aye | Aye | 4 | Nay |
| Drake | VA | | | Aye | | 1 | |
| Dreier | CA | | | Aye | | 1 | |
| Duncan | TN | Aye | Aye | Aye | Aye | 4 | Nay |
| Ehlers | MI | | Aye | | | 1 | |
| Emerson | MO | | | Aye | | 1 | |
| Everett | AL | Aye | Aye | Aye | Aye | 4 | Nay |
| Feeney | FL | | Aye | Aye | | 2 | |
| Flake | AZ | Aye | Aye | | Aye | 3 | |
| Forbes | VA | | | Aye | | 1 | |
| Fortenberry | NE | Aye | Aye | Aye | Aye | 4 | |
| Fossella | NY | | | Aye | | 1 | |
| Foxx | NC | Aye | Aye | Aye | Aye | 4 | Nay |
| Franks | AZ | Aye | Aye | Aye | Aye | 4 | Nay |
| Gallegly | CA | | | Aye | | 1 | |
| Garrett | NJ | Aye | Aye | Aye | Aye | 4 | Nay |
| Gibbons | NV | | Aye | Aye | Aye | 3 | |
| Gillmor | OH | | Aye | Aye | | 2 | |
| Gingrey | GA | Aye | Aye | Aye | Aye | 4 | Nay |
| Gohmert | TX | Aye | Aye | Aye | Aye | 4 | |
| Goode | VA | Aye | Aye | Aye | Aye | 4 | |
| Goodlatte | VA | Aye | Aye | Aye | Aye | 4 | |
| Granger | TX | Aye | Aye | Aye | Aye | 4 | |
| Gutknecht | MN | Aye | Aye | Aye | Aye | 4 | |
| Hall | TX | Aye | Aye | Aye | Aye | 4 | |
| Harris | FL | | | Aye | | 1 | |
| Hart | PA | | Aye | Aye | Aye | 3 | |
| Hastings | WA | Aye | Aye | Aye | Aye | 4 | |
| Hayes | NC | | | Aye | | 1 | |
| Hayworth | AZ | Aye | Aye | Aye | Aye | 4 | |
| Hefley | CO | Aye | Aye | Aye | Aye | 4 | Nay |
| Hensarling | TX | Aye | Aye | Aye | Aye | 4 | Nay |
| Herger | CA | | Aye | Aye | Aye | 3 | Nay |
| Hobson | OH | | | Aye | | 1 | |
| Hoekstra | MI | Aye | Aye | Aye | Aye | 4 | |
| *Holden* | PA | | | Aye | | 1 | |
| Hostettler | IN | Aye | Aye | Aye | Aye | 4 | |
| Hulshof | MO | | | Aye | | 1 | |
| Hunter | CA | | | Aye | | 1 | |
| Hyde | IL | Aye | | Aye | | 2 | |
| Inglis | SC | | | Aye | | 1 | |
| Issa | CA | | | Aye | | 1 | |
| Istook | OK | Aye | Aye | Aye | Aye | 4 | |

TABLE 5.5 Who voted to amend the Voting Rights Act in 2006? (*continued*)

| Lawmaker | State | Amd. 1183 | Amd. 1184 | Amd. 1185 | Amd. 1186 | Amendments supported | Vote on final passage |
|---|---|---|---|---|---|---|---|
| Jenkins | TN | Aye | Aye | Aye | Aye | 4 | |
| Jindal | **LA** | Aye | Aye | Aye | Aye | 4 | |
| Johnson | CT | | | Aye | | 1 | |
| Johnson | IL | | | Aye | | 1 | |
| Johnson, Sam | **TX** | Aye | Aye | Aye | Aye | 4 | Nay |
| Jones | NC | Aye | Aye | Aye | Aye | 4 | |
| Keller | **FL** | Aye | Aye | Aye | Aye | 4 | |
| Kelly | **NY** | | | Aye | | 1 | |
| Kennedy | MN | | | Aye | | 1 | |
| King | IA | Aye | Aye | Aye | Aye | 4 | Nay |
| King | **NY** | | | Aye | | 1 | |
| Kingston | **GA** | Aye | Aye | Aye | Aye | 4 | |
| Kline | MN | Aye | Aye | Aye | Aye | 4 | |
| Knollenberg | **MI** | | | Aye | | 1 | |
| Kolbe | **AZ** | Aye | Aye | | Aye | 3 | |
| Kuhl | **NY** | | | Aye | | 1 | |
| LaHood | IL | | | Aye | | 1 | |
| Latham | IA | | | Aye | | 1 | |
| LaTourette | OH | | | Aye | | 1 | |
| Lewis | KY | | Aye | Aye | | 2 | |
| Linder | **GA** | Aye | Aye | Aye | Aye | 4 | Nay |
| Lucas | OK | Aye | Aye | Aye | Aye | 4 | |
| Lungren, Daniel E. | **CA** | | Aye | Aye | Aye | 3 | |
| Mack | **FL** | Aye | Aye | Aye | Aye | 4 | |
| Manzullo | IL | Aye | Aye | Aye | Aye | 4 | |
| Marchant | **TX** | Aye | Aye | Aye | Aye | 4 | |
| *Marshall* | **GA** | | Aye | | | 1 | |
| McCaul | **TX** | Aye | Aye | Aye | Aye | 4 | |
| McCotter | **MI** | | | Aye | | 1 | |
| McCrery | LA | | | Aye | Aye | 2 | |
| McHenry | **NC** | Aye | Aye | Aye | Aye | 4 | Nay |
| McHugh | **NY** | | | Aye | | 1 | |
| McKeon | **CA** | Aye | Aye | Aye | Aye | 4 | |
| McMorris | WA | | Aye | Aye | Aye | 3 | |
| Mica | **FL** | | Aye | Aye | Aye | 3 | |
| Miller | **FL** | | Aye | Aye | | 2 | |
| Miller | **MI** | | | Aye | | 1 | |
| Miller, Gary | **CA** | Aye | Aye | Aye | Aye | 4 | Nay |
| Moran | KS | | | Aye | | 1 | |
| Murphy | PA | | Aye | Aye | | 2 | |
| Musgrave | CO | Aye | Aye | Aye | Aye | 4 | |
| Myrick | **NC** | Aye | Aye | Aye | Aye | 4 | |

TABLE 5.5  Who voted to amend the Voting Rights Act in 2006? (*continued*)

| Lawmaker | State | Amd. 1183 | Amd. 1184 | Amd. 1185 | Amd. 1186 | Amendments supported | Vote on final passage |
|---|---|---|---|---|---|---|---|
| Neugebauer | **TX** | Aye | Aye | Aye | Aye | 4 | |
| Ney | OH | | | Aye | | 1 | |
| Norwood | **GA** | Aye | Aye | Aye | Aye | 4 | Nay |
| Nunes | **CA** | | | Aye | Aye | 2 | |
| Nussle | IA | | | Aye | | 1 | |
| Otter | ID | | Aye | Aye | Aye | 3 | |
| Oxley | OH | | Aye | Aye | | 2 | |
| Paul | **TX** | Aye | Aye | Aye | Aye | 4 | Nay |
| Pearce | NM | | Aye | | Aye | 2 | |
| Pence | IN | | Aye | | Aye | 2 | |
| *Peterson* | MN | | | Aye | | 1 | |
| Peterson | PA | | Aye | Aye | Aye | 3 | |
| Petri | WI | | | Aye | | 1 | |
| Pickering | **MS** | Aye | Aye | Aye | Aye | 4 | |
| Pitts | PA | Aye | Aye | Aye | Aye | 4 | |
| Platts | PA | | | Aye | | 1 | |
| Poe | **TX** | Aye | Aye | Aye | Aye | 4 | |
| Pombo | **CA** | | | Aye | | 1 | |
| Porter | NV | | | Aye | | 1 | |
| Price | **GA** | Aye | Aye | Aye | Aye | 4 | Nay |
| Pryce | OH | | | Aye | | 1 | |
| Putnam | **FL** | Aye | Aye | Aye | Aye | 4 | |
| Radanovich | **CA** | Aye | Aye | Aye | | 3 | |
| Regula | **CA** | | | Aye | | 1 | |
| Rehberg | MT | | Aye | Aye | Aye | 3 | |
| Reynolds | **NY** | | | Aye | | 1 | |
| Rogers | **AL** | | Aye | Aye | Aye | 3 | |
| Rogers | KY | | Aye | Aye | Aye | 3 | |
| Rogers | **MI** | | | Aye | | 1 | |
| Rohrabacher | **CA** | Aye | Aye | Aye | Aye | 4 | Nay |
| Royce | **CA** | Aye | Aye | Aye | Aye | 4 | Nay |
| Ryan | WI | | | Aye | | 1 | |
| Ryun | KS | Aye | Aye | Aye | Aye | 4 | |
| Schmidt | OH | | | Aye | | 1 | |
| Shadegg | **AZ** | Aye | Aye | | Aye | 3 | |
| Shaw | **FL** | | Aye | | | 1 | |
| Sherwood | PA | | Aye | Aye | | 2 | |
| Shimkus | IL | Aye | Aye | Aye | Aye | 4 | |
| Shuster | PA | Aye | Aye | Aye | Aye | 4 | |
| Simpson | ID | | Aye | Aye | Aye | 3 | |
| Smith | **TX** | Aye | Aye | Aye | Aye | 4 | |
| Sodrel | IN | | Aye | Aye | Aye | 3 | |
| Souder | IN | | Aye | Aye | | 2 | |

TABLE 5.5    Who voted to amend the Voting Rights Act in 2006? (*continued*)

| Lawmaker | State | Amd. 1183 | Amd. 1184 | Amd. 1185 | Amd. 1186 | Amendments supported | Vote on final passage |
|---|---|---|---|---|---|---|---|
| Stearns | **FL** | Aye | Aye | Aye | Aye | 4 | |
| Sullivan | OK | | Aye | Aye | Aye | 3 | |
| Sweeney | **NY** | | | Aye | | 1 | |
| Tancredo | CO | Aye | Aye | Aye | Aye | 4 | Nay |
| *Taylor* | **MS** | Aye | Aye | Aye | Aye | 4 | |
| Taylor | NC | Aye | Aye | Aye | Aye | 4 | |
| Terry | NE | | | Aye | | 1 | |
| Thomas | **CA** | | | Aye | | 1 | |
| Thornberry | **TX** | Aye | Aye | Aye | Aye | 4 | Nay |
| Tiberi | OH | | | Aye | | 1 | |
| Turner | OH | | | Aye | | 1 | |
| Upton | **MI** | | | Aye | | 1 | |
| Walden | OR | | | Aye | | 1 | |
| Wamp | TN | Aye | Aye | Aye | Aye | 4 | |
| Weldon | **FL** | Aye | Aye | Aye | Aye | 4 | |
| Weldon | PA | | | Aye | | 1 | |
| Weller | IL | Aye | | Aye | | 2 | |
| Westmoreland | **GA** | Aye | Aye | Aye | Aye | 4 | Nay |
| Whitfield | KY | Aye | Aye | Aye | Aye | 4 | |
| Wicker | **MS** | Aye | Aye | Aye | Aye | 4 | |
| Wilson | **SC** | Aye | Aye | Aye | Aye | 4 | |
| Wolf | **VA** | | | Aye | | 1 | |
| Young | **AK** | | Aye | | | 1 | |
| Young | FL | | Aye | Aye | Aye | 3 | |

*Note:* **Bold** indicates Section 5 coverage. *Italic* indicates Democratic lawmakers.

voted for one or no amendments and only 23 percent backed all four. Table 5.6 makes clear that the more extensive a legislator's district's experience with Section 5, the more eager the legislator was to change the law.

Table 5.7 presents a model of support for amending the VRA with the dependent variable being the number of amendments a Republican supported. As reported in the table, both coverage since 1965 and representing a district brought wholly or partially under Section 5 by the 1970 or 1975 triggers were related to the representative voting for a greater number of amendments.[35] Junior legislators were also likely to back a greater number of amendments. There is no relationship between the percentage of African Americans in the district and the number of amendments supported.

TABLE 5.6   Amendments supported by type of Section 5 coverage

| No. of amendments supported | Type of Section 5 coverage (%) | | | | |
|---|---|---|---|---|---|
| | Section 5 state but none | Section 5 state not district | Section 5 district Level 1 | Section 5 since 1965 Level 2 | Level 3 |
| 0 | 23 | 14 | 8 | 5 | 3 |
| 1 | 28 | 42 | 24 | 14 | 16 |
| 2 | 10 | 14 | 7 | 3 | 3 |
| 3 | 13 | 7 | 12 | 15 | 5 |
| 4 | 26 | 23 | 49 | 63 | 73 |
| No. of districts | 104 | 43 | 121 | 78 | 37 |

TABLE 5.7   Model of number of amendments supported

| | Slope coefficient | Std. error |
|---|---|---|
| Coverage since 1965 | 1.467 | .341 |
| District covered since 1970 | 1.170 | .253 |
| Member seniority | -.057 | .025 |
| Percent black | -.007 | .013 |
| Constant | 2.248 | |
| Adj. $R^2$ | .16 | |

The Voting Rights Act renewal was approved in the House on final passage with an overwhelming majority. Just thirty-three lawmakers—all Republicans, with twenty-six of them from Section 5 states—voted "Nay" on final passage. Twelve of the Nay votes came from legislators in states covered by Section 5 since 1965. Another nine opponents represented districts brought under coverage by later triggers, five came from states but not districts partially covered by Section 5, and the remaining seven votes came from legislators whose states did not need preclearance. Again the extent of Section 5 experience was related to the vote, with 32 percent of the Republicans from states covered by Section 5 since its onset, 27 percent of the Republicans from districts subsequently covered, but only 11 percent of those from states but not districts covered by Section 5 opposing the 2006 extension. Only 6.7 percent of Republicans from states not covered by a trigger opposed the 2006 legislation. Of the lawmakers voting against the renewal and extension of the Act on final passage, thirty-one of thirty-three had supported all four amendments and the remaining two had backed three of four amendments. Of eleven Republicans from the original Section 5 states who voted against final passage, six were Georgians. Neither Republican from Mississippi opposed final passage, nor did the Democrat who consistently voted to amend the legislation, Gene Taylor.

The VRA as passed in the House was held together largely by a minority of Republicans and a majority of Democrats. There was a definite geographic and partisan structure to the vote on the amendments. And, as a significant piece of legislation, it forced Speaker Hastert to abandon his desire for a closed rule and his stated practice of passing bills with at least majority Republican support.

## SENATE RESPONSES

In the Senate, after extensive and detailed hearings, the Judiciary Committee adopted the House version of the VRA renewal (H.R. 9) and sent it to the floor. The statement of freshman senator Barack Obama, the second African American to represent Illinois in the Senate, captured the content and spirit of the emotional appeal of the Voting Rights Act renewal and reminded listeners of a different Alabama, an Alabama from the time of Bull Connor and George Wallace:

> The most striking evidence of our progress can be found right across this building, in my dear friend, Congressman John Lewis, who was on the front lines of the civil rights movement, risking life and limb for freedom. And on March 7, 1965, he led 600 peaceful protestors demanding the right to vote across the Edmund Pettus Bridge in Selma, Alabama . . . blacks and whites, teenagers and children, teachers and bankers and shopkeepers—a beloved community of God's children ready to stand for freedom. . . . I wonder, where did they find that kind of courage? When you're facing row after row of state troopers on horseback armed with billy clubs and tear gas . . . when they're coming toward you spewing hatred and violence, how do you simply stop, kneel down, and pray to the Lord for salvation? But the most amazing thing of all is that after that day—after John Lewis was beaten within an inch of his life, after people's heads were gashed open and

their eyes were burned and they watched their children's inno-cence literally beaten out of them . . . after all that, they went back to march again. . . . They awakened a nation's conscience, and not five months later, the Voting Rights Act of 1965 was signed into law. And it was reauthorized in 1970, 1975, and 1982. Now, in 2006, John Lewis, the physical scars from those marches still visible, is an original cosponsor of the fourth reauthori-zation of the Voting Rights Act, and he was joined last week by 389 of his House colleagues in voting for its passage.[36]

The House had rejected the four amendments offered to the VRA and then passed it by an overwhelming margin of 390–33. Even less opposition surfaced in the Senate, where no one offered an amendment or voted against the bill. Representative Westmoreland sought to drum up interest in the Senate but found little receptivity. Sen. Tom Coburn (R-Okla.) did take the lead in including a minority statement in the Senate Committee report. We uncovered no reports of lobbying from the White House on this issue in the Senate or the House.

Despite the unanimity registered by the Senate on passage, the consensus hid notable dissent inside the chamber's majority party. Conservative senator Jeff Sessions (R-Ala.), though more circum-spect about the need for blanket renewal of the Act, nonetheless spoke for the legislation. His support was the equal to Rep. Melvin Watt's appeal to history:

The results of the Voting Rights Act of 1965 were some of the best things that ever happened to Alabama. . . . voter registra-tion rates for Blacks and Whites in Alabama are now virtually identical. In fact, in the last presidential election, according to the Census Bureau, a larger percentage of African Americans voted than Whites in the State of Alabama. Now, that was the goal of the act—to have this kind of progress occur. In fact, over the past 15 years, Alabama has not had a single court find the State guilty of violating the 15th amendment or the very broad pro-tections afforded by section 2 of the Voting Rights Act. . . . The people of Alabama understand that these changes in our State are good, and they do not want to do anything that would suggest that there is any interest in moving away from the great right to vote. We want to reauthorize the Voting Rights Act.[37]

Sessions's support was not without caveat. The junior senator from Alabama spoke not just for the progress of Alabama. He also rose to advance the more controversial aspect of the renewal debate, the prospect for revision of the Act. In doing so, he sounded a need for careful conversation regarding the nature of the renewal of the Act, noting that "how we reauthorize the act is something that is worthy of discussion. . . . The witnesses we have heard in the Judiciary Committee over the past couple of months have had many different ideas, and after hearing from them, I am concerned that we should have listened more carefully to the recommendations."

Although no senators cast a vote that put them on record as opposing the renewal of the Act as passed by the House, several did pursue an alternative strategy for registering concerns. The vehicle for their concerns was the report issued by the Senate Judiciary Committee. The Senate report on the legislation contained an expansive record of statistics and statements regarding political change in the South and progress on voting rights and minority access. This record also documented potential vulnerabilities in the coverage formula, thereby writing into the permanent record a large, critical minority report. The actual legislative report of the committee runs some twenty-one pages.[38] A larger component, some thirty-one pages, is given over to the additional views of senators Jon Kyle (R-Ariz.), Tom Coburn (R-Okla.), and John Cornyn (R-Tex.). Kyle focused on his belief that the Act could not be used to compel states to create "influence" or coalitional districts as a remedy to retrogression. The Coburn/Cornyn additions were far more critical and called attention to the speed and lack of debate in the Senate regarding the bill. The senators noted at the outset of their minority report, "We regret that these views will be filed post-enactment. The expedited process prohibited normal order, but we believe the following considerations should accompany the Act's passage." Even though they voted for the bill, they proceeded to criticize it, thereby creating a legislative record of vulnerabilities and doubts regarding the renewed bill. The criticism are summarized at the front of the minority report at pages 21–22:

> We do hold some significant reservations about a number of important issues. These concerns can generally be categorized as follows: (1) the record of evidence does not appear to reasonably

underscore the decision to simply reauthorize the existing Section 5 coverage formula—a formula that is based on 33 to 41 year old data, and (2) the seemingly rushed, somewhat incomplete legislative process involved in passing the legislation prevented the full consideration of numerous suggested improvements to the Act. In short, while we support reauthorization generally, we reluctantly conclude that the final product is not the best product we might have produced had we engaged in a more thorough debate about possible improvements. We also conclude that it would have been beneficial if the Section 4 coverage formula had been updated in order to adhere to constitutional requirements—an update that would have preserved, strengthened and expanded the Act to ensure its future success.

The minority report engaged each issue in turn. In arguing that the coverage formula needed to be revised and updated, the senators drew on data on registration and voting and also declining instances of DOJ objections to preclearance submissions as evidence of change. The report criticized much of the evidence offered by proponents of unamended renewal as nothing more than anecdotal evidence that did not apply to most of the jurisdictions affected by Section 5. In response to House Judiciary chairman Sensenbrenner's characterization of the 8,000 pages of witness testimony describing discrimination and Sen. Dick Durbin's (D-Ill.) observation in markup that "we have gathered thousands of pages of reports and evidence," Cornyn and Coburn described these pages as containing "a limited number of examples of discrimination." They then noted that, "of 893 covered counties, 139 are directly implicated in the accounts of discrimination scattered throughout those 'thousands of pages.'"

The report went further, characterizing the legislative process used to pass the bill as being "not deliberative." It then took a veiled swipe at the motivations of the House majority in passing the legislation and embraced one of Issacharoff's recommendations, noting that "we cannot help but fear that the driving force behind this rushed reauthorization process was the reality that the Voting Rights Act has evolved into a tool for political and racial gerrymandering. We believe that is unfortunate and that political re-districting should be driven by objective parameters and should not use race to further the objectives of political parties." Seven years later, the characterization of the evidence used in the renewal of the Act, and also the concerns of Senators Cornyn and Coburn, would make their way into the language of the *Shelby County* decision.

The concerns raised in the additional views of Senate Judiciary Committee members were shared by some Republicans not on the committee, as we discovered in interviews with staffers of southern GOP senators. One senior Senate staffer observed that Westmoreland was "dead-on right. The formula needed to be updated. The intimidation of the 1960s was horrendous. It was entirely unjust. However, it is also unjust to continue to punish some states for the sins of the past."[39]

Although some GOP senators from Section 5 states may have agreed privately with Norwood and Westmoreland that the trigger mechanism needed updating, the criticisms directed at House members who supported amending the VRA dissuaded senators from registering public opposition. "Senators did not want to look like they were anti-minority, that they were anti–civil rights, explained a senior staffer. "Senators saw what happened to the opponents [of renewing without change] in the House. Those who supported modernizing the Voting Rights Act got vilified. Why take a political hit? The senators were not willing to lie on the train tracks." "There was serious backlash on the House members who voted for the amendments and voted against the legislation. They had to defend themselves from charges like 'You're for voter intimidation,'" explained a second staffer. Another staffer explained that for Republicans to support extension "there was no downside. The opponents of the renewal were labeled as racists. Politically it was easiest to be for the legislation. Voting against renewal would be like voting to stop the cost of living adjustment for Social Security." Another staffer explained, "Prior to the Supreme Court ruling in *Shelby County* you couldn't be a southern senator and vote against the Voting Rights Act. Even a Republican senator couldn't oppose extending the VRA. To do such a vote was a bridge too far." One of the Senate staffers with whom we spoke lamented, "We had the chance to modernize the Voting Rights Act. The political environment did not allow that conversation to take place. . . . We had the opportunity to modernize the legislation and to do the right thing. But now that the courts have acted, no one will be covered."

A Senate staffer described the coalition that renewed Section 5 as a "bipartisan coalition that consisted of the minorities who argued

that 'You have got to keep it just as it is.' They were joined by legislators from states like Iowa and California who didn't want to see
Section 5 coming into their states."

That no southern Republican senator joined colleagues from the
House and took a public stand against extending Section 5 or in favor
of modifying Section 4 is at least partially due to the nature of
their constituencies. Senators represent states and thus have a diverse
constituency. In some House districts where the population overwhelmingly comprises conservative, white Republicans, voting to
amend or even terminate Section 5 would play very well. Even if
the legislators became subjects of editorial criticism and civil rights
leaders charged them with racism, the incumbents' reelection chances
would not be harmed.[40]

## PROBABILITY NEGLECT

An intriguing question in light of the Supreme Court's *Shelby County*
decision is why Congress did not act to avoid the gutting of preclearance. The hearings on renewal generated clear warnings from
leading scholars concerned that the legislation continue to focus
scrutiny on noncompliant jurisdictions. Although VRA supporters
might discount the efforts of southerners like those who offered
amendments as nothing more than a lingering and outmoded commitment to white supremacy, that could not be the reason to ignore
law professors like Hasen and Issacharoff. These scholars' close attention to Supreme Court decisions convinced them that reliance on
generations-old data to identify the location of current problems
would not pass constitutional muster. As we see in the next chapter,
the head-in-the-sand reaction to warnings that the triggers needed
updating persisted even when the Supreme Court expressed concerns.

The unwillingness of the congressional, bipartisan majority to
consider updating the Section 4 triggers in 2006 can be explained, at
least in part, by the phenomenon of probability neglect. When confronting a greatly feared event, even when the potential that the cala-
mity will occur may be tiny, most people will go to great lengths to
avoid the risk. This kind of behavior is contrary to utility theory, which
predicts that in the case of an unlikely occurrence a person will do
little to avoid it. For example, those extremely afraid of flying may
opt to drive to a distant location even though the likelihood of death

on the highway exceeds the likelihood of death in the sky. A lab experiment found that subjects were willing to pay roughly equal amounts to avoid a greatly feared outcome—in the experiment the risk of an electric shock—regardless of the likelihood of being shocked.[41] Another experiment asked law students about willingness to pay to remove arsenic from water given various odds of developing cancer. The relationship between the risk of developing cancer and willingness to pay to avoid was dramatically less when the description of the ravishing impact of cancer evoked a more emotional response.[42] Events that trigger a strong emotional response result in widespread fear even when there is minimal likelihood of the event taking place.

Acquisition of the right to vote did not come easily in much of the area covered by Section 5. Moreover, access to the ballot box was part of the larger effort to transform a society that denied many African Americans access to good jobs, good schools, good housing, and an opportunity to improve their status. Even the slightest prospect that the bad old days might return obscured arguments that the clock would not be turned back. Lessons from history showing that during the last quarter of the nineteenth century inattentive northern members of Congress and the judiciary allowed unreconstructed southerners to undo many of the gains made under the Fifteenth Amendment compounded fears that even modest changes to the VRA could lead to disastrous consequences.

Activists who stand to benefit from an energized following fanned the fears that recalibrating the trigger mechanism could prove catastrophic. Even more than forty years after the initial enactment of the Voting Rights Act, Congress confronted claims that widespread backsliding would result should it fail to reenact the statute with the trigger mechanism intact. Similar claims of likely backsliding had been made each time the VRA came up for renewal, and the likelihood of attempts to resurrect barriers to voting were more likely in 1970 or 1975. By 2006, most if not all of the public officials who had discriminated against prospective black registrants had passed from the scene and two generations had come of age in integrated environments.

Further minimizing the potential of a second Reconstruction, scores of African Americans now hold elective office at every level from the tiniest towns to state legislatures, Congress, and the presidency. African Americans constitute the core constituency of the Democratic Party, a component of the electorate so significant that it could not be abandoned by the party if it hoped to maintain its strong position vis-à-vis the Electoral College. Republicans may have forsaken their black supporters in the South in the 1890s, but Democrats could not hope to win the presidency or have success in many states without enthusiastic support from African American and other minority voters. Nonetheless, fear that the gains made since the 1960s could be lost proved paralyzing, and Congress ignored the warnings about the vulnerability of the Section 4 triggers.

## CONCLUSION

As the defendants in *Shelby County v. Holder* pointed out, Congress renewed the Voting Rights Act with unanimous Senate support and the backing of more than 90 percent of the House. How dare the Supreme Court go against a piece of legislation lauded on all sides as the most successful civil rights law ever, the renewal of which attracted near unanimous backing from a rarely harmonious Congress? The experience of Section 4 and 5 renewal provides a classic example of how those who lost the battle nonetheless won the war.

Congressional opponents to extending Section 5 without modification failed in their efforts, but the groundwork for the successful challenge in *Shelby County* was laid in Congress. Edward Blum had no more success in shaping the decisions taken by Congress than he had when trying to become a member of that body. He failed to get support for his concerns in the White House or the Senate and found few allies in the House. His efforts to limit the extension of Section 5 to a decade or less, to modernize the Section 4 triggers, or to end preclearance were all rebuffed. Yet the research that he funded provided evidence that the law had transformed Section 5 jurisdictions such that by 2006 black political participation at the mass level and in terms of office holding in those states differed little from that in states not required to get preclearance for changes. If the states that had been singled out in the 1965 legislation for their repressive practices now were indistinguishable from other states, and even offered some examples of black political activity outstripping states elsewhere, what justification existed for extending the Section 4 triggers as they had been for more than three decades? The Senate Judiciary Committee report's minority views contained data that highlighted the advances made in preclearance states.

Committee hearings on renewal provided a forum at which to offer evidence of the successes achieved by previous versions of the VRA. It was important to get that material into the record even if claims of persistent problems in the preclearance areas far outnumbered assertions that Section 5 had served its purpose and now needed to be retired.

The House took up renewal first, and critics won a skirmish when they succeeded in offering four amendments. These failed in the face of near unanimous Democratic opposition coupled with divisions in the GOP ranks. Republicans whose districts had experienced preclearance strongly favored modernizing the triggers, shortening the length of the renewal, facilitating bailouts, and, especially, eliminating the requirement that election materials be printed in languages other than English. Nevertheless, even if House Republicans had united sufficiently to pass one or more of the amendments, these modifications would probably have died in the Senate. If change was to come, it would have to be at the hands of judges.

# 6   Pushback

The Voting Rights Act accomplished much by guaranteeing minority voter access and facilitating the election of minority officeholders. Recognition of the accomplishments of this legislation validated the postwar democratic rhetoric of the United States. The VRA is regularly referred to as the most important civil rights legislation ever enacted. Underscoring its importance, as part of an assessment of thirty-six democracies political scientist Arend Lijphart asserted that "universal suffrage was not firmly established in the United States until the passage of the Voting Rights Act in 1965."[1] These gains did not occur in a vacuum but in a dynamic political environment that dramatically and permanently changed American party politics. The 1965 statute came just one year after Barry Goldwater's presidential campaign had initiated political realignment in the Deep South as the subregion began down the path Rim South states had set out on a decade earlier. Conservatives of various stripes left the Democratic Party in search of a new avenue for political expression.

Physics teaches that for every action there is a reaction, and so it was with the VRA. By the first decade of the twenty-first century the political reaction became manifest as pushback against the emergency provisions of the Act. The unsuccessful legislative attempt at pushback, described in chapter 5, took the form of amendments that deviated from blanket renewal. But there was other pushback, which took three forms and contributed to the creation of an environment that impedes meaningful new voting rights legislation.

First, political empowerment accompanied the emergence of the Republican Party as a viable alternative in the South. The implementation of the Voting Rights Act and its subsequent renewals and amendments coincided with nothing less than a dramatic realignment of southern politics.[2] In light of the overwhelming dominance of the GOP in the South today, it can be overlooked how entrenched the Democratic Party was until the mid-1960s. Prior to the Goldwater election, only once had a Deep South state given its electors to a Republican presidential candidate since 1876.[3] No Republican had represented any of these states in Congress in the twentieth century. Similar statements could have been made for most of the Rim South states, except that the onset of change began during the Eisenhower presidency. Conservative whites decamped first from the Democratic Party; later moderate whites followed their lead. By the 1980s, Democratic presidential nominees attracted no more than a third of the white vote, a level of frustration that has persisted.[4] White support for GOP candidates other than president came later, with the Reagan presidency playing a major role in moving less conservative whites away from their traditional party moorings. By 1996 the white share of the vote for Democratic congressional candidates in the South had fallen to the level registered for Democratic presidential candidates. With realignment came the reemergence of conservative legislative and electoral majorities more resistant to national government authority than at any time since 1964. The return of anti-federalism as a viable political vehicle found its feet, most visibly, in resistance to the Patient Protection Affordable Care Act (PPACA, also known as ObamaCare), but it also extended to other issues including the preclearance provision of the Voting Rights Act.

Second, starting with the post-2000 census redistricting, states pushed back against Section 5 implementation. This pushback was not confined to one party but instead took the form of local legislative majorities seeking to comply with Section 5 while minimizing the detrimental political consequences of compliance. Georgia, which had a long, difficult history with the Department of Justice when submitting statewide districting plans, broke with tradition and submitted its plans to the district court of the District of Columbia. Although time consuming and costly, the judicial approach succeeded. In contrast with 1992, when DOJ rejected Georgia's maps for Congress and both legislative chambers multiple times, the D.C. trial court approved the 2001 plans for Congress and the state house. The trial court rejected three state senate districts even though the Legislative Black Caucus had agreed to reductions in black concentrations, but on appeal the Supreme Court found the reductions acceptable despite a seeming violation of the nonretrogression standard.[5] A decade later, Georgia and several other states pursued a novel strategy of "simultaneous submission"—seeking administrative preclearance while initiating litigation, as Georgia had done successfully in 2001. The dual-submission strategy may have placed pressure on DOJ to act expeditiously; it approved Georgia's 2011 plans before the D.C. court could hold a hearing.

Third, opponents of the existing voting rights regime sought judicial remedies to achieve what they failed to secure in the legislative process, challenging the regime directly through the bailout provision and the preclearance coverage formula. The first effort, the *NAMUDNO* case, set the stage for the subsequent *Shelby County* litigation that would fell the most powerful provision of the Act.

## SOUTHERN REALIGNMENT AND ANTI-FEDERALISM IN AMERICAN POLITICS, 2007–2013

Erosion of the one-party Democratic South, bastion of white supremacy and defender of states' rights, started in the 1960s and finally collapsed under the combined weight of economic, cultural, and racial pressures. This regional realignment, which proceeded at different speeds among the eleven southern states, produced a permanent change in the politics and coalitional bases of both major parties. Four decades of implementing voting rights policy in the South witnessed heightened minority political participation. In the wake of increased black voting for Democrats came a wholesale movement of white voters to the Republican Party over the course of two generations. Shrewd politicians in both parties anticipated the role of race in the movement of southern whites to the GOP.[6] A year before passage of the VRA, Lyndon Johnson observed to Bill Moyers that, by signing the 1964 Civil Rights Act, "I think we have just delivered the South to the Republican Party for a long time to come."[7] A similar assessment provided the basis for Richard Nixon's southern strategy.[8]

Political scientists who study the South generally conclude that a realignment of the region began in the 1950s with the civil rights revolution acting as a catalyst. Rather than a critical realignment occurring across an election or two, the transformation of the white South from Democrat to Republican took decades. Change in terms of presidential voting came rapidly. The Rim South except Arkansas and North Carolina voted for Eisenhower. Although the Rim South returned to the Democratic fold in 1964, the Deep South flocked to Goldwater's banner. Since 1964 only one Democrat has captured a majority of the region's electoral votes (Jimmy Carter in 1976) and none has won most of the white vote for president. Down-ticket, the loss of the national Democratic Party in Congress as a vehicle for racial conservatism followed a creeping realignment, making its way in fits and starts, gaining occasional momentum from the candidacy of Ronald Reagan in 1980 and Newt Gingrich's (R-Ga.) 1994 "Contract with America" campaign. Earl Black and Merle Black conclude that by the end of the Reagan presidency the South had essentially become Republican not just in its presidential preferences but further down-ticket. Conservative voters had decamped from the Democratic Party in droves, and moderates were following suit, although some remained true to the party of their ancestors.[9] The manifestation of this realignment at the congressional level became obvious in 1994 as Republicans took the bulk of the southern seats in both chambers of Congress.

The race issue and civil rights were not the only accelerant for realignment in the South. The in-migration of voters from other regions, urbanization and suburbanization, and the increase in incomes and literacy also contributed to the growth of the nascent Republican Party.[10] Generational replacement also played a role as New Deal Democrats died and their Reagan-era grandchildren began going to the ballot box. As a consequence of partisan realignment, the Democratic Party primary ceased to be the decisive election for statewide offices in the South. As competition shifted to the general election, party voting acquired a racial structure. Black voters and Latinos, except Cuban Americans, now overwhelming supported Democratic candidates, while large majorities of white voters favored Republicans. The critical infusion of black votes into the Democratic Party and the opening up of the opportunity structure in politics to black candidates helped propel white voters and some aspirant white candidates to the GOP. What now varied across most states was the intensity of support for Republicans among the white electorate and the range of offices for which whites preferred Republicans. Trey Hood,

Quentin Kidd, and Irwin Morris argue in their book *The Rational Southerner* that conservative whites exited the Democratic Party for the GOP because the cost structure was lower. The GOP offered white voters and politicians the possibility of winning as a conservative without having to share the political party with liberals and African Americans.[11]

Survey data, election results, and trends in office holding support the notion of white realignment to the GOP across the South. Data compiled in the American National Election Study indicate that Republicans went from a net 50-point disadvantage among southern white identifiers in the 1950s and early 1960s to parity in party identification among white southerners by 1992.[12] Exit poll data from the 1990s and 2000s show that whites continued to realign toward the GOP, and in some southern states today fewer than 20 percent of whites remain with the Democratic Party.[13] White defections from the Democratic Party were paralleled by reductions in the number of white Democratic officeholders. Republicans and black Democrats shared the spoils of the offices previously held by white Democrats. In 1969 fewer than four hundred African Americans held elective office in the South; by 2001 the number exceeded 5,500. Republican officeholders made even more impressive gains; as of 2013 they commanded congressional majorities in every southern state, held all statewide offices in Alabama, Georgia, and Texas, and dominated every southern legislative chamber save for the Virginia senate.

One consequence of the realignment of the South and the emergence of a viable GOP alternative was the creation of a "race-party-incumbency" structure to southern politics. Put simply, partisan realignment impedes black political success above the local level. Throughout the South, when black candidates lose general elections, they typically lose because they run as Democrats and not because they are minority candidates.[14] Republican administrations, specifically the first Bush administration, used the Voting Rights Act to encourage creation of majority-minority districts and to limit the opportunities to create cross-racial coalitions supporting Democrats. White Democrats preferred districts with sizable (but not majority) minority populations because biracial coalitions could win more seats. The aggressive use of Section 2 of the VRA to create majority-minority districts in the early 1990s resulted in electoral maps that helped shift one-third of all southern congressional districts to the GOP over the course of the next three elections. Concentrating the most loyal Democratic voters into the fewest districts possible helped elect Republicans as well as minorities.

Partisan realignment has consequences not just for the electorate but also for minority officeholders. As more white politicians win office as Republicans, the ranks of Democratic legislators and party leaders, especially the most senior ones, become increasingly black. Movement of whites to the GOP gives black politicians increased institutional clout within state party organizations and in state and national legislatures. Senior black legislators have accrued significant legislative leadership and committee positions in Congress and, for a time, in southern legislatures. However, when Republicans achieve majority status in a legislative chamber, black influence becomes marginalized. Since most southern legislatures follow the congressional model and limit committee chairs to members of the majority party, even senior black Democrats have little clout in today's GOP-dominated legislatures.

By the time the Voting Rights Act as renewed in 2006 was being challenged in the federal courts, Republicans had largely gained control of the southern states. After the 2013 elections, of the nine southern states covered by Section 5, eight had unified Republican government. Virginia had the only Democratic governor, and its upper chamber had equal numbers of Democrats and Republicans. These nine states sent thirty-eight Democrats (of whom fourteen were Anglo whites) and eighty-seven Republicans to Congress. Just four of the eighteen U.S. senators from these states were Democrats. Whether through election or threat of primary challenge, Republican state and federal lawmakers in these states increasingly engaged in hardened states' rights rhetoric.

Between 2007 and 2013 the Tea Party movement erupted in reaction to initiatives of the Obama administration and a widespread malaise sparked by concerns about the scope and competence of federal authority. This loosely connected, multiheaded protest fueled growing disenchantment with all manner of government regulations, which were widely seen as interference. Since preclearance is unique, the only aspect of state and local decision making required to get federal approval before implementation, opposition to it fits within this broader context of a call to have the federal government back off and allow citizens to make their own decisions—or, if government was to be involved, have it be authorities closer to the public.

## PUSHBACK IN PRECLEARANCE:
## THE SIMULTANEOUS SUBMISSION STRATEGY

The initial pushback strategy developed by southern states against the preclearance regime turned to judicial approval rather than administrative preclearance to satisfy Section 5. Prior to 2001, when Georgia asked the district court of the District of Columbia (DCDC) for preclearance of the Democratic gerrymander of congressional and state legislative districts rather than trust the Bush Justice Department, the judicial alternative had usually been pursued only after an unsuccessful bout with DOJ. The DCDC approved Georgia's congressional and state house maps, but the state had to appeal its senate map to the Supreme Court. In approving the state senate plan, *Georgia v. Ashcroft* made a hash of the presumed standards applied in baselining and measuring retrogression (see chap. 2).

Georgia's success set the stage for a new strategy after release of the 2010 census. Instead of testing the waters with DOJ, several Section 5 jurisdictions undertook "simultaneous submission," which involved seeking judicial preclearance in conjunction with the submission of new maps for the more traditional administrative preclearance. In part these states had a motivation similar to Georgia's a decade earlier. The partisan plans favored the party (Republicans) that did not control DOJ (Democrats); going to court avoided what Republicans perceived to be a hostile administration. Republicans had enjoyed the advantages of politically motivated, creative, unconstitutional applications of Section 5 in the past. Fearing a political reaction from the Obama regime, they were "looking for an escape hatch from dealing with the DOJ."[15]

Conservative attorney Hans von Spakovsky, an alumnus of the George W. Bush Justice Department, recommended simultaneous submission early in the 2011–2012 redistricting cycle. Prior to coming to Washington, he had served on the Fulton County (Atlanta), Georgia, Board of Elections and so had watched as Gov. Roy Barnes, often referred to as the smartest member of the general assembly during his long tenure there, seemingly outfoxed DOJ by sending plans directly to the DCDC in 2001. Just as Barnes wondered whether a Republican DOJ would accept a Democratic gerrymander, von Spakovsky warned, "Republican-controlled legislatures that have drawn up redistricting plans that Democrats don't like would be foolish to submit those plans to the Civil Rights Division for administrative review. Instead, they should go straight to the federal district court in D.C., the alternative procedure set forth in the Voting Rights Act."[16] A partisan gerrymander, no matter how extreme, would not violate Section 5, but politicians feared that the need for preclearance could open the door for an administration to intercede on behalf of its aggrieved copartisans since the burden of proof under Section 5 falls on the submitting authority.

In addition to suspicions about the evenhandedness of DOJ, other explanations emerged for the dual-submission strategy. Von Spakovsky's advice could also be seen as foreshadowing a strategy to tie up the DCDC with a logjam of preclearance requests. In the February/March 2011 issue of *James* magazine, Bullock and Gaddie speculated about the potential consequences of this strategy, if taken to extreme. Imagining several hundred jurisdictions all filing suit in the DCDC, they described a potential docket nightmare:

In the wake of the 2010 elections, Republicans enjoy the greatest potential they have had to shape new maps. In the preclearance states, they will control redistricting in Alabama, Arizona, Florida, Georgia, Louisiana, North Carolina, South Carolina, and Texas. In most of these states the new plans will supplant ones drawn by Democrats or judges. . . . If each of these states opts to seek preclearance through the DCDC it will add to the court's already busy workload. The need to review plans for Congress and the legislatures of eight states would require weeks of court time, but could be just the tip of the iceberg. What if a number of local governments that also need to secure preclearance choose to litigate their plans? Georgia, to cite one example, has 159 counties, 179 school districts and more than 500 municipalities. While not all of these will have new plans since some elect members of their governing bodies at-large, if each of these entities that draws new districts turned to the DCDC for preclearance it could lead to well over 700 suits. Texas provides an even greater threat to clog the DC courts with its 254 counties, more than 1000 school districts, approximately 1200 municipalities, and numerous municipal utility districts. Even Florida, with just five covered counties, could generate up to 32 lawsuits when the state legislative, congressional, and possible local government maps are all counted. In sum, there are as many as

5,500–6,000 local, county, and state government maps that could be submitted for bench review.

The politics of standing up against DOJ offered advantages for Republican lawmakers in Dixie. The emerging political environment of Tea Party politics had Republicans rediscovering the Tenth Amendment, so going to court "to fight national government interposition into state election administration has political cache."[17]

An argument advanced initially during the 2003 Texas redistricting trial contributed to Republican fears. DOJ and other plaintiffs in that case contended that districts that did not have a majority-minority population but that elected Democrats with strong minority support should constitute part of the retrogression baseline and therefore be protected from changes detrimental to the preferences of minority voters. The claim that districts in which white Democrats won thanks to strong minority-group support and that reducing concentrations of minority voters in these districts would contravene Section 2 of the VRA failed in the Texas litigation and elsewhere but remained a concern for GOP mapmakers. The basis for the claim came largely from dicta in *Georgia v. Ashcroft*, but it still resonated with Democrats and Republicans for different reasons. Democrats could plausibly increase their competitiveness in the South if minority votes were efficiently spread around and not segregated by mapmakers. Packing minority voters had helped Republicans in the South. The *Ashcroft* dicta allowed jurisdictions to decide how to maintain the retrogression baseline. Simultaneous submission left open an expedient avenue to pursue relief if the states disagreed with DOJ's demands during preclearance. Having a suit already docketed in the District of Columbia would expedite the process should DOJ balk at the new plans.

Was dual submission part of a cynical strategy to bog down preclearance? No. The "docket creaking strategy" was not completely pursued by most states or jurisdictions.[18] Eight of sixteen states filed preclearance cases in the DCDC. For local governments, many of which had built working relationships with DOJ over time, it was easier and less expensive to pursue the traditional path.

Of sixteen states covered in whole or in part by Section 5, eight pursued simultaneous judicial and administrative preclearance for congressional and legislative maps: Alabama, Arizona, Georgia, Louisiana, North Carolina, South Carolina, Texas, and Virginia. All of these states secured preclearance from DOJ except Texas, which failed to obtain approval both there and in the federal court. Alaska, California, Florida, Michigan, Mississippi, New Hampshire, New York, and South Dakota did not file suit with the DCDC but successfully pursued administrative preclearance. Only Mississippi's state legislative maps went through preclearance review since a federal district court had crafted the congressional plan, which, therefore, did not need to be approved.

As noted earlier, von Spakovsky had warned Republicans against trying to get approval from the Democratic-led DOJ. States in which Republicans drew plans usually followed this advice. Of the eight states pursuing dual submission, Republicans controlled six, the Virginia legislature split between the parties, and an independent commission redistricted Arizona. Of the eight states that followed the traditional administrative route, Republicans drew the maps in Florida, Michigan, and South Dakota; four others had split partisan control; and in California, like Arizona, an independent commission drew the new districts. A relationship exists between partisan control of the redistricting process and the approach taken to achieve approval. The tendency not to rely exclusively on DOJ is especially strong among states fully covered by Section 5. Of nine states wholly subject to preclearance, all but Alaska and Mississippi pursued the dual strategy, including all five with Republicans in control of the legislature and governorship.[19]

Von Spakovsky's prediction that Republican-drawn plans would "run into a buzz saw of Voting Section opposition based not on the legal standards set forth under Section 5, but on whether the Section's lawyers think the plan will hurt or help Democratic candidates" was not born out. Simultaneous submission generally worked for the states pursuing it. Seven of eight states precleared a total of twenty-one maps. Courts rejected three maps—all from Texas. Louisiana for the first time successfully precleared a state house map on the initial effort, and for the first time Georgia got *all* three maps approved on initial submission. In the previous four decades the states that pursued dual submission had had fifty-four statewide redistricting plans rejected by DOJ. But in 2011–2012 simultaneous submission was not *more* successful as a strategy submitting than submitting only to administrative review by DOJ. The only maps to fail preclearance in the most recent redistricting cycle were rejected by a three-judge panel.

There is still reason to suspect politics in the use of simultaneous submission. Of the eight dual-submission states, six were covered by the original Act in 1965 and, as noted above, they had a long record of preclearance failure with DOJ. The other two, Arizona and Texas, also had a history of voting rights and preclearance problems despite not coming under Section 5 until 1975. All of them also had previous or pending challenges involving their voter identification laws—though so, too, did Florida, which did not pursue simultaneous submission.

Whether the goal of simultaneous submission was to prod DOJ to action or to secure a favorable review is beyond our ken. The U.S. Commission on Civil Rights, in its analysis of preclearance in 2012, concluded that there was "no particular evidence that filing simultaneously increased the chances of a prompt positive resolution, since the rates of approval during this cycle are only marginally different from what they were in the 2001–2002 cycle in which judicial and dual submission were uncommon. However, the Commission also has no particular evidence that filing simultaneously did not increase the chances of a prompt positive resolution."[20] And since DOJ rejected no plan, the rationale that dual submission would expedite a judicial assessment never came into play.

Supporting the proposition that dual submission encouraged DOJ to preclear is the observation of a former DOJ attorney whom we interviewed. The lawyer acknowledged that during this time the attorney general was making litigation decisions with an eye toward what might get to the Supreme Court and how the high court might react, and this concern was not limited to voting rights. Nathaniel Persily, a leading legal scholar of the Voting Rights Act, stressed that "each preclearance determination, especially concerning statewide redistricting, is seen as a zero sum game between the political parties with great political and policy consequences." DOJ, consequently, "must view each decision 'as a potential vehicle [for a court decision] that would destroy Section 5 itself.'"[21]

One voting rights case widely thought to have been settled in order to avoid a Supreme Court review of a "fact situation" unfavorable to DOJ came from eastern North Carolina. In 2009 almost two-thirds of the voters in Kinston, North Carolina, approved a proposal to make municipal elections nonpartisan, the approach used by 98 percent of the state's cities. More than 60 percent of Kinston's voters were black, and the change won approval in five of seven majority-black precincts. The city had an all-Democratic council, but in denying the proposed change DOJ explained that the party label prompted a few white voters to support black nominees, often as a result of casting a straight-party ballot.[22] Removing the party identifier would, according to the acting assistant attorney general, make it harder for African American candidates to succeed since it would likely reduce white support and also eliminate Democratic Party campaign funds.

The city decided not to contest DOJ's ruling, but a group of citizens who had worked to put the referendum on the ballot to change to nonpartisan elections secured the pro bono services of Michael Carvin, an experienced hand in voting rights litigation. The lawsuit Carvin filed contended that Kinston should be allowed to change its electoral format but also challenged the extension of the VRA in 2006. A judge in the DCDC dismissed the challenge on the ground that the plaintiffs lacked standing. Carvin's appeal to the court of appeals in the District of Columbia was scheduled for a hearing when DOJ suddenly withdrew its objection. In explaining this unprecedented about-face, DOJ noted that in 2011 for the first time the city elected a black majority to the council and that the African American percentage among registered voters had increased from 65 to 65.4 percent.[23] Others attribute the withdrawal to fear that the Supreme Court would use this case to strike down pre-clearance. Even though the court of appeals had dismissed the case since nonpartisan elections could now proceed, the plaintiffs filed a writ of certiorari with the Supreme Court arguing that the case provided an ideal opportunity to examine the expansion of the scope of the Voting Rights Act in 2006. The expansion consisted of provisions overturning two Supreme Court opinions. In *Georgia v. Ashcroft* the Court had accepted new ways to satisfy the nonretrogression standard. In *Reno v. Bossier Parish School Board (Bossier II)* the Court had ruled that the sole purpose of Section 5 was to prevent backsliding; it could not be used as a tool to force affirmative action.[24] The cert petition failed, the Supreme Court opting instead to hear the case from Shelby County, Alabama. But before it got to Shelby County, the Supreme Court ruled on the *NAMUDNO* case.

## NAMUDNO

Subsequent to the renewal of the Voting Rights Act, the opponents of the maintenance of the legislative status quo moved from legislation to litigation. In early 2007 the first of a pair of cases questioning the constitutionality of the renewed Act was filed in the DCDC. The plaintiff in *North Austin Municipal Utility District Number One [NAMUDNO] v. Mukasey* (restyled *NAMUDNO v. Holder*) was a small metropolitan utility district (the "MUD") in Travis County, Texas, incorporated in 1987. The MUD specifically sought to exercise Section 4 to bail out from having to comply with Section 5 preclearance requirements.[25]

The 1982 extension of the VRA supposedly made it easier for jurisdictions to escape Section 5. In 1980, Rome, Georgia, had tried to remove itself from preclearance but failed because the law did not allow parts of a state subject to Section 5 to bail out.[26] The 1982 changes that supposedly facilitated bailing out by political units within covered states proved largely illusionary. As of 2008, only seventeen jurisdictions (all in Virginia) had exited Section 5.

*NAMUDNO* focused on two questions, one statutory, the other constitutional. The statutory issue related to a technical matter: what is a "jurisdiction" under the Voting Rights Act? The constitutional question involved fundamental issues of federalism—specifically, the preemption of state authority by the national government, and the scope of evidence and timeliness of wrongdoing necessary to allow the Congress to enforce the Fifteenth Amendment.

Three-judge panels of the DCDC hear bail-out requests. To bail out from under Section 5 coverage, a jurisdiction must meet many stringent criteria:

> It must show that during the previous 10 years: (A) no "test or device has been used within such State or political subdivision for the purpose or with the effect of denying or abridging the right to vote on account of race or color"; (B) "no final judgment of any court of the United States . . . has determined that denials or abridgments of the right to vote on account of race or color have occurred anywhere in the territory of" the covered jurisdiction; (C) "no Federal examiners or observers . . . have been assigned to" the covered jurisdiction; (D) the covered jurisdiction has fully complied with §5; and (E) "the Attorney General has not interposed any objection (that has not been overturned by a final judgment of a court) and no declaratory judgment has been denied under [§5]." . . . the jurisdiction also has the burden of presenting "evidence of minority participation, including evidence of the levels of minority group registration and voting, changes in such levels over time, and disparities between

minority-group and non-minority-group participation." . . . a covered jurisdiction seeking bailout must also meet subjective criteria: it must "(i) have eliminated voting procedures and methods of election which inhibit or dilute equal access to the electoral process; (ii) have engaged in constructive efforts to eliminate intimidation and harassment of persons exercising rights protected [under the Act]; and (iii) have engaged in other constructive efforts, such as expanded opportunity for convenient registration and voting for every person of voting age and the appointment of minority persons as election officials throughout the jurisdiction and at all stages of the election and registration process."[27]

Jurisdictions seeking to escape Section 5 requirements have a substantial burden. In *NAMUDNO*, the lower court denied bailout not because the MUD failed to satisfy the criteria, noted above, but because it did not register voters, which made it ineligible for bailout. The plaintiffs appealed to the Supreme Court. In its appeal, the MUD pointed out that the Act imposes no such limitation on bailout. Being a jurisdiction for the purpose of coverage made the MUD one for the purpose of bailout. If it lost on the statutory challenge, the MUD asked the Court to invalidate Section 5 on constitutional grounds.

Disagreements over the need to continue preclearance illuminate the differences in the evaluation of minority-white relations early in the new millennium. Hearings held prior to the 2006 Voting Rights Act renewal celebrated the dramatic improvements in the political status of African Americans and other minorities. The hearings took place in the context of a changed, two-party South. Opponents of any modification of the VRA triggers viewed changes wrought by the Act as tenuous and requiring constant monitoring. They feared that, based on the historical precedent of the first Reconstruction, any dimming of DOJ's watchful eye would trigger an avalanche of backsliding by an unreconstructed South. Second-generation discriminatory effects are on par with the insidious evil of Jim Crow in their reading of the South and other jurisdictions covered by Section 5.

Advocates for revised VRA coverage pointed to the same transformed landscape as evidence of changes in white attitudes and the ability of minorities to secure their rights with less federal involvement. The *NAMUDNO* plaintiff/appellant asserted that the time for national preemption of state and local electoral authority had expired with the passing of the emergency. The plaintiff and supporters filing amicus briefs pointed to data on registration, voting, and minority descriptive representation to challenge the need for continuing federal oversight for another quarter-century.[28]

The politics of the Supreme Court loomed large over this test case, as it would also in the *Shelby County* case. Pre-opinion speculation in *NAMUDNO* focused on Justice Anthony Kennedy, who regularly moved between the conservative and liberal blocs of the court, often authoring 5–4 decisions in which he was the critical vote. *NAMUDNO* fit the mold of a case where Kennedy's preferences would be decisive.

The *NAMUDNO* decision was full of surprises for the composition of its majority, the author of the Court's opinion, and the scope of the decision. When *NAMUDNO* came down on June 22, the Court voted 8–1 rather than 5–4 to reverse the finding of the DCDC panel and to remand the case. Chief Justice John Roberts and not Kennedy delivered the opinion of the Court, and the lone partial dissent came from Justice Clarence Thomas. The majority opinion focused entirely on the statutory issue, allowing the Court to avoid the constitutional issues (an application of the doctrine of constitutional avoidance). However, both the majority opinion and the Thomas dissent prompted widespread concerns and cautions regarding the continuing constitutionality of Section 5.

Chief Justice Roberts noted that the MUD sought constitutional relief *only* if it lost the statutory challenge to bail out under Section 4. Seizing on this opening, he observed that the larger constitutional questions "attracted ardent briefs from dozens of interested parties, but the importance of the question does not justify our rushing to decide it." Roberts and seven of his colleagues demonstrated their own restraint, noting that the "usual practice [of the Court] is to avoid the unnecessary resolution of constitutional questions."[29] The Supreme Court reversed the lower court and found NAMUDNO eligible to seek bailout.

Despite not reaching the constitutional question, the Court took time to engage the constitutional question on an intellectual level. Roberts's opinion explored constitutional issues related to Section 5, all the while declining to rule on these issues. Some justices had expressed concerns about the constitutionality of Section 5, a concern first articulated by Justice Hugo Black in 1966 in *Katzenbach,* later echoed by Justice John Harlan in *Allen* and by Justice Lewis Powell in *City of Rome.*[30] Justices Kennedy and Thomas had indicated concerns about the constitutionality of Section 5, most recently in the *LULAC* decision involving the Texas congressional redistricting of 2003.[31]

Justice Roberts advanced a strong argument for reassessing Section 5's constitutionality:

> Some of the conditions that we relied upon in upholding this statutory scheme in *Katzenbach* and *City of Rome* have unquestionably improved. Things have changed in the South. Voter turnout and registration rates now approach parity. Blatantly discriminatory evasions of federal decrees are rare. And minority candidates hold office at unprecedented levels. . . . these improvements are no doubt due in significant part to the Voting Rights Act itself, and stand as a monument to its success. . . . the Act imposes current burdens and must be justified by current needs.[32]

Roberts also noted concerns regarding equal sovereignty among the states, guaranteed by the Constitution, and questioned the scope of coverage of the Section 4 trigger:

> A departure from the fundamental principle of equal sovereignty requires a showing that a statute's disparate geographic coverage is sufficiently related to the problem that it targets. . . . The evil that §5 is meant to address may no longer be concentrated in the jurisdictions singled out for preclearance. The statute's coverage formula is based on data that is now more than 35 years old, and there is considerable evidence that it fails to account for current political conditions.[33]

Roberts referenced the Project Fair Vote analyses incorporated into the Senate Judiciary Committee minority report by Senators John Cornyn (R-Tex.) and Tom Coburn (R-Okla.), showing that "the racial gap in voter registration and turnout is lower in the States originally covered by §5 than it is nationwide," and also evidence from several amicus briefs filed in support of the MUD.[34]

The cautions directed at lawmakers even from supporters of the Act during reauthorization hearings (see chap. 5) loomed large in the majority's opinion. Justice Roberts cast light on an issue well documented in the journals after the renewal, that "Congress heard warnings from supporters of extending §5 that the evidence in the record did not address 'systematic differences between the covered and the non-covered areas of the United States . . . and, in fact, the evidence that is in the record suggests that there is more similarity than difference."[35] The Court, when assessing the balance of the evidentiary record against the scope of coverage and impact of the Act on federalism, was circumspect but skeptical:

> The Act's preclearance requirements and its coverage formula raise serious constitutional questions under either test. . . . More than 40 years ago, this Court concluded that "exceptional conditions" prevailing in certain parts of the country justified extraordinary legislation otherwise unfamiliar to our federal system. *Katzenbach*, 383 U.S., at 334. In part due to the success of that legislation, we are now a very different Nation. Whether conditions continue to justify such legislation is a difficult constitutional question we do not answer today. We conclude instead that the Voting Rights Act permits all political subdivisions, including the district in this case, to seek relief from its preclearance requirements.[36]

Justice Thomas, concurring in part and dissenting in part, criticized the majority's circumspect constitutional approach. The "appeal presents two questions: first, whether appellant is entitled to bail out from coverage under the Voting Rights Act of 1965 (VRA); and second, whether the preclearance requirement of §5 of the VRA is unconstitutional." The majority opinion dissatisfied Thomas because it "does not provide appellant with full relief," making it "inappropriate to apply the constitutional avoidance doctrine in this case. . . . Regardless of the Court's resolution of the statutory question . . . this case raises serious questions concerning the constitutionality of §5 of the VRA. . . . The ultimate relief sought in this case is not bailout eligibility—it is bailout itself." Justice Thomas argued that, because the Court could not afford final relief in the form of bailout, the Court needed to decide the larger constitutional issue: "To the extent that constitutional avoidance is a worthwhile tool of statutory construction, it is because it allows a court to dispose of an entire case on grounds that do not require the court to pass on a statute's constitutionality. . . . The doctrine of constitutional avoidance is also unavailable here because an interpretation of §4(a) that merely makes more political subdivisions eligible for bailout does not render §5 constitutional and the Court notably does not suggest otherwise."[37]

Thomas was skeptical about the potential for most jurisdictions to make use of the bailout provision, terming it a "distant prospect." He observed that "all 17 covered jurisdictions that have been awarded bailout are from Virginia . . . and all 17 were represented by the same attorney—a former lawyer in the Voting Rights Section of the Department of Justice [Gerry Hebert]." Of some 12,000 government jurisdictions conducting elections within more than nine hundred covered jurisdictions that registered voters, only seventeen had successfully exited Section 5. Justice Thomas continued, opining that "whatever the reason for this anomaly, it only underscores how little relationship there is between the existence of bailout and the constitutionality of §5."[38]

Beyond this issue of limited success in bailing out, Justice Thomas forcefully took to task the evidentiary record advanced by Congress for supporting the 2006 renewal:

> The lack of current evidence of intentional discrimination with respect to voting renders §5 unconstitutional. The provision can no longer be justified as an appropriate mechanism for enforcement of the Fifteenth Amendment. . . . The Court has never deviated from this understanding. . . . Congress must establish a "history and pattern" of constitutional violations to establish the need for §5 by justifying a remedy that pushes the limits of its constitutional authority. . . . for §5 to withstand renewed constitutional scrutiny, there must be a demonstrated connection between the "remedial measures" chosen and the "evil presented" in the record made by Congress when it renewed the Act. . . . The extensive pattern of discrimination that led the Court to previously uphold §5 as enforcing the Fifteenth Amendment no longer exists.[39]

The evidence was inadequate to the task in Justice Thomas's opinion, and the majority opinion also raised questions about the weight of discrimination relative to the constitutional issue. As we explore further below, this issue of data and evidence in context is not merely a technical one for social science but also a substantive one for lawmakers and judges who make determinations about the law and the Constitution based on empirics. Good intentions, it seems, also require impressive and very good data regarding the social biases that are at work.

Context matters when determining how evidence is considered when making law. In his *NAMUDNO* dissent, Justice Thomas echoed many witnesses and scholars who contended that the evidence of problems was thin compared to the continued scope of the federal intervention. Much as it is increasingly difficult to distinguish a racial vote from a party vote in a general election, it is also important to remember that a racial vote does not rise to the level of unconstitutional discrimination, and that the evidence that warrants overturning just politics under our constitutional system must be compelling. According to Justice Thomas:

> when reenacting §5 in 2006, Congress evidently understood that the emergency conditions which prompted §5's original enactment no longer exist. . . . Instead of relying on the kind of evidence that the *Katzenbach* Court had found so persuasive, Congress instead based reenactment on evidence of what it termed "second generation barriers" constructed to prevent minority voters from fully participating in the electoral process. . . . Congress relied upon evidence of racially polarized voting within the covered jurisdictions. But racially polarized voting is not evidence of unconstitutional discrimination . . . is not state action . . . and is not a problem unique to the South. . . . The other evidence relied on by Congress, such as §5 enforcement actions, §2 and 4 lawsuits, and federal examiner and observer coverage, also bears no resemblance to the record initially supporting §5, and is plainly insufficient to sustain such an extraordinary remedy.[40]

In sum, evidence of "second generation barriers" did not compare to the prevalent and pervasive voting discrimination of the 1960s. Moreover, it stood up poorly to evidence of dramatically declining federal intervention, growth in minority office holding, voter participation, and the emergence of a politics in which the South and the rest of the nation were now more alike than different. The text of Thomas's dissent read, in many ways, like the draft of a majority opinion or a warning shot to Congress to deal with the defects identified in the opinion of the Court and also the minority dissent.

NAMUDNO did not prompt the Supreme Court to invalidate any portion of the Voting Rights Act, but it did set off an unprecedented level of activity by jurisdictions seeking to bail out. After NAMUDNO, additional jurisdictions succeeded in escaping Section 5 review as of the end of May 2013. Although some of these jurisdictions were independent cities or counties in Virginia, they also included the nine covered towns in New Hampshire. Other successful bailout efforts were launched by a city in Georgia, a town in Alabama, a drainage district in Texas, a city in North Carolina, and Merced County, California. But it would be the unsuccessful efforts wherein the danger lay for the VRA. Writing in the immediate aftermath of the NAMUDNO decision in 2009, Bullock and Gaddie indicated concern for the viability of the preclearance regime: "[NAMUDNO] opens the way for jurisdictions other than states and counties to seek bailout from Section 5. But, it also illuminates the constitutional vulnerability of the legislation, and in so doing, offers no ready hope for retention in a direct challenge. The lack of a concurrence defending the constitutionality of Section 5 is surprising, and seems to invite additional challenges in the near future. Supporters and opponents of Section 5 await that challenge, likely from one or more southern counties seeking bailout."[41]

The challenge came quickly from Shelby County, Alabama.

# 7    *Shelby County* and Equal Sovereignty

In this chapter we look at the rationale for the litigation brought that led to *Shelby County*, a case that is in itself a continuation of the political pushback described in chapter 6 and which led to the *NAMUDNO* decision. Then we explore the environment prevailing in the Court leading up to *Shelby County* and explain the creation of an appellate environment that made the Voting Rights Act ripe for challenge. We look at the Court's applied logic in *Shelby County* through multiple theoretical lenses and in particular situate the case among several other recent, controversial cases. In the latter, the Court has actively pursued an aggressive approach to constraining Congress and especially congressional authority that relies on the Commerce Clause—and by extension its application of that authority through the Fourteenth Amendment.

*Shelby County v. Holder* did more than strike down the Section 4 coverage formula of the Voting Rights Act. The decision effectively ended close scrutiny of the conduct of state elections. And, possibly of greater importance, the Court in *Shelby County* also entrenched as precedent an idea that conservatives on the Court had been floating since the *NAMUDNO* case—namely, that each state in the union enjoys "equal sovereignty." Equal sovereignty is a nebulous concept, but the Court brought it full bore in *Shelby County*. The Court also signaled its continued defense of a conservative notion of federalism, one that seems to preclude all national congressional efforts to regulate elections except those specifically mentioned in Article I of the Constitution. Finally, the Court employed the theme of time and temporality to explain and defend its decision to strike down Section 4. According to the Court's majority, the Act was a temporary and extraordinary action taken by Congress in 1965, even despite continued renewals by subsequent congresses. And, based on the Court's reading of the evidence and the burden the Act placed on states and their "equal sovereignty," the Act's day had literally passed.

These several themes are of a piece with the Roberts Court and also the Rehnquist Court that preceded it. Since the early 1990s the conservative bloc of the Supreme Court had been moving in step with these themes, even apart from voting rights cases. These efforts from the conservative bloc have not always been successful. But they prevailed in *Shelby County*, not in a novel way but in a fashion that followed several previous decisions from this bloc on the Court. In this sense, as momentous as *Shelby County* is, it is just one more case that is following a conservative path set decades earlier.

## THE CHALLENGE: WHY *SHELBY COUNTY*?

Congressional refusal to modernize the Voting Rights Act triggers convinced critics such as Edward Blum that litigation held the only hope for eliminating Section 5 or getting a recalibration of the triggers in Section 4. By the time he refocused his attention from an effort to get Congress to revisit the components of the Act that did not apply nationwide, Blum had extensive experience in filing test cases in voting rights and civil rights cases. In addition to the successful challenges to the 1990s race-based congressional districts in Texas, New York, South Carolina, and Virginia, he had funded efforts to eliminate affirmative action. He succeeded in preventing the use of race when selecting children for Houston's gifted program.

Blum used his American Enterprise Institute connections to tap donors to sponsor, initially, three suits, although he ultimately launched a four-case legal effort, all but one of which countered congressional action renewing Section 5. Three of these cases made it to the Supreme Court. This is an extraordinary rate of success, since the Court agrees to hear fewer than one hundred of the thousands of cases requesting review each term. Blum's previous successes fueled these new efforts. "By getting cases to the Supreme Court it makes donors more generous," Blum observed. "I can tell them I am going to take a case to the Supreme Court and now they believe me."[1]

Just as civil rights lawyers had looked for cases with which to test changing attitudes on the Supreme Court when attacking discriminatory practices a couple of generations earlier, Blum set out to identify a jurisdiction he could use to force the high court to revisit Sections 4 and 5 of the Act. He explained the process:

> I needed a jurisdiction. I looked at each county subject to Section 5. I looked at election results from 2000 and 2004. I looked at counties with wide Bush margins. I called the chair or judge of the county commission and board of supervisors. I needed a relatively small jurisdiction so that my phone calls would get through directly to the decision maker. If I went to a big county some secretary would intercept the message and write "kook" underneath my name. In Texas I looked at counties that had between 1,400 and 10,000 people. Otherwise the layers of bureaucracy are too great. I offered legal help to challengers. I spoke to Federalist Societies and friends through my network. Finally I came across Greg Coleman who had clerked with Justice Thomas when the *Vera* case went up. He was living in Austin. He was the one who pointed to NAMUDNO. As it was being litigated, since it was clear that granting a bailout was a possibility, I looked for a backup.

The outcome of the *NAMUDNO* case (see chap. 6) left Blum to activate his backup. When the Supreme Court dodged the question of the constitutionality of Section 5, Blum was ready with Shelby County, Alabama. He explained this choice. "Shelby County was attractive because it couldn't bail out. There had been objections in the county [by DOJ]." Alex Dudchock, the county manager for Shelby County, identified some of the features that made his county an attractive choice for a test case. African Americans had won elections in heavily white jurisdictions including the mayor's office in Pelham, which is only 7 percent black. As further evidence that black candidates could succeed, Dudchock pointed to a county board of education contest in which the white female incumbent who held a doctorate lost to by a black male. Moreover, the county had a history of hiring African Americans for a variety of administrative positions.[2]

As a first step, Blum approached Frank "Butch" Ellis, a former legislator who has served as Shelby County attorney since 1964. "It was not hard to convince the county attorney in Shelby County," Blum recollected. "He hated Section 5. He was angered at the difficulties in getting preclearance. He represented a number of other jurisdiction in the county. As a result of Section 5 objections they had to cancel elections. He was thrilled when I called. Challenging Section 5 was expensive. But since I would come up with the funding, the county would not have to divert hundreds of thousands of dollars or even one million." County manager Dudchock agreed: "It wasn't a hard sell for me. Section 5 made no sense to me. I never thought Section 5 would hold up. The only rationale for its maintenance was a political one."

Ellis put it this way: "For several years we had thought that Section 4B and Section 5 were unjustified. They were unfair. We had to preclear every little thing that we did."[3] He pointed to a specific difficulty that he, as attorney not just for the county but for several jurisdictions within the county, confronted. As he laid out the case, local communities could create medical, fire, and protection districts, which was done in a grassroots movement when the local volunteer fire department became overwhelmed as a result of population growth. The fire districts provided both fire protection and EMS services and had the power to tax in order to fund these services. Alabama law required that an election occur within forty-five days of the creation of such a unit, but the creation of such entities required preclearance and therein lay a potential problem. DOJ had sixty days during which to object to a submission. Moreover, DOJ required separate requests for preclearance of the action creating the administrative unit and the scheduling of a special election to choose trustees for the new unit. Ellis noted that because of delays in securing preclearance some elections had to be delayed, and the need for two rounds of approval added greatly to the cost.

The experience with annexations to the City of Calera along Shelby County's southern border especially galled Ellis. Like many municipalities, Calera allows property owners adjacent to the city boundary to petition for inclusion. When he became city attorney, Ellis discovered that the city had failed to seek preclearance for annexations during the previous thirteen years, allowing 177 annexations to go unapproved. When the city sought preclearance, DOJ denied the request on the grounds that the city had failed to provide reliable data on its current population, its voting age population, and the racial composition.[4] Specifically, the denial letter challenged the city's estimates of its total population and the current black percentage. In this, the last Section 5 objection registered in Alabama, DOJ asserted that adding these parcels to the city would eliminate the only majority-black council district, a district that had elected an African American for two decades. DOJ wondered why the city council had not considered alternative methods of election. Ellis was angered because, had the annexations been submitted when first made and before being developed with housing, he believed DOJ would have found no fault. Calera resolved the issue by switching from single-member districts to an at-large, limited voting system akin to that used for most of the postwar period in Japan, in which each voter registers a single preference and the six most popular candidates constitute the council. Under this system, the council's black member won reelection.

Ellis readily joined in the chorus that included critics of the extension of preclearance in the 2006 legislation: "I support the Voting Rights Act. . . . It has done a good job. It corrected inequities which existed in the past. But Section 5 has outlived its relevancy. Congress never intended for Section 5 to be permanent. It was approved initially for five years. Now Section 2 is intended to be permanent and we didn't attack it. In the early days Section 5 was justified. It matched the wrong with the remedy. Things now have changed." As evidence of the changes in Shelby County, Ellis pointed to the election of black candidates, some of whom, he said, have succeeded in predominantly white districts. He referenced a city about three-fourths white that had elected a black mayor on more than one occasion. Voters in another city had elected a black council member from a district Ellis described as 97 percent white. The school board, elected countywide in this approximately 25 percent black county, had a black member.

Ellis and Dudchock recommended to the county board that it become the test case. The commission voted 9–0 to serve as plaintiff so long as the county did not incur any cost.

## UNDERSTANDING SHELBY COUNTY

Until *Shelby County*, the most salient case to come before the Roberts Court was *National Federation of Independent Business v. Sebelius*— the ObamaCare decision.[5] But here, the chief justice seemed to take an about-face. So how do we make sense of this? One explanation could simply be that Roberts followed the law. According to the "legal model" of judicial behavior, judges are guided by legal norms, precedent, rules, and constitutional and statutory text to resolve cases. *Sebelius* does and does not conform to this model. From one perspective, Roberts's rationale for upholding the ObamaCare legislation—Congress' taxing power—could be seen as a mechanical application of the law in that it could be construed, as he suggested, as "construing a statute to save it."[6] But on the Commerce Clause question, which the Roberts rejected, he went to great lengths to hew his opinion to the Court's post-1995 arguments. More than likely, then, something other than the legal model was at work.

Attitudinal models of politics assume that judges are like other politicians, who just vote their political preferences or tastes. From this perspective the assumption would be that Roberts simply votes his policy preference, unencumbered by legal rules and precedent. This reduces, for example, Justice Roberts to being just another Republican and Justice Ginsburg to just another Democrat. Particularly in civil liberties cases (Fourth Amendment), there is evidence that this model is persuasive. But this cannot be the whole story in this case, because every justice *but* Roberts voted the way the attitudinal model would have predicted.

Related to the attitudinal model is the strategic model.[7] The strategic approach to judicial decision making largely agrees with the attitudinal model, in that justices vote their policy preferences. But strategic theorists believe that justices also want to *win*. A simple roll call of attitudes can always lose, so justices often modify their ideal preferences to achieve a minimal winning coalition. This trimming of ideology (or of logic) allows them to accomplish the broader goal in an adversarial system where there is more than one play in the game. The attitudinal and strategic models are powerful and persuasive models, but we are asking about the conditions under which these variables are more or less helpful. Even if reports of Roberts switching his vote are wrong, the strategic model does not explain *Sebelius* either, because the conservatives would not need to adjust their preferences *at all* to achieve their desired result.

Another explanation could be "regime theory," which might arguably have been the perspective from which opponents of the VRA hoped would predict their preferred outcome.[8] Without rejecting attitudinal and strategic explanations outright, regime theory seeks to explain long-term judicial outcomes as part of the larger political process, particularly critical election theory. Justices are appointed by presidents and confirmed by the Senate, so over time we get judicial outcomes from courts that largely uphold the core political commitments and values of the regimes that appointed them. Again, Roberts's vote in this case is not explained by regime theory.

A more "historical-institutional" approach, on the other hand, might give us something close to a valid explanation. Although this perspective certainly admits that judges are often solicitous of their policy preferences and concedes that at times they might act strategically to achieve those preferences, it also sees justices as solicitous of their own peculiar institutional roles as well. This means that the institution itself might produce incentives or preferences (e.g., concern for its independence or legitimacy). Institutions, as Rogers M. Smith argues, can "influence the self-conception of those who occupy roles defined by them in ways that can give those persons distinctively 'institutional' perspectives."[9] Among the various approaches, then, this explanation might have the most explanatory power.

Alexander Hamilton declared the judiciary to be the "least dangerous branch," largely because it had neither the "power of the purse or of the sword" to enforce its opinions.[10] It only has judgment, and that judgment cannot have any meaningful effect if the institution's independence is threatened, especially if it is threatened because other institutions doubt its legitimacy. Robert McCloskey persuasively argues that "the judges have usually known what students have sometimes not known—that their tribunal must be a court, as well as seem one, if it is to retain its power."[11] If there are to be politics, they are to be tempered by the acceptance of the court's legitimacy and primacy by other political actors who come before it. Here, then, we can start to see how and why some judges—and in the health care decision Chief Justice Roberts seems to be one of them—might vote in ways that are different from, and even diametrically opposed to, their own preferences, or the preferences of the regime from which they were appointed.

To understand *Shelby County*, it helps to first understand the signals from the Court that precede the case. The political aspects of this larger trend are instructive to how constitutional politics actually work. Political science research finds myriad reasons political parties often use the courts to get their work done.[12] One obvious way is when a party—like the Republicans in early 2008—is on the losing end in the election: it can attempt to overcome this institutional reality by appealing to a seemingly sympathetic Court, in the hopes that the Court might change the rules and, by extension, the political outcome. The courts become an extension of the political fight that most citizens presumed was resolved either at the ballot box or in the legislative process.

There are recent examples of this phenomenon. One is the pursuit of litigation and then the subsequent Court decision in *National Federation of Independent Business v. Sebelius.* Despite *legal* speculation that the Patient Protection Affordable Care Act (PPACA) would be upheld based upon the Court's post-1937 deference to a broad conception of Congress's Commerce Clause powers, the reality was that this had been a reliably conservative court, made up of a majority of justices appointed by Republican presidents. With few exceptions, then, opponents of the Act had good reason to believe that the Roberts Court would sustain their objections to the PPACA, if only because it and the Rehnquist Court before it had been unabashed in their willingness to advance a conservative vision of constitutional governance.

This conservative vision made a Commerce Clause–based defense of PPACA potentially suspect. With respect to Commerce Clause cases, both the Rehnquist and Roberts courts had signaled a line in the post-1937 sand in two cases—*U.S. v. Lopez* (1995), striking down the Gun-Free School Zones Act, and *U.S. v. Morrison* (2000), striking down the Violence Against Women Act)—that they were willing to constrain Congress's expansive use of the Commerce Clause.[13] And when Congress's powers have been upheld by these courts, the substantive area in question has been criminal law, an area that is central to the conservative agenda. For example, in *Gonzales v. Raich* (2005) the Court upheld Congress's ability to criminalize the production of marijuana in states that allowed such production. It also upheld Congress's power to require civil commitment for sex offenders in *U.S. v. Comstock* (2010).[14] Similarly, in the equal protection arena, the Roberts Court struck down even minimal attempts by school districts to achieve racial integration, with the chief justice arguing that "the way to stop discrimination on the basis of race is to stop discriminating on the basis of race."[15] And though the Court had never come close to overturning the *Roe* decision, with respect to abortion, the Roberts Court upheld the Partial Birth Abortion Act in *Gonzales v. Carhart* (2007).[16] The conservatives on the Court seem to have had little "taste" for the flavor of arguments invested in the Commerce Clause if they resided outside the policy preferences of their ideology. Recent history revealed a political dimension to constitutional interpretation that defied abstract theories vested solely in the assumption that construction and interpretation need be only politically convenient, rather than intellectually consistent.

Roberts wrote in *NAMUDNO* for a near-unanimous court in allowing a political subdivision to bail out from the Voting Rights Act's preclearance requirements, but ground was also laid in that case for potentially overturning large portions of the Act (see chap. 6). The chief justice signaled that, though he was not asked to strike down portions of the Act specifically (citing the doctrine of "constitutional avoidance"), another Court might do so. The Court had already acted in such a fashion when confronted with challenges to handgun ownership in Chicago. Toeing the party line as close as the chalk allowed, the Court not only (re)interpreted the Second Amendment as guaranteeing an individual right to own a firearm but incorporated this right against the states.[17] These were not new arguments, at least from the perspective of an increasingly conservative Court.

The Roberts Court behavior was not new, and it was not a departure in the behavior of the conservative majority. The previous Supreme Court, led by William Rehnquist, had also been moving in these directions. In *Seminole Tribe v. Florida*, the Court addressed a law that required states to negotiate with Indian tribes who were pursuing casino and gaming ventures.[18] The Rehnquist Court ruled that Congress could not abrogate the sovereign immunity of states under the Commerce Clause even though legal intercourse with the tribes is conducted by Congress only according to Article I. In *Alden v. Maine*, the Court held that states were immune from challenges that they (the states) violated federal laws that were identical to state laws. And maybe most important for the issues in *NAMUDNO* and later *Shelby County*, in *City of Boerne v. Flores* the Rehnquist Court held that Congress could use its Section 5 powers under the Fourteenth Amendment only to remedy supposed constitutional violations as the Court understood them. Moreover, Congress's remedies were limited to what the Court deemed "congruent and proportional" remedies.[19]

Arguably the biggest signal of the Roberts Court's overlap with these conservative visions of constitutional governance was *Citizens United v. FEC*.[20] Many saw this case as clear evidence that the Roberts

Court—and the chief justice himself—was truly on board and unafraid of advancing the conservative agenda. Even though in *Gonzales v. Carhart* the door was left open for future as-applied challenges, the Court (with Roberts) nevertheless declined to overrule *Roe* and *Casey*.[21] Moreover, in *District of Columbia v. Heller* the Court announced that the Second Amendment included a personal right to firearms, and just two years later in *McDonald v. City of Chicago* the Court selectively incorporated Second Amendment against the states, which has largely been part of the liberal agenda.[22]

In *Citizens United*, the initial argument made by the nonprofit Citizens United (represented by former George W. Bush solicitor general Ted Olson) was that it should simply be exempt from existing campaign finance regulations. During oral arguments, though, it quickly became clear that the conservative justices were, according to Jeffrey Toobin, "disappointed by the modesty of Olson's claim."[23] This was confirmed when the deputy solicitor general, Malcolm Stewart, addressed the Court. Alito, Scalia, and Roberts pushed the argument further, asking Stewart if he believed existing regulations would also require a ban on other forms of advocacy beyond commercial and broadcast media, including books. Seemingly flummoxed, Stewart responded: "Well, if it says vote for X, it would be express advocacy and it would be covered by the pre-existing Federal Election Campaign Act provision."[24]

The initial conference vote was unsurprising, with a 5–4 conservative majority. The initial draft opinions, though, began to change when circulated among the justices. Roberts's opinion was limited to the narrow question of exemption, but Kennedy's went further, arguing that McCain-Feingold was unconstitutional. Soon, Scalia, Alito, and Thomas indicated their support for Kennedy's opinion. Roberts then assigned the majority opinion to Kennedy. Angered, Justice Souter (who had just announced his impending retirement) wrote in dissent an argument that was not just a critique of the legal issues but a broadside leveled against what he perceived as a disingenuous attempt by the conservatives to achieve a result in the case that even the petitioners had not advanced. Maybe recognizing the potential damage to the Court's legitimacy and reputation, Roberts jettisoned the majority opinion and ordered another round of arguments to consider whether to overrule *Austin v. Michigan Chamber of Commerce* (1990), *McConnell v. Federal Election Commission* (2003), or both.[25]

The final decision—which did indeed overturn both cases and also characterized corporations as citizens—was highly controversial. For our purposes, though, the fact that the chief justice was moved to issue a concurring opinion addressing "the important principles of judicial restraint and *stare decisis* implicated in this case" is most significant.[26] Unmoved by the chief justice's attempt to defend the decision, though, Justice John Paul Stevens railed against the majority: "The Court's ruling threatens to undermine the integrity of elected institutions across the country. The path it has taken to reach this outcome will, I fear, *do damage to this institution*" (emphasis added).[27] And, of course, six days later President Obama criticized the Court in his State of the Union Address, which led to Justice Alito angrily mouthing, "Not true!" in response. It did indeed seem that even if "damage" had not been done to the institution as a result of the decision, it was, at the very least, in the crosshairs.

## RESULT: *SHELBY COUNTY V. HOLDER*

This case does not present the same competing considerations as cases like *Sebelius*. Unlike *Sebelius*, the *Shelby County* decision was decided on familiar ideological grounds, not on a sense of duty to the legitimacy of the court as an institution. Roberts wrote the majority opinion, in which Scalia, Thomas, Kennedy, and Alito joined. Justice Ginsburg's dissent was joined by Justices Kagan, Sotomayor, and Breyer. This is the familiar 5–4 breakdown that we are used to seeing for well over a decade now.

As we have argued so far in this chapter, issues of federalism and state sovereignty have motivated both the previous Rehnquist Court and certainly the Roberts Court. As we explain the *Shelby County* decision below, these two issues again form a large part of the Court's reasoning in striking down Section 4 of the Voting Rights Act, especially as the majority argues for the unique notion of a fundamental principle of "equal state sovereignty among states."[28] There is one other important idea, though—one that the Court utilizes in analyzing not just this most recent case but *all* of the voting rights cases over the previous fifty years: temporality. The Voting Rights Act of 1965 has permanent provisions, but the most powerful component in particular was only ever meant to be a *temporary* legislative power, not a permanent one. Congress, in effectively taking over the conduct of all state authority to conduct elections, had stepped outside the ordinary bounds of the Constitution. This extraconstitutional assertion of power was based on the assumption of extraordinary circumstances so dire that they constituted an emergency and required extreme action to ensure the rights and sovereignty of American citizens. It was not meant to be a permanent regulatory regime. The evidence relied on by the *Shelby County* majority in overturning the key provision of the Act asserted a change in circumstance and attempted to belie the emergency.

Chief Justice John Roberts begins his majority opinion by using language that characterizes the original VRA as employing "extraordinary measures to address an extraordinary problem." Section 5, he explains, requires federal approval of any change in or enactment of a voting—"an equally dramatic departure from the principle that all states enjoy equal sovereignty." Although this was "strong medicine," the Court in 1965 had determined that "exceptional conditions can justify legislative measures not otherwise appropriate." Already Roberts is making familiar federalism and state sovereignty arguments buttressed by the notion that the Act was a temporary anomaly. For the Court, even though the Act had been extended many times, with the most recent extension expiring in 2031, the conditions that produced the anomaly of the Act in 1965 had changed. Roberts makes this argument by citing statistics that show that the "racial gap" in voter registration and voter turnout in 2009 was lower in states originally covered by the Act than it was nationwide. He also argues that census data showed the African American voter turnout exceeded white voter turnout in five of the six states originally covered. Though Roberts does concede that discrimination "still exists; no one doubts that," the Act still had to pass constitutional muster, "including its disparate treatment of states."[29]

The heart of decision begins with a brief history of the challenges to minority voting. The Fifteenth Amendment, passed during Reconstruction to prohibit the denial of voting on account of race, color, or previous condition of servitude, quickly failed to achieve its stated goal, as congressional enforcement of the amendment was a "failure."[30] With the ugly rise of Jim Crow in the 1890s, states such as Alabama, Georgia, Louisiana, Mississippi, North Carolina, South Carolina, and Virginia enacted creative measures to disfranchise African Americans. The most onerous off these measures were the notoriously inscrutable literacy tests. And early congressional legislation to combat the measures only slightly improved access to the vote.

Skipping to the middle of the twentieth century, Roberts then lays out the provisions of the original Act as passed in 1965 and as renewed and expanded over the next forty-one years. Of particular concern for Roberts in his explanation of the Act is that the baselines for covered jurisdictions never extended past the 1972 election cycle and that each renewal was only intended to be temporary, evidenced by Congress extending, not making permanent, the Voting Rights Act. As a result, Section 5, in particular, "imposes substantial federalism costs" and "differentiates between the States, despite our historic tradition that all the States enjoy equal sovereignty."[31]

After reviewing the rulings of lower federal courts with respect to Shelby County's (the county lost all of its claims), Roberts then continues his federalism arguments and also invokes both the Supremacy Clause in Article 6 and the federal elections clause in Article I in explaining further how the Act fails constitutional muster. First, although "State legislation cannot contravene federal law," the federal cannot as a general rule "review and veto" state legislation before it goes into effect. Second, consistent with the already developing jurisprudence of federalism of the Roberts and Rehnquist courts, the chief justice argues that states retain broad powers in determining the election procedures of their own states, with the Tenth Amendment buttressing these state election powers. He even asserts that this "allocation of powers in our federal system preserves the integrity, dignity, and residual sovereignty of the States."[32]

Of course, the federal elections clause in Article I establishes certain enumerated federal powers over state elections, like determining the time and manner of state elections for Congress. Nevertheless, according to Roberts, the founders envisioned the states controlling the "power to regulate elections," including the power to determine "the conditions under which the right of suffrage may be exercised," the power to "prescribe the qualifications of its officers and the manner in which they shall be chosen," and the power of drawing congressional districts, which is "primarily the duty and responsibility of the State."[33]

Most fundamentally for the Court, though, is a "fundamental principle of *equal* sovereignty among the states."[34] Even though this "principle" seems only to have applied to the admission of new states to the union, and even thought the Warren Court rejected its use outside of this context, Roberts and his majority nevertheless resurrected it as dicta in *NAMUDNO* and finally apply it here in *Shelby*.

The "principle of equal sovereignty" seems to require that the Court apply strict scrutiny—the highest level of review by the Court—to any legislation affecting this sovereignty. For Roberts and the majority, the Act does not meet these requirements; legislation that gets strict scrutiny must meet a compelling government interest, be narrowly tailored to address the exact problem, and be designed to be the least restrictive alternative among other legislative options. For the reasons we have highlighted—temporality, equal sovereignty among the states, and the purported changing conditions in which minorities vote—the majority asserts that it has the awesome privilege of striking down an Act of Congress, "the gravest and most delicate duty that this Court is called on to perform."[35] Roberts argues that the Court warned Congress in *NAMUDNO* that the provisions and requirements in Section 4 were suspect. Since no changes had been made in accord with the Court majority's suggestions, they had no other choice than to rule Section 4 unconstitutional. Summing up his argument, Roberts states, "Our country has changed, and while any racial discrimination in voting is too much, Congress must ensure that the legislation it passes to remedy that problem speaks to current conditions."[36]

## CONTRA *SHELBY COUNTY*: THE OLD ORDER IN DISSENT?

The dissent, written by Justice Ruth Bader Ginsburg, proceeds along three important arguments. The first is the admittedly difficult challenge of defending the Voting Rights Act when conditions have improved across many dimensions. Does this then mean that the Act is no longer needed, or is it the case that it is still needed in order to maintain these positive changes? Second, although the majority has argued that gains have been made in voting access with the Act over the past fifty years, the minority will argue that these are only one kind of voter discrimination that the Act is meant to protect. These "first-generation" obstacles—voting registration and participation—pale in comparison to newer, "second-generation" forms of discrimination that continue to rear their heads. Finally, the dissent will attack the judicial activism of the majority in striking down a piece of congressional legislation—the Voting Rights Act—

which has time and again been justified and reauthorized. This last point, in particular, pits the increasingly conservative Court majority against what is likely to be a permanent minority of liberal justices in the near future.

Leading the dissent, Justice Ginsburg begins her opinion by attacking the very notion that the Act is no longer needed because it has reduced some forms of voter discrimination: "In the [majority's] view, the very success of §5 of the Voting Rights Act demands its dormancy." Congress, though, thought differently, she argues, not only because have they reauthorized the Act as recently as 2006, but also because they have added more provisions to the Act. With each reauthorization, moreover, Congress has provided voluminous evidence to justify its actions. These congressional actions over the past five decades would ensure that the gains in voting were buttressed and that these rights would not be lost by cessation of the Act. Congress's "assessments were well within [its] province to make and should elicit this Court's unstinting approbation."[37]

Ginsburg certainly recognizes that dramatic improvements had been realized as a result of the Act, but unlike the majority she believes that the Act is still needed to prevent and protect against myriad types of discrimination that voters still face. For example, each year the U.S. attorney general declines to accept numerous types of voting changes submitted by jurisdictions covered by Section 4, suggesting that these jurisdictions are still trying to interfere with voting rights. One congressional finding, for example, suggested that as minority voting registration increased other kinds of attempts to dilute minority voting quickly took their place.

These "second-generation" barriers to voting rights lie at the heart of the minority's argument. Second-generation barriers continue to take many forms. One example is racial gerrymandering of state legislative districts, which is an "effort to segregate the races for the purposes of voting." Another example is at-large voting. At-large, as opposed, to single-member districts, can effectively dilute minority voting power by subjecting an otherwise successful candidate in a minority district to the votes of the larger majority in a district that now includes the minority voters, thus diluting their voting preferences. Minority voting dilution can also be achieved by annexing a majority-white municipality into a neighboring majority-black municipality; again, white votes would dilute the voting strength of black votes. Moreover, the Court has consistently accepted these

arguments that "voting dilution, when adopted with a discriminatory purpose, cuts down the right to vote as certainly as denial of
the ballot." Indeed, the House report in support of the 2006 VRA
reauthorization found that "discrimination today is more subtle than
the visible methods used in 1965 . . . and the effect and results are
the same, namely a diminishing of the minority community's ability to fully participate in the electoral process and to elect their
preferred candidates."[38]

Over the years, these findings—and others—were fully accepted
by Congress, as it continued to "amass a sizeable" record of continued
barriers to voting discrimination. The only question that remains,
Ginsburg argues, is whether Congress had, and continues to have, the
constitutional authority to pass legislation that seeks to remedy these
barriers. The majority's use of strict scrutiny, she argues, flies in the
face of these well-grounded findings over the past fifty years—a
period of time in which no Court found Congress's authority lacking. Congress's power to pass legislation under the Fourteenth and
Fifteenth Amendments, she argues, "warrants substantial deference"
from the judiciary. Moreover, because the Act addresses the right to
vote, a right that is "preservative" of all other rights and racial discrimination, Congress's power to act through legislation is at its "height."
The Fourteenth and Fifteenth Amendments, which in their last
clauses explicitly provide that "Congress shall have power to enforce,
through appropriate legislation, the provisions of this article," are
fundamentally different than previous amendments, which only prevent or prohibit Congress from passing certain kinds of legislation.
Quoting constitutional scholar Akhil Amar, Ginsburg argues that
the Civil War amendments used "language that authorized trans-
formative new federal statutes to uproot all vestiges of unfreedom
and inequality" through "sweeping enforcement powers . . . to enact
appropriate legislation targeting state abuses." This means that, contrary to the use of strict scrutiny by the majority, the Court should
not ask whether the Congress's VRA is wise but whether "Congress
has rationally selected means appropriate to a legitimate end."[39]

The majority's level of analysis, then, is not only misapplied in
this case, it is created out of whole cloth. Ginsburg further points
out that in the first challenge to the constitutionality of the Voting
Rights Act, in *South Carolina v. Katzenbach* (1965), the standard of
review for Congress's power to remedy voting discrimination was

announced and accepted up until now: "As against the reserved power of the States, Congress may use any rational means to effectuate the constitutional prohibition of racial discrimination in voting."[40]

Ginsburg continues: The majority then develops three reasons why the reauthorization of existing legislation—like the Act—almost always satisfies rational-basis analysis. First, the many reauthorizations of the VRA over the past fifty years have resulted in a massive record of evidence detailing the necessity and propriety of congressional legislation in this area. Just as important as the evidence, though, is that during this time the Court has never voted down the basis for the Act, that is, Congress's power or approach to their legislative remedies. Second, and related to our arguments about temporality and the Act, the very fact that each reauthorization has a sunset provision suggests that Congress deserves great deference from the Court. Finally, the record obtained by Congress before each reauthorization should either show more or less racial discrimination in voting during the statute's lifetime, as indeed the record has shown.

Ginsburg is mindful, however, to argue that Congress's power is not limitless in the area of voting rights. Those limits are partly found in a judicial review that simply makes sure that Congress uses the appropriate means to remedy voting discrimination. More specifically, and in response to the majority, the Court's role in this situation "is not to substitute its judgment for that of Congress, but to determine whether the legislative record sufficed to show that 'Congress could rationally have determined that its chosen provisions were appropriate methods.'"[41] In sum, Congress has a wide berth to remedy voter discrimination, and the Court should give it great deference in determining evidence and in crafting remedial means in this area of the law.

## CONCLUSION

Taken in sum, the Roberts Court used (1) the temporal nature of the Voting Rights Act (its characterization as temporary and extraordinary legislation), (2) evidence of changing levels of African American voting participation and office holding, and (3) its conception of "equal state sovereignty" to strike down the key coverage provision of the Act. But the reasons it did this, and was able to do so, are the product of a long trajectory in the shaping and repositioning of the Court.

An identifiably conservative Supreme Court developed in the United States over the past twenty-five years. The individual legal and ideological views of the various Republican-appointed justices do vary, but there is nevertheless a clear agenda this conservative majority serves. The Rehnquist and Roberts Courts revived states' rights and Tenth Amendment arguments to limit federal power and regulation over states. In service of these arguments the Court in *Shelby County* went so far as to resurrect the doctrine of "equal state sovereignty." In doing so it was able not only to override vital parts of the Voting Rights Act but also to assert itself as a political institution into important legislative and executive decision making.

This trajectory of elevating states' rights over federal power is not new. What is new is the Court's successful use of the "equal state sovereignty" doctrine. The most prominent of recent criticisms of this doctrine comes from James Blacksher and Lani Guinier.[42] These two respected voting rights experts and litigators make the uncomfortable argument that the equal sovereignty doctrine has its roots in the infamous *Dred Scott* decision, and that it is specifically derived from Chief Justice Taney's majority opinion that ruled not only that blacks could never be citizens but also that the Missouri Compromise was unconstitutional in its ban on slavery in the territories.[43]

In advancing their thesis, Blacksher and Guinier use Taney's discussion of the privileges and immunities clause of Article IV of the Constitution (and then subsequently from the Fourteenth Amendment) as a vehicle. For the reader who might not have recently read *Dred Scott*, Justice Taney's understanding of the privileges and immunities clause was one that recognized a large swath of state sovereignty to determine exactly what citizens' privileges and immunities *were* that other states had to recognize. As applied by Taney in the *Dred Scott* case, this meant that blacks could not become citizens of a free state or territory merely by being present in them—whatever these privileges and immunities were, blacks were never meant to be entitled to them. States, through their sovereignty, had power to determine what these privileges and immunities were for their own citizens against any federal pronouncement. Interestingly, the privileges and immunities clause of the post–Civil War Fourteenth Amendment would be understood by Reconstruction courts to provide little help to freed blacks as well. Blacksher and Guinier also argue that the correct understanding of the term "equal state sovereignty" is limited to an equal sovereignty of states in their admission to the union; in this sense, then, the idea is a threshold one, not a perpetual limit on federal action against states—and therefore the Roberts doctrine infuses substantially more meaning into this phrase.

# 8 The Voting Rights Act after *Shelby County*

For advocates of the Voting Rights Act, these are the crucial questions: How can the preclearance regime of the Act be restored? How does the Department of Justice defend against potential abuses of voting rights absent a powerful lever to compel state and local governments to comply with the Fourteenth and Fifteenth Amendment guarantees of voting rights? As the debate is engaged over how to restore the regime, other voting rights questions might be taken up and weighed by Congress if legislators revisit the consequences of *Shelby County*: What does *Shelby County* tell us about the high court and how it will act when asked to review any law that seeks to reestablish preclearance? Can Congress craft a law that simultaneously satisfies the political needs of the coalition advancing the law *and* a majority on the Supreme Court?

Overturning the coverage trigger left the Voting Rights Act largely ineffective. Preclearance remains a legitimate exercise of Congress's authority to protect equal access to the ballot. But, like any weapon, it is only as effective as the ability of the bearer to trigger it. The *Shelby County* decision stripped the Act of its trigger. If, however, Congress should design an acceptable trigger mechanism, preclearance would be reinstated for those jurisdictions subject to the new trigger.

This chapter takes up these questions by examining potential solutions to the coverage formula problem in the wake of the *Shelby County* decision, including various coverage formulae and the application of the Section 3 pocket trigger as both a coverage solution and a means for DOJ to defend voting rights. We discuss ongoing debates in voting rights not addressed by the most recent update of the Act, in 2006, but which might return to Congress's attention in an effort to restore Section 4. We offer our assessment of the Court's majority in the wake of *Shelby County* and suggest what to expect from future voting rights cases.

## RESTORING THE PRECLEARANCE REGIME
## OF THE VOTING RIGHTS ACT

The crafting of a coverage formula to restore the preclearance regime can follow several avenues. Regardless of the approach, a new trigger must satisfactorily answer two questions: What is the evidence of contemporary government practice that offends the Constitution and requires an extraordinary federal solution? How does the coverage formula match the problem subject to remediation, that identified by the first question? Or, put more simply: What is the problem? What can a new trigger look like?

In the initial challenge to the constitutionality of Congress's authority to design and implement Section 5, the 1966 *Katzenbach* case, the Warren Court recognized by an 8–1 majority that the coverage trigger was a proxy for a set of political circumstances that rose to the level of intentional racial discrimination that violated the Fifteenth Amendment.[1] These old problems are described in chapter 1. In the *Shelby County* case, the Court made clear its conclusion that the test—and also, implicitly, the problem—should be contemporary rather than historical. The problem was not just that the data used to determine the trigger were over forty years old; the Court majority emphasized that the problem must be measured in contemporary terms. The decision described the political change and the lack of congruence between the historical test and contemporary circumstances. In the process, the opinion asked Congress not only to redefine the test but also to deal with the problem in the current context.

In the wake of *Shelby County*, journalists and legal analysts renewed a conversation initially undertaken during the *NAMUDNO* litigation: what is a constitutional coverage formula? To that end, the most common solution advanced was either an updated formula based on voter turnout or a dynamic, self-updating formula based on voter turnout combined with other evidence of recent use of discriminatory devices. If discrimination impeding participation is the problem, then a participation-based formula as proxy is reasonable. This was the reasoning of the Warren Court in *Katzenbach* and also the contemporary reasoning of those seeking to restore the pre-clearance regime.

The choice of proxy lay at the heart of the debate over coverage in 2005 and 2006, and also in determining the final outcome of the *Shelby County* litigation. *Shelby County* trial court judge John D. Bates concluded that the recent nature of turnout data as irrelevant to coverage, because the elections chosen "were never selected because of something special that occurred in those years; instead, they were chosen as mere proxies for identifying those jurisdictions with established histories of discriminating against racial and language minority voters."[2] A half-century of history since 1964 has unfolded and substantially changed the political environment of the South and especially in the covered jurisdictions. Where should the target of legal coverage be placed? Do the election results from 1964, 1968, and 1972 remain appropriate indicators? Or should the Act be more discriminating, homing in on places where conditions remain little changed and places where new concerns have emerged since 1964 (or 1975, or even 2006)? Justice Roberts posed this very question in the majority opinion in *Shelby County:* "In 1965, the States could be divided into two groups: those with a recent history of voting tests and low voter registration and turnout, and those without those characteristics. Congress based its coverage formula on that distinction. Today the Nation is no longer divided along those lines, yet the Voting Rights Act continues to treat it as if it were."[3]

How might Congress proceed, should it take up the Court's challenge to craft a new coverage formula? There are alternatives from the past, and also from different applications of findings from social science.

### The 2006 Norwood Amendment Alternative

Charlie Norwood (R-Ga.) offered the most prominent alternative coverage formula advanced during the 2006 renewal debate. Critics of the Act, led by southern Republicans, questioned the appropriateness of continuing to rely on participation data from 1964, 1968, and 1972 as the bases for requiring federal approval of changes related to voting through 2031. Those urging change saw the unprecedented federal oversight of election activities as a temporary expedient to correct a persistent injustice. Despite three recent attempts to open the ballot box to African Americans, most black adults in the South remained unregistered in 1965. The barriers of literacy tests and hostility from local registrars made the ballot a difficult objective, as it had been for decades in the portions of the South made subject to preclearance by the Section 4 trigger mechanism. However, as detailed in the previous chapters, by 1970 most African Americans in Section 5 states had registered to vote, and for decades turnout in presidential elections in covered states had usually involved a majority of the adult citizens.

Norwood advanced an amendment that proposed to "update the formula in Section 4 of the Voting Rights Act that determines which states and jurisdictions will be covered under Section 5 of the act. This updated formula would be a rolling test based off of the last three presidential elections. Any state would be subject to Section 5 if it currently has a discriminatory test in place or voter turnout of less than 50% in any of the three most recent presidential elections."[4] This amendment would have restored the timeliness of the coverage formula and allowed for automatic updates. Norwood's formula would have extended preclearance to jurisdictions in which fewer than half the adult citizens had voted in any of the three most recent presidential elections. Had the new trigger been implemented in 2006, Section 5 coverage would have decreased substantially in Texas, Virginia, Louisiana, Alabama, and Mississippi, whereas most Georgia and South Carolina jurisdictions would have remained covered. Current and additional southern counties and independent cities that would have been picked up for preclearance coverage by the Norwood proposal appear in map 8.1.

In *The Triumph of Voting Rights in the South*, we presented the coverage formula and affected areas picked up by Norwood's proposal. At that time, we determined that the application of the amendment using turnout data from 2000 to 2004 would have released 340 counties, Alaska, and ten townships of New Hampshire from Section 5 coverage.[5] Of the 340 counties exempted by the amendment until such time as their turnout fell below 50 percent of the voting age population, forty-three were in Mississippi, thirty-one in Alabama, and fifty-eight in Virginia, a 55 percent reduction in covered counties in these three states. Of sixty-four Louisiana parishes, fifty-eight would not get picked up. These four states account for more than half of the current Section 5 counties that would have escaped

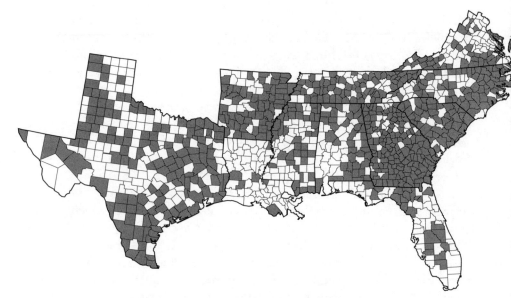

Map 8.1 Possible preclearance coverage using the Norwood amendment trigger (shaded). First published in *The Triumph of Voting Rights in the South*, by Charles S. Bullock III and Ronald Keith Gaddie; © 2009, University of Oklahoma Press. See also Charles S. Bullock III and Ronald Keith Gaddie, "Good Intentions and Bad Social Science Meet in the Renewal of the Voting Rights Act," *Georgetown Journal of Law and Public Policy* 5 (Winter 2007): 1–27.

coverage. An additional 118 counties came from Texas, though among major urban counties only Tarrant County (Fort Worth) met the Norwood turnout threshold to discontinue Section 5 oversight. In Dallas, Harris (Houston), El Paso, and Bexar (San Antonio) Counties and most of the South Rio Grande Valley, Section 5 would continue in place. The excluded counties tended to be in sparsely populated West Texas. Twenty-two of 159 Georgia counties and nine of forty-six South Carolina counties would not have been picked up by the new trigger. Most of the Georgia dropouts were in the Atlanta urban doughnut or outside the Black Belt. Norwood would have continued Section 5 coverage in four of Alabama's fourteen Black Belt counties and about half of the rural, majority-black counties of Mississippi. The Norwood amendment would have continued coverage of 524 Section 5 counties.

Opponents offered two critiques of Norwood. First, Norwood's trigger would have removed coverage from jurisdictions that some voting rights activists considered problematic in terms of compliance despite increased voter participation and a decline in Department of Justice challenges. The second concern about Norwood focused on the potential expansion of coverage to new jurisdictions. An examination of turnout data from 2000 and 2004 shows how the Norwood amendment would have expanded coverage. Norwood's trigger would have imposed Section 5 on 486 counties not previously covered. Of these, fifty-seven are in states already covered in part by Section 5: twelve in California, eighteen in Florida, five in Michigan, sixteen in North Carolina, and six in New York State. Another 121 are in Arkansas and Tennessee. The border states Kentucky, Missouri, Oklahoma, and West Virginia account for another 155 counties, including many rural Appalachian counties or, in the case of Oklahoma, counties with sizable American Indian populations. In sum, 334 new counties come from former Confederate or Border South states or from current Section 5 states.

Another twenty-one counties come from New Mexico, where a state court in 2001 and 2002 found the presence of racially polarized voting in the southern part of the state and in the areas populated by Navajos and Jicarilla Apaches. Of the remaining 131 new, covered counties, sixty-seven are in Indiana and Pennsylvania. This leaves sixty-four counties scattered over sixteen states, including very populous counties like rapidly growing Clark County, Nevada (Las Vegas) but also sparsely populated places such as Glacier County, Montana, the home of the Blackfeet Indian Nation and about 14,000 residents. Many of the counties that are picked up in the new states with few covered counties host Indian reservations, including counties in Nebraska, Michigan, Idaho, Montana, North Dakota, and Oregon.

More recent elections bode even less well for non-southern states when applying Norwood. In eleven states a majority of the voter eligible population failed to turn out in either 2008 or 2012. Of these states, four were picked up in whole or in part by the 1972 Section 4 trigger—Arizona, California, Texas, and New York—and a fifth had been bailed in under Section 3 in the 1980s. Of the remaining six, four are in the greater South—Arkansas, Oklahoma, Tennessee, and West Virginia. Nevada and Hawaii are also unable to satisfy the Norwood trigger on a statewide basis in 2008 and 2012.

Adopting the Norwood amendment or some variant would acknowledge two uncomfortable political truths: the application of Section 5 worked in the South to such an extent that it eradicated the facially neutral legislative rationale that triggered emergency national government preemption of state authority;[6] and, beyond the South, the problem of declining participation is growing, and this declining participation is evident in non-southern areas populated with minorities who have historic concerns about voting rights.

The second finding would challenge the implicit sectional moral authority that underlay the debate over the use of Section 5 and other voting rights issues. The stark differences between southern and national politics in terms of partisan competition, the need for administrative oversight, and the scale of resistance to minority participation have receded, even if not wholly eliminated. The Norwood trigger showed that turnout problems were not just southern problems.

A related concern that other trigger proposals would have to deal with, and which Norwood did not address, is the lack of immediacy of the use of tests, devices, or other discriminatory practices to the coverage formula. The problem with the election-based coverage formula rejected by the *Shelby County* court was not just that the data in the trigger were old; the precondition to consider those data, the use of tests and devices, were also old. Literacy tests have been gone since 1970, along with good character tests and understanding tests. Even the poll tax, which was not a triggering feature in the earlier legislation, was eliminated in the mid-1960s. Although low turnout could be linked to discriminatory government action half a century ago, that is much more challenging today. The Norwood data component did not align easily with the places that had historic turnout problems due to tests and devices. The data component also did not align well with any other theory of nonparticipation. Consequently, the Norwood trigger might not have been accepted by the *Shelby County* court, simply because the cause to be remedied was deemed antiquated.

## A Racial Disparity Coverage Trigger

An alternative approach to updating the coverage formula would capture places having observable and significant differences in the voter participation rates of whites and minorities. During the oral argument for the *Shelby County* case, Justice Roberts asked, "Do you know which state has the worst ratio of white voter turnout to African-American voter turnout? . . . Massachusetts. Do you know what has the best, where African-American turnout actually exceeds white turnout? Mississippi." Roberts was criticized for using data that evidently came from the Current Population Survey (CPS); he did not cite the source.[7] CPS data are the only source of racial registration and turnout data across all fifty states. These surveys, taken after each election, have margins of sampling error, as does any survey, and the error margins for minority populations are quite large in states with small minority populations. Nevertheless, these data serve as one basis for Congress and the courts to assess potential racial discrepancies or racial trends in participation, and they are collected for that very reason. Exit polls are another potential source for data on turnout by race or ethnicity. As with the CPS data, though, in states having a small population of any one particular ethnic group, estimates would be less reliable. Moreover, in recent years the number of states in which exit polls have been conducted has been sharply reduced in the face of market forces.

We used state-level American Community Survey data from 2012 to determine the rates of voter registration among citizen-eligible Anglo whites, Hispanics, African Americans, and Asian Americans. In some states, samples for some nonwhite groups are too small to make any meaningful estimate of registration. An examination of the data show that Anglo whites nationally have higher registration rates than African Americans, Hispanics, or Asian Americans (data for Native Americans are not available). The data affirm the observation made by Justice Roberts regarding black and white voter participation. In thirteen states, as shown in map 8.2, the estimated black voter registration rate is actually higher than the white rate. Six of these states (Georgia, Mississippi, New York, North Carolina, South Carolina, Texas) were covered in whole or part by Section 5, and two others (Kentucky and Tennessee) are part of the greater South. The rest (Illinois, Indiana, Missouri, Ohio, Wisconsin) are in the industrial Midwest. Of the eleven former Confederate states, six have higher black than white voter registration rates.

In another eight states white rates are less than 5 percentage points higher than for blacks. Three of these states were Section 5 states in the South (Florida, Louisiana, Virginia), and another (California) had counties covered by Section 5. The remaining states are Maryland, Nevada, New Jersey, and Pennsylvania.

Eleven other states had sufficiently large black samples to compare registration rates with Anglo whites. In all of these states, the difference between the black and white samples fell outside of a

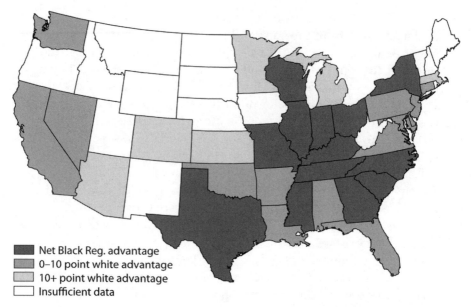

Net Black Reg. advantage
0–10 point white advantage
10+ point white advantage
Insufficient data

MAP 8.2 Relative black and Anglo white registration rates, 2012, according to American Community Survey data.

5-point confidence interval. The largest estimated differences, in excess of 15 points, occurred in Colorado and Kansas. In Arizona, Massachusetts, Michigan, and Minnesota, white registration exceeded black registration by at least 10 percentage points. Alabama, Arkansas, Connecticut, Oklahoma, and Washington each had estimated registration differences greater than 5 points (Alabama and Arizona were covered by Section 5).

National data from the American Community Survey demonstrate an ongoing gap in racial voting. But this gap does not disadvantage African Americans. Instead, on one side of the gap are high-registration and high-turnout Africa American and Anglo whites; on the other side are low-registration and low-turnout Hispanics and Asian Americans (table 8.1). The registration and turnout gap between blacks and whites nationally has largely disappeared, led by black voter mobilization in the South and Midwest. The overall turnout gap was 10.4 points in 1992 but fell to 1.4 points in 2008, and in 2012 black turnout exceeded the white rate by 2.1 points. Meanwhile, the turnout rate among citizen-eligible Hispanics and

TABLE 8.1    Reported voting and registration for citizen voting age
population, by race and Hispanic origin, 1980–2012

| | Registration (%) | | | |
| | White non-Hispanic | Black | Asian | Hispanic |
|---|---|---|---|---|
| 1980 | 84.7 | 64.1 | | 56.0 |
| 1984 | 75.1 | 72.0 | | 61.4 |
| 1988 | 73.6 | 68.8 | | 59.1 |
| 1992 | 77.1 | 70.0 | 61.3 | 62.5 |
| 1996 | 73.0 | 66.4 | 57.2 | 58.6 |
| 2000 | 71.6 | 67.5 | 52.4 | 57.3 |
| 2004 | 75.1 | 68.7 | 51.8 | 57.9 |
| 2008 | 73.5 | 69.7 | 55.3 | 59.4 |
| 2012 | 73.7 | 73.1 | 56.3 | 58.7 |

| | Turnout (%) | | | |
| | White non-Hispanic | Black | Asian | Hispanic |
|---|---|---|---|---|
| 1980 | 66.2 | 53.9 | | 46.1 |
| 1984 | 66.4 | 60.6 | | 50.0 |
| 1988 | 64.2 | 55.0 | | 48.0 |
| 1992 | 70.2 | 59.8 | 53.9 | 51.6 |
| 1996 | 60.7 | 53.0 | 45.0 | 44.0 |
| 2000 | 61.8 | 56.8 | 43.4 | 45.1 |
| 2004 | 67.2 | 60.0 | 44.1 | 47.2 |
| 2008 | 66.1 | 64.7 | 47.6 | 49.9 |
| 2012 | 64.1 | 66.2 | 47.3 | 48.0 |

*Source*: American Community Survey.

Asian Americans has remained large, with Hispanic and Asian American turnout 16.1 points and 16.8 points, respectively, below that for Anglos in 2012.

When we look at the geography of citizen-eligible registration, we run into sample size issues for nearly every minority voting group in some state or the other. Therefore, we cannot make comparisons across all racial and ethnic groups to Anglo whites in several states. But in every state we do have a sufficiently large, self-identified population of Anglo whites that we can net out from the total sample; that which remains is some combination of African American, Hispanic, Asian American, and American Indian. And in many of these states there are sufficient numbers of nonwhites to generate an Anglo white/non-Anglo white estimate of voter registration.

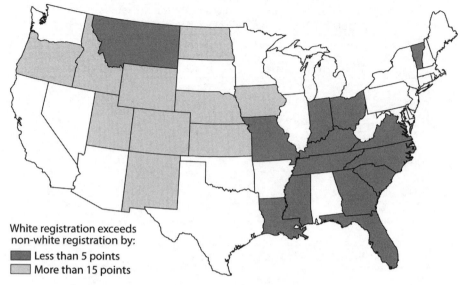

MAP 8.3 Relative Anglo white and non–Anglo white registration rates, 2012, according to the American Community Survey data.

There are fifteen states where the rate of Anglo white registration is less than 5 points higher than the minority, nonwhite registration (map 8.3). Of these, seven are former Section 5 states and eight are in the South: Florida, Georgia, Louisiana, Mississippi, North Carolina, South Carolina, Tennessee, and Virginia. No southern state has a white-nonwhite registration disparity of over 15 points (Texas and Arkansas come the closest), and even Alabama's differential is under 10 points, largely driven by a very low citizen Hispanic voter registration estimate.

The highest rates of white-nonwhite citizen registration disparities are in the Plains states, the Mountain West, and on the Pacific Rim. Colorado, Hawaii, Idaho, Iowa, Kansas, Utah, and Wyoming all have nonwhite citizen registration rates that are at least 20 points lower than for Anglo white citizens. Alaska, Nebraska, New Mexico, North Dakota, and Oregon have nonwhite citizen registration rates that are at least 15 points lower than for Anglo white citizens. Overall, the South east of the Mississippi River and the states of the Ohio River Valley have smaller racial differences in voter registration rates among citizens than the trans-Mississippi South, the West, or New England.

TABLE 8.2　Black turnout in Section 5
states and nationwide, ranked

| 2008 | | 2012 | |
|---|---|---|---|
| MISSISSIPPI | 72.9 | MISSISSIPPI | 82.0 |
| SOUTH CAROLINA | 72.0 | NORTH CAROLINA | 78.7 |
| *Michigan* | *70.2* | LOUISIANA | 69.5 |
| NORTH CAROLINA | 67.2 | SOUTH CAROLINA | 68.7 |
| VIRGINIA | 66.6 | VIRGINIA | 63.1 |
| LOUISIANA | 66.2 | ALABAMA | 62.8 |
| GEORGIA | 65.0 | GEORGIA | 62.3 |
| *California* | *63.8* | U.S. | **62.0** |
| ALABAMA | 62.5 | TEXAS | 61.1 |
| *Texas* | *61.8* | *Michigan* | *61.0* |
| U.S. | **60.8** | *California* | *58.7* |
| *Arizona* | *51.5* | *New York* | *58.7* |
| *Florida* | *50.1* | *Florida* | *49.2* |
| *New York* | *45.7* | *Arizona* | *45.1* |

*Source:* "Reported Voting and Registration of the Voting-Act Population by Sex, Race, and Hispanic Origin," for states: November 2008 and November 2012, released by the U.S. Bureau of the Census.

*Note:* States in italics were only partially covered by Section 5 of the Voting Rights Act. States subject to Section 5 since 1965 are in ALL CAPS. Three states subjected in whole or part to the Voting Rights Act's Section 5 (Alaska, New Hampshire and South Dakota) had too few African Americans to make reliable estimates of their turnout rates.

Using disparities in racial registration, when comparing Anglo whites to everyone else, identifies a very different set of states with participation problems than those picked up by the trigger used in the 2006 renewal of the Act. We observe intersection with those states that generally have problems with voter participation identified when applying the Norwood amendment to the 2008 and 2012 election—mainly in the Southwest. But, even then, many states with substantial registration disparities between whites and non-whites are not picked up by a Norwood-style trigger.

Table 8.2 ranks Section 5 states in terms of their black turnout rates in 2008 and 2012. In 2008 all seven of the states covered by the 1965 Voting Rights Act had higher rates of black turnout than did the nation as a whole. Indeed, in 2008 only three of the thirteen Section 5 states had lower rates of black participation than did the nation. In 2012 the seven states with the highest rates of participation were those covered by the initial version of the Act. Each of these states had higher African American turnout than did the nation as a whole. In the more recent election, four of the five states with the lowest rates of black participation were states only partially covered by Section 5.

## A Social Science Trigger

Writing in the wake of the *Shelby County* decision, political scientist Bernard Grofman advances a trigger based on social science evidence to identify where heightened scrutiny of election law changes should occur. Grofman first acknowledges what was previously an argument made only by critics of the law or by those few willing to say it during the renewal debate in 2006: "The data used for the trigger were not just stale, they were incredibly stale. . . . the data led to over-inclusion (at least below the level of the states) and under-inclusion."[8] The coverage formula was continued, according to Grofman, because it avoided confronting the possibility of current problems with voter participation and voter discrimination. The consequence was a flawed law that was invalidated because of a defect plainly evident to observers at the time, a matter we have discussed.

The problem with the old trigger, a lack of currency and over-coverage, stemmed from the nature of discriminatory practice and effect in 1965. Back then, the extensive use of discriminatory practices and their consequences were largely isolated to one part of the country, which was picked by the original formula as if so much low-hanging fruit. But it does not necessarily follow that these same areas still need Section 5 coverage because of remote and facially obvious discriminatory practices.

Grofman proposes a two-step solution for identifying candidate areas for Section 5 coverage: first, identify the rate of Section 2 violations by jurisdiction and state; then, place multiple offenders under Section 5 coverage on the basis of a yet-undetermined rate of offense. In his examination of the record from the renewal hearings and subsequent litigation, Grofman turns to data collected by Ellen Katz (used in chap. 2 of this volume) and also the analysis of DOJ staff historian Peyton McCrary regarding Section 2 litigation.[9] McCrary's data show that successful Section 2 cases are far more likely to occur in states picked up by the old coverage trigger. They also show that there are some jurisdictions with an even worse record of Section 2 complaints that were nevertheless not covered by Section 5. Applying a cut-point of ten cases with an outcome favorable to a minority plaintiff, he identifies "seven Southern states in need of Section 5 scrutiny: Alabama, Georgia, Louisiana, Mississippi, South Carolina, Texas, and Virginia . . . while Arkansas and Illinois may be new candidates for coverage." Alaska and Arizona drop out under this coverage model. Grofman also observes that "Louisiana and Virginia . . . are borderline cases and may need further analysis" and might therefore not be picked up for Section 5's enhanced scrutiny.[10]

Grofman then notes that even this formula might have too broad-based coverage, leading to overinclusion and that "problems may be highly localized, independent of statewide issues." Instead, triggers might only be highly localized, for example, picking up local election practices only in portions of states where there are large minority populations (e.g., East Saint Louis or Chicago) or where there is other evidence that the states have "unclean hands.'"[11] Rather than use a single figure of ten cases per state, an alternative would be to calculate the number of cases based on the number of political subdivisions (counties, cities, etc.) within a state or the population of the state. Ten successful Section 2 cases in Texas could involve a far smaller share of that state than in Arkansas or South Carolina.

The Grofman social science trigger overlaps substantially the general geography of the original trigger from 1965 that was continued into the 2006 Act. But it acknowledges the importance of granularity and the need for further analysis when applying the extraordinary power of Section 5. Incorporating a history of more recent bad acts, and also returning to a shortened sunset horizon, compels Congress to return more frequently to the issue of preclearance coverage and to ascertain how, where, or even whether preclearance should be continued in the future. Grofman's trigger would expire seven years after enactment.

## The Sensenbrenner-Conyers-Leahy Trigger

In early 2014, Sen. Patrick Leahy (D-Vt.) and Reps. James Sensenbrenner (R-Wis.) and John Conyers (D-Mich.) offered legislation designed to rehabilitate Section 4 of the 1965 Act. Applying this trigger, any state with five or more violations of federal voting law during the previous fifteen years would have to submit subsequent election changes for federal approval. Once a jurisdiction ran afoul of Section 4, it would have to obtain preclearance for the next ten years before implementing new election-related legislation. As of January 2014, this trigger provision would include the Deep South states Georgia, Louisiana, and Mississippi and also Texas. Localities would be picked up if they had three or more violations in the previous fifteen years or one violation in conjunction with "persistent, extremely low minority turnout" in the previous fifteen years. This trigger proposed a rolling calendar. Previous preclearance objections would not count as violations. By considering only violations from the previous fifteen years, the proposal substantially shortens the period on which Section 4 had relied previously, that is, election results from 1964, 1968, or 1972. The time considered would roll forward and apply nationwide, so future misdeeds could extend the preclearance requirement well beyond the confines of areas subject to preclearance in the past. In an effort to secure a degree of Republican support, voter ID objections registered by DOJ would not count as violations, although losing a judicial challenge to a voter ID law would get counted.

The legislation would also facilitate implementation of the Section 3 pocket trigger by eliminating the need to prove intent to discriminate. If this proposed legislation passes, a single bad act even in the absence of intent to discriminate could subject a jurisdiction to preclearance. The legislation does not specify the length of time a jurisdiction would have to secure preclearance under Section 3. Past experience with Section 3 bail-ins indicates that the courts can set the period for which preclearance is necessary. A finding of intentional discrimination would still be necessary before a voter ID case could be used to bail in a jurisdiction using Section 3.

Another provision would require that every jurisdiction in the country publish announcements of changes affecting elections, such as moving a voting precinct, redistricting, or a change in election procedures. Making this information public would allow federal authorities or local activists to have the opportunity to seek to enjoin changes they fear would have a discriminatory effect. A fourth aspect of the bill would make it easier to enjoin a proposed action. All that plaintiffs need prove would be that the change would be more harmful to them than the harm the government would suffer as a result of having the change blocked. A final component of the proposal would renew the attorney general's authorization to send election monitors to a jurisdiction, with a broader scope permitting the observers to go to areas with a history of discrimination against language minorities.

The proposal has drawn criticism from both the left and the right. Liberals complain that the new trigger misses Alabama, North Carolina, South Carolina, and Virginia. North Carolina was one of the first states to take advantage of *Shelby County* and enacted a voter ID law to which DOJ would have denied preclearance and which DOJ has challenged under Section 2. Another complaint involves the decision not to count rejections of voter ID requirements when applying Sections 3 or 4, since challenges to these new requirements have constituted a major effort of civil rights groups in recent years.

Conservatives worry that DOJ and civil rights groups would be encouraged to file suits in order to create the number of violations needed to meet the proposed Section 4 trigger.[12] The Heritage Foundation characterizes the proposed hardship comparison for determining whether a court would enjoin a change as "a novel legal standard for injunctive relief that is unknown in modern jurisprudence." A third criticism from the Heritage Foundation points to the expanded authority of the attorney general to bring suit. Going back to the 1957 Civil Rights Act, the attorney general has been authorized to sue on behalf of individuals denied the right to vote. The Heritage Foundation worries that broadening the types of cases for attorney general involvement could allow DOJ involvement in cases involving elections even if not involving minorities. Finally, the Heritage Foundation assessment frets that, although low levels of participation by minorities might set off the Section 4 trigger for local jurisdictions, the bill says nothing about low levels of participation among whites. In reality, DOJ has shown little interest in prosecuting instances in which whites have experienced problems voting, and the one DOJ attorney who took such action became a pariah in the Obama Justice Department.[13]

## Loosening the Pocket Trigger

Another approach that might be taken would be to loosen the conditions for applying the Section 3 pocket trigger to states when pursuing Section 2 litigation. Under Section 3, jurisdictions losing a challenge where a constitutional violation has been found can be placed under Section 5 preclearance. Congress might consider amending Section 3 to permit a finding of discriminatory effect to be sufficient to compel bail-in to Section 5 coverage.

There are two potential problems with this approach. First, as we noted previously, Section 3 requires that DOJ has successfully sued states and jurisdictions. DOJ will have to take on the states one by one and then prevail. The Act, as redesigned in the 1982 renewal, changed the standard of evidence in Section 2 litigation from an intent standard to an effects standard. Since then, according to the data presented in chapter 2, of 330 cases tried under Section 2 there were 123 successful challenges. Of the suits brought, forty-four were successful challenges to congressional, state legislative, or local redistricting and apportionment plans. Most suits invalidated only part of the plan, affecting a third or fewer of the districts in the map.

Second, the intent standard currently codified in Section 3 finds strong precedent and support for being constitutional—intent to discriminate violates the Fourteenth Amendment. But it is not certain that a finding of a discriminatory effect suffices to disrupt federalism by making states preclear their election law changes. In any case, absent amending Section 3 to provide for a lower standard for bail-in, this option does not open up broad new authority for Congress to seek to rein in state behavior through extended oversight.

## Status Quo Post-bellum

DOJ could just apply Section 3 as is. Three years before the *Shelby County* decision, Travis Crum penned a note for the *Yale Law Journal* in which he described how to continue Section 5 coverage even if the high court overturned the Section 4 coverage formula. In his note, Crum argued for the use of the Section 3 bail-in authority as a means to maintain preclearance where it is required. His argument for using the pocket trigger is threefold. First, it has been successfully applied in both localities and statewide jurisdictions. Second, the pocket trigger likely satisfies the congruence and proportionality test: it reacts to current circumstances where a finding of discriminatory intent is demonstrated and does so while treating all states or jurisdictions the same under the law. Third, there is no politics involved: Congress does not have to create additional legislation to use the pocket trigger. Crum observed on his election law blog subsequent to the *Shelby County* decision that "the pocket trigger also reduces preclearance's federalism costs. Courts have often required jurisdictions to preclear only certain problematic changes. . . . Courts have further tailored Section 3 preclearance by setting temporal limitations. Instead of mandating preclearance for a twenty-five year period, courts have fashioned more limited sunset dates."[14]

The Holder Justice Department demonstrated awareness of this argument in the aftermath of the *Shelby County* decision. Very soon after the high court axed Section 4, several jurisdictions moved forward with election changes that were at various stages of preclearance submission, review, or litigation. Texas sought to change its voter registration and identification law and adopted a new congressional district map. DOJ initiated litigation in August 2013 to bail Texas back in under Section 5 preclearance authority.[15]

As we note in chapter 2, the use of bail-in is costly and cumbersome as an alternative to Sections 4 and 5. The costs of litigation to establish a Section 3 bail-in are substantial, running into millions of dollars for states and plaintiffs. The process is reactive. DOJ has to identify the state or jurisdiction to sue and then affirmatively make the case for bail-in to coverage. The evidentiary standard needed to activate the pocket trigger is different. Moreover, the burden of proof has shifted. Under the old Section 4/5 regime, there was a presumption of bad behavior by the state, and the state had to demonstrate its lack of discriminatory intent or effect to the courts or DOJ. Invoking Section 3 returns to the more conservative and demanding standard in voting rights, which is evidence of discriminatory intent (a constitutional violation) where the burden is born by the plaintiff. Further, the determination is made on a case basis, meaning that DOJ would have preclearance coverage by winning suits one jurisdiction at a time.

## A Different Perspective

The proposals just discussed all, in some way or other, seek to bring back under preclearance the southern jurisdictions that had been covered by the Section 4 triggers. New York University law professor Richard Pildes has spent years thinking about voting problems and how the Voting Rights Act relates to those issues. Rather than simply applying a patch to Section 4, Pildes calls for a more innovative approach that moves beyond the racial and ethnic focus of the past. He observes that "Section 4 long ago in practice became more about racial redistricting than access to the ballot box." Without opera-tionalizing a new trigger, Pildes urges those who assume the chal-lenge to come up with standards that do "not try to predict in advance the areas of the county in which inappropriate voting rights barriers might arise, and which does not require proof of racial discrimina-tion but protects the right to vote robustly regardless of where those barriers might emerge and which voters are wrongly denied access."[16]

Nathaniel Persily, another voting rights scholar, also questions the appropriateness of trying to craft a workable Section 4 trigger. He observes that Section 2 provided a better defense against discri-minatory redistricting plans than Section 5 since the latter has at times been infected by the partisanship of the administration in charge of DOJ enforcement. Turning his attention to more current voting issues, Persily questions the utility of resurrecting Section 5 and observes that "disenfranchisement of felons, the discriminatory application of voter ID laws, and partisan or incompetent adminis-tration of elections present greater nationwide challenges to minority voting rights than the voting charges ordinarily denied preclearance in the covered jurisdictions."[17]

Political scientist Bruce Cain also sees problems with simply reenacting an updated version of Section 4 that continues to focus on the black-white context that characterized the South half a century ago. Cain notes the growing ethnic diversity that increasingly charac-terizes parts of the South as well as the nation. Racial polarization as a key element in litigation made sense in a bivariate world but is strained in a multiethnic setting.[18]

## OTHER ISSUES IN VOTING RIGHTS

There are other issues of concern in voting rights. Some existed prior to the latest renewal of the Act and continue. Others emerged since the renewal of the Act and have been brought to the attention of the Court and Congress. None has yet to receive any systematic atten-tion from lawmakers.

### Measuring Racially Polarized Voting

One challenge involves measurement of racially polarized voting. The methods of measuring voting preferences of racial groups are well established and not subject to debate. But the larger question of the contextual measure of racially polarized voting remains. The concept of racially polarized voting as a source of legal concern arises when white and minority voters have contrary interests, and white voters act to defeat candidates preferred by minority voters.[19] In Democratic Party primaries, the traditional avenue to political empowerment in the South for liberals and conservatives alike,[20] white conservative interests had sought to narrow the franchise and control access to party elections in violation of the Fourteenth and Fifteenth Amendments.

Having lost their avenue for expression through the Democratic Party, racial, economic, and eventually social conservatives and many moderates gravitated to the Republican Party in the South,[21] which made general elections the elections of consequence in the region. These contests still pit white and black voters against each other, since they have different partisan preferences. But increasingly throughout the South the racial policy motive for whites has disappeared in structuring their voting.[22] The core political ideologies of blacks and whites are not distributed in the same fashion, and this ideological distribution influences policy preferences, party preferences, and voting behavior.[23] A question for the courts is whether political differences that are racially distributed, but do not find their basis in racial attitudes or racial motivations, rise to a level of constitutional violation?

## Representatives of Choice versus Candidates of Choice

Both Sections 5 and 2 of the Voting Rights Act include a term of art used by political science expert witnesses and attorneys: "candidate of choice." Section 2 as amended in 1982 focuses on whether minority voters "have less opportunity than other members of the electorate to participate in the political process and to elect representatives of their choice."[24] In establishing the basis for assessing changes using Section 5, the Supreme Court said that nonretrogression required "that the minority's opportunity to elect representatives of its choice not be diminished, directly or indirectly, by the state's actions."[25] A critical difference exists between the law as written and the term of art as analyzed, and this difference underlies the debate over the application of both Section 2 and Section 5: *candidate* versus *representative.*

A candidate of choice is a candidate, regardless of race or ethnicity, who is the choice of a particular racial or ethnic voting bloc. The threshold for defining "candidate of choice" is subject to debate, though a minimum standard of a majority preference for *one* candidate from a racial voting bloc has been accepted as sufficient. David Epstein and Sharyn O'Halloran note that "the Supreme Court has made it clear that a candidate of choice need not be a member of any particular minority group. But beyond that, definitions are notoriously vague and hard to apply in specific circumstances so that too often only minority officeholders are considered to be a candidate of choice."[26]

One question remains unanswered: is a representative different from a candidate? On a technical level the answer is no, because an elected candidate becomes a representative. If one thinks of descriptive representation as a prerequisite for successful representation in a racially divided political environment, then a candidate is not necessarily a *representative* if he or she does not come from the minority community. The community of policy interest is the collection of persons presumed to be the affirmative target of the policy, in this case a minority group receiving legal protection from the implementation of the Act. David Canon illuminates the substantive importance of this distinction in his book *Race, Redistricting, and Representation*, and it is this distinction that continues to merit exploration.[27] Canon found that controlling for the racial composition of a congressional district, African American Democrats were more likely than white Democrats to introduce legislation and offer amendments dealing with race and to do more press releases focused on race. Christian Grose concludes, based on a multivariate model, that controlling for the racial makeup of the district, and the party of a member of Congress, a black Democrat votes for civil rights issues about 5 percent more than does a comparable white Democrat.[28]

## Coalition Politics and the "Performance" of Election Laws

The Voting Rights Act initially sought to provide access to the ballot and to ensure that jurisdictions did not throw up new impediments to African American participation. In the late 1960s, the Supreme Court's expansive interpretation broadened the Act's scope. More recently, the Court in *Georgia v. Ashcroft* offered a different model for assessing the ability of redistricting plans to perform on behalf of minority voters.[29] The *Ashcroft* decision moved away from a fairly narrow model of minority success—majority-minority districts that guaranteed minority control of the election. *Ashcroft* offered an alternative model of coalition districts in which black voters could coalesce with enough whites to control non–majority-minority districts. This approach can result in unintended consequences both in the effort to baseline performance and access for minority voters and in possible remedies to ensure minority access and nonretrogression.

Congress rejected the *Ashcroft* suggestion of alternative approaches to satisfy Section 5. Did the broadening of solutions also expand the scope of districts protected from retrogression? Before *Ashcroft*, had Section 5 become primarily a vehicle for the pursuit of partisan advantage rather than ensuring minority-group access to the political process? Does a broad definition of the retrogression baseline and remedies draw Section 5 closer to "just politics"?

Republican administrations, specifically the first Bush administration, used the Act to encourage creation of majority-minority districts and to limit the opportunities to create cross-racial coalitions supporting Democrats. White Democrats preferred districts with sizable (but not majority) minority populations because biracial coalitions could win more seats. The aggressive use of Section 2 to create majority-minority districts in the early 1990s resulted in electoral maps that helped shift one-third of all southern congressional districts to the GOP over the course of the next three elections. Concentrating the most loyal Democratic voters into the fewest districts possible helped elect Republicans as well as minorities.

Relying on the Equal Protection Clause, courts upheld challenges to several of the new majority-minority districts, and this reduced minority concentrations. Ultimately the Supreme Court suggested that, as long as jurisdictions justified their actions in partisan rather than racial terms, redistricting plans could probably survive judicial challengers. Maps drawn using the 2000 census resulted in shapes as bizarre as those a decade earlier and allocated minority concentrations with the same care as in the 1990s but without overt acknowledgment of the role race played. After 2000, in the declining number of states they still controlled, Democrats sought to maximize the number of districts they could win, a goal endorsed by both the party's black and white legislators. This signaled an abrupt about-face for black legislators who in the past had criticized Democratic plans that distributed black voters to shore up white Democrats rather than aggregate black population concentrations to enhance the likelihood of black legislators being elected. By 2001, however, Republicans had assumed control by three states. Even in the states where

Democrats drew the new maps, they frequently experienced losses. The new plans saw Republicans win majorities in both chambers of the Texas legislature and in the Georgia senate. Elsewhere, Republicans made gains in the North Carolina senate and the Alabama, Arkansas, and Tennessee lower chambers.

A significant difference between 1991 and 2001 was the growing recognition that heightened black participation rates coupled with increased numbers of whites willing to support black candidates meant that African Americans could win in districts with lower black concentrations. The success of black candidates in the whiter districts drawn after the courts invalidated the racially gerrymandered 1990s districts showed that such heavy black-voter concentrations were unnecessary. After the 2000 census, some legislatures reduced black percentages in minority districts to barely half the voting age population. In the 1980s, DOJ and courts often demanded that a district be at least 65 percent black in its total population in order to enable African Americans to elect their preferences.[30] In the 1990s, DOJ reinforced black aspirations and required maximizing the number of districts likely to elect minorities. A decade later, neither DOJ nor minority groups pushed for the creation of additional districts designed to elect minorities, and the Supreme Court articulated a new standard for assessing compliance with Section 5. Despite plans lowering black concentrations, the number of African Americans serving in southern legislatures has continued to grow, albeit gradually.[31]

Assuming that minority-representation guarantees can be achieved through biracial coalitions, another question arises: can minority candidates and candidates of choice be elected from districts with minority voting age population (VAP) percentages at or below 50 percent? In an analysis embraced by Georgia's Legislative Black Caucus, David Epstein estimated that a black-preferred candidate has a 50:50 chance of winning in a district where the black VAP is 44.3 percent.[32] For a black preference to have an "even chance" at winning a 44.3 percent black VAP district, assuming equal rates of black and white turnout with 90 percent minority-voter cohesion, a candidate of choice needs 18.1 percent of the Anglo vote to win. To have an even chance at winning a 40 percent minority VAP district requires 23.3 percent of the Anglo vote. To have an even chance at winning with 30 percent minority VAP and 90 percent cohesion requires 32.8 percent of the Anglo vote. These thresholds for white crossover voting increase as the rate of minority turnout falls.

Racial voting patterns demonstrate that these thresholds are often met in most former Section 5 states in major elections. As more and more whites participate in Republican primaries, the influence of black voters in Democratic primaries becomes greater. Consequently the black vote can determine the Democratic nominee in districts in which the black population falls well below 50 percent. In districts in which the black vote dominates the primary selection process, the runoff requirement found in most southern states also works to the advantage of African Americans. In a situation in which one white candidate faces multiple black candidates, if a runoff involves a single white and a single black, the black electorate is often sufficient to determine the winner.[33] Then, in the general election, a near unanimous black vote coupled with the remaining whites who identify with the Democratic Party can suffice to win in districts that have small white majorities.

On the other hand, by overturning the *Ashcroft* attempt to reduce minority concentrations, even when the minority community approves such redistribution, Congress endorsed ratcheting up minority percentages in heavy minority districts with each round of redistricting. An obvious consequence of that approach is a reduction of the number of districts where minorities acting alone or in collaboration with white voters can elect candidates preferred by the minority electorate.

In renewing the Act, Congress sided with DOJ in favoring districts with higher concentrations of minorities. The Supreme Court, beginning with *Shaw v. Reno* in 1993, has issued rulings that reduce minority concentrations and encourage the development of cross-racial coalitions. Though lowering the minority percentage in a district involves some risk for minority candidates, coalitions that elect Democrats promote the likelihood of legislatures controlled by Democrats, which, in turn, increase the potential for policy outputs preferred by minority voters. The Supreme Court's discussion of coalitional possibilities in *Ashcroft* indicates the extent of change among southern white voters. At the time of the adoption of the Act, so few whites would vote for a black candidate, regardless of the individual's qualifications, that only in districts in which minorities dominated the electorate could a minority candidate hope for success. Now minority voters control Democratic primaries in majority-white jurisdictions when whites participate in the Republican primary. Once nominated, minority candidates can win if they fashion a coalition as noted above.

The initial goals of the Act—removing barriers to black registration and turnout—have long since been attained. The more recent goal of facilitating the election of candidates preferred by minority voters has also achieved great success. The remaining concern is whether in the absence of the federal oversight authorized by Section 5 subject jurisdictions will unravel the advances of the past two generations. The potential for that happening seems slight. Suit can be brought under Section 2, a tool used extensively in jurisdictions far beyond the sixteen states wholly or partially covered by Section 5. But those suits are rare, expensive, and largely unsuccessful. This is in no small sense because habits of egregious conduct were caught early and often in the Voting Rights Act regime by Section 5.

In the context of redistricting, and it is this activity that has most frequently drawn numerous DOJ objections of recent years, the political situation militates against backsliding. As noted repeatedly in *The Triumph of Voting Rights in the South*, Republicans benefit from drawing majority-minority districts, so GOP-controlled legislatures gladly pump up minority percentages in selected districts; this is the action at issue in the Alabama case before the Supreme Court in 2014, which we discuss shortly. Since the 2014 elections, Republicans control every legislative chamber in the South and in more than a dozen other states. Further, states in which Democrats could carry out redistricting pose no threat to majority-minority districts. Members of a legislature's black caucus can block any actions viewed as harmful to minority representation in a Democratic-controlled chamber in which minorities constitute a sizable share of the Democratic Party membership. Any temptation by Democrats to eliminate majority-minority districts in order to maximize the numbers of districts likely to elect white Democrats would face tough sledding in southern legislatures given the size of their black caucuses. In 2008, in the lower chambers of six southern states, along with three upper chambers, at least 40 percent of Democrats were black, and in both Texas chambers most Democrats were either Hispanic or black. The chambers in which fewer than 40 percent of Democrats were minorities include Arkansas and Tennessee, states not under Section 5. North Carolina and Virginia, two other states with lower percentages of blacks among Democratic legislators, voted for Obama in 2008.

## The Party-Race Nexus

It is increasingly difficult to distinguish a racial vote from a party vote in the South. Most elections, at least above the local level and

TABLE 8.3    2014 racial/ethnic partisan divisions

| | | Democratic support (%) | | Republican support (%) | | |
|---|---|---|---|---|---|---|
| State/office | | Black | Hispanic | White male | White female | White evangelical |
| AR | Sen. | 97 | — | 69 | 61 | 73 |
| | Gov. | 90 | — | 67 | 59 | 71 |
| FL | Gov.* | 85 | 58 | 58 | 57 | 73*** |
| GA | Sen. | 92 | 57 | 79 | 69 | 86 |
| | Gov. | 90 | 53 | 77 | 67 | 82 |
| LA | Sen. | 94 | — | 64 | 55 | 59*** |
| MS | Sen. | 92 | — | 82 | 79 | 82 |
| NC | Sen. | 96 | — | 69 | 57 | 78 |
| SC | Sen.** | 89 | — | 74 | 73 | 81 |
| | Gov. | 92 | — | 81 | 71 | 84 |
| TX | Sen. | 87 | 47 | 77 | 71 | 86 |
| | Gov. | 92 | 55 | 79 | 66 | 84 |
| VA | Sen. | 90 | — | 63 | 57 | 76 |

*Source*: Exit polls for Nov. 4, 2014 election.

*Florida did not have a Senate contest.

**Results are for the Lindsay Graham and not the Tim Scott contest.

***Figures are for white Protestants and not for white evangelicals, since the latter breakout was not available.

especially in the absence of a Democratic incumbent, are racially polarized, regardless of the race of the candidates or the role of race as an issue in campaigns. Whites vote for Republicans, and African Americans massively prefer Democrats. The media cooperative included nine southern states in its exit polls of the November 2014 general election. As shown in table 8.3, African Americans overwhelmingly opted for Democratic candidates, with all but three winning at least 90 percent of the black vote. Most states have too few Hispanics to provide a reliable sample, but in four of five contests surveyed a majority of the Hispanic vote went to the Democrat. In Texas, Sen. John Cornyn (R) split the Hispanic vote, taking 48 percent to the Democrat's 47 percent.[34]

White voters voted for Republicans by landslide proportions in every state. The strongest performance occurred in Mississippi, where Thad Cochran won a seventh term with 82 percent of the white male vote and 79 percent from white females. In eight other contests at least 69 percent of white men chose the Republican, with the weakest performances registered by Florida governor Rick Scott (58 percent), Virginia's Ed Gillespie (63 percent), and Louisiana Senate challenger Bill Cassidy (64 percent). White women's enthusiasm for GOP candidates never exceeded that of men, although in the Florida gubernatorial and South Carolina Senate contests the two were essentially equal. The presence of a sitting female Democrat reduced white female support for the GOP challenger in Louisiana and North Carolina, and the presence of a woman nominee may have held down the female backing for David Perdue in Georgia. The one GOP female, South Carolina governor Nikki Haley, had one of the strongest showings with white women, attracting 71 percent of their votes, but still ran 10 points lower than among white men. The median figure for white female GOP support was 66 percent, compared with 74 percent for white males. Although among Democratic incumbents only Mark Warner (Va.) survived, the presence of a sitting Democrat depressed white support for the GOP Senate nominee.

The strongest GOP support came from white evangelicals, the core constituency of the GOP in the South. These socially conservative whites gave 86 percent of their votes to the GOP candidates in Georgia, Mississippi, South Carolina, and Texas. In the Texas Senate contest white evangelical support for the GOP equaled the African American vote for the Democrat, and in Georgia, Mississippi, and South Carolina the difference in the two figures was no greater than 10 points. In the seven states in which the exit polls separated out white evangelicals or born-again Christians, the median Republican support stood at 82 percent.

Is it appropriate to ascribe sinister motives to voters who make a choice governed by partisanship? Perhaps, but to do so raises the concept of party and free association to an uncomfortable level of scrutiny, with the partisanship preferences of many whites assumed to be discriminatory behavior.

Partisan bias is permissible under the Constitution, as long as a superior principle is not violated in the process—electoral systems that discriminate by party are permissible if they do not violate equal protection and racial equality standards.[35] The movement of elections of consequence in the South out of the Democratic Party primary and to the general election shifts the location of the assessment of both the value of the vote and assessment of racially polarized voting. When whites and minorities have different preferences in a general election, is it due to racial animus or to partisanship? If white Democratic candidates have no more success in general elections than minority members on the Democratic ticket, do conditions merit judicial relief?

Recent election results show African Americans losing statewide contests across the South just as do white Democrats. For example, Georgia's 2014 statewide Democratic ticket general election ballot consisted of five African Americans and five whites. Democrats lost every contest, with their vote shares ranging from 41.7 to 45.21 percent (table 8.4). Two of the three weakest performances in which the Democrat failed to break 42 percent featured white nominees. Excluding the vote for the Libertarian candidate shows that the poorest performing African American, Liz Johnson, who ran for insurance commissioner, actually had the median share of the two-party vote at 43.19 percent. The three best-performing Democrats included the African American who ran for state school superintendent. The candidates with the largest shares of the two-party vote, both of whom are white, had advantages not enjoyed by the other Democrats. Michelle Nunn is the daughter of former four-term senator Sam Nunn, and Jason Carter's grandfather was president. Moreover, these were the only Democrats able to fund major television campaigns.[36] Yet even name recognition and funding did little to boost the vote share for these two. At the other end of the two-party vote, the candidate for agriculture commissioner was the grandson of Tommy Irvin, who had served in that post from 1969 to 2011.

On the GOP side, few African Americans have run statewide. In 2014, though, the South Carolina ballot included Tim Scott, who, having been appointed to the Senate to fill the vacancy caused by the resignation of Jim DeMint, sought the remainder of the term. In addition, Lindsay Graham was running for reelection in the other Senate seat, and Nikki Haley was seeking a second term as governor. South Carolina, like Georgia, elected a full complement of statewide officers. Scott, the only African American, led the GOP ticket with 61.1 percent of the vote. His colleague Graham got 54.3 percent, slightly less than Haley's 55.9 percent of the vote. These South

TABLE 8.4    Performance of Georgia statewide Democratic candidates, 2014

| Office | Democrat | Race | Vote % | Open seat | Libertarian candidate | % Two-party vo |
|---|---|---|---|---|---|---|
| Senate | Michelle Nunn | W | 45.21 | Yes | Yes | 46.08 |
| Governor | Jason Carter | W | 44.89 | No | Yes | 45.98 |
| Lt. governor | Connie Stokes | B | 42.01 | No | No | 42.01 |
| Sec. of state | Doreen Carter | B | 42.53 | No | No | 42.53 |
| Attorney gen. | Greg Hecht | W | 43.07 | No | No | 43.07 |
| Agriculture comm. | Christopher Irvin | W | 41.74 | No | No | 41.74 |
| Insurance comm. | Liz Johnson | B | 41.70 | No | Yes | 43.19 |
| School supt. | Valarie Wilson | B | 44.89 | Yes | No | 44.89 |
| Labor comm. | Robbin Shipp | B | 43.07 | No | No | 43.07 |
| Pub. service comm. | David Blackman | W | 41.75 | No | Yes | 43.88 |

Source: Georgia Office of the Secretary of State website.

Carolina and Georgia examples from the 2014 election cycle suggest that southerners' candidate preferences reflect partisan ties far more strongly than racial attitudes. This marks a dramatic change from forty years ago, when white voters rejected African American candidates regardless of those candidates' partisanship or experience.

### New Issues

Whereas many Section 5 objections in recent years have involved redistricting plans, two new items triggered DOJ denials in the years immediately before the *Shelby County* decision and remain the subject of Section 2 challenges. One of these involves requirements that voters provide proof of their identity as a condition for in-person voting in more than thirty states. Particularly troubling for Democrats and many civil rights activists are requirements in a growing number of states that the perspective voter produce a state-issued photo ID. Critics contend that photo ID requirements disadvantage minorities because as a group they are less affluent. Being poorer, members of minority groups less often own cars and therefore are less likely to have a driver's license, the most widely available government-issued photo ID. The youngest and oldest voters are other groups who disproportionately lack driver's licenses. Almost all of the states enacting photo ID requirements are controlled by Republicans, and Democrats see those demands as but faintly disguised ploys to reduce the ranks of prospective Democratic voters.

Defenders point to the widespread popularity of photo ID requirements, with large majorities regardless of party and across ethnic groups supporting this as a precondition for casting a ballot.[37] Photo ID advocates claim that they reduce voter fraud. They counter assertions that this requirement will keep large numbers of individuals from casting votes by noting the various venues requiring photo IDs, including the courthouses in which these cases are tried.

The Supreme Court upheld a photo ID requirement in an Indiana case.[38] Georgia was the first Section 5 state to adopt a similar provision, and it secured DOJ approval. A federal judge in Georgia delayed implementation until the state provided IDs free of charge. Initially, when voters had to purchase the document, the judge had likened it to a poll tax and blocked implementation. Ultimately challenges in both federal and state court failed when plaintiffs could not produce a single witness who testified that she or he either did not already have an appropriate ID or could not have gotten one. Despite judicial approval of the photo ID requirement, DOJ and private plaintiffs have fought these requirements in North Carolina, South Carolina, Texas, and northern states such as Pennsylvania and Wisconsin. DOJ had filed Section 5 objections to the Texas and South Carolina plans and sought to prohibit implementation once these states went ahead with their plans after *Shelby County.*

In rejecting the South Carolina and Texas plans, DOJ acknowledged that states have a legitimate interest in ensuring the integrity of the ballot, as the Supreme Court had noted in upholding Indiana's photo ID requirement in *Crawford v. Marion County Election Board.* The DOJ rejection letters articulated concerns that plaintiffs raised in challenging the statutes in these two states and in others. First, DOJ noted the absence of evidence that voter impersonation— which a photo ID would prevent—is widespread.[39] Going beyond questioning the need for a photo ID (and that issue alone would not sustain a Section 5 objection), DOJ emphasized the differential impact on minorities. The South Carolina objection letter noted that non-whites were almost 20 percent more likely than whites to lack a driver's license or photo ID in lieu of a license issued by the Department of Motor Vehicles. The Texas objection letter referenced a data set that indicated that Hispanic voters might be twice as likely as non-Hispanics to lack the necessary ID. In the Texas letter, DOJ went on to note that, even though the state would provide an ID at no charge, Texans who lacked a birth certificate or other documentation would have to pay at least $22 to get materials needed for the free ID. Another concern registered by DOJ was the lack of a driver's license office in some counties, the failure of some offices to have extended hours of operation, and the higher incidence of Hispanics in households that have no car, which could make it harder to get to locations offering the free ID.

After the demise of Section 4, a federal court upheld South Carolina's photo ID law scheduled to take effect in 2016. The three-judge panel observed that, not only does South Carolina make free IDs available, a person can vote without one by invoking the "reasonable impediment" exemption under which voters explain why they did not find it convenient to get a photo ID.[40]

The trial court judge in Texas found that the statute disadvantaged minorities, but almost immediately the 5th Circuit overturned the trial court. The Texas photo ID requirement, which had already been used in several elections, had its first application in a statewide general election in 2014. On the other hand, a federal judge in Wisconsin struck down a similar photo ID requirement, contending that Hispanics and blacks would be disproportionately represented among the 300,000 voters affected. The 7th Circuit Court of Appeals reversed the trial court but was itself overruled by the Supreme Court. By a 6–3 vote the high court blocked implementation of Wisconsin's photo ID requirement on the grounds that five weeks was insufficient for voters to acquire the requisite ID.[41] With lower courts coming to opposing conclusions on the legality of photo ID requirements and with the Supreme Court allowing the Texas law to proceed since it had already been implemented whereas Wisconsin was not allowed to implement its law for the 2014 election, it seems likely that the Supreme Court will need to provide further guidance on when these requirements are acceptable.

Reducing the time for early voting has also triggered opposition. Not that long ago states strictly limited the conditions under which one could vote at any time other than election day. By 2014, twenty-seven states and the District of Columbia had liberal rules allowing no-fault absentee voting, and Oregon, Washington, and Colorado had universal vote-by-mail with the state sending ballots out to all registrants.[42] Beginning with Texas, thirty-three states have adopted in-person early voting. The number of days prior to the election during which early voting is allowed varies from state to state. When states that have embraced early voting subsequently seek to reduce the time available, those efforts have drawn outrage primarily from minority groups. When Florida reduced the window for early voting from fifteen to ten days, it sought a declaratory judgment from the district court of the District of Columbia. DOJ objected on the grounds that minorities more often vote early than do whites, so that reducing the days for early voting would be retrogressive.[43] Ohio's legislature shortened the early voting period from thirty-five to twenty-eight days and eliminated the possibility that a person could register and immediately cast a ballot—same-day registration and voting. The 6th Circuit Court of Appeals blocked the proposed reduction on the grounds that it would disadvantage African Americans and the poor. In a per curiam opinion the Supreme Court by a 5–4 vote reversed the court of appeals and upheld the statute.[44] A related concern that draws objections comes if a state proposes to cease allowing early voting on one or more Sundays prior to election day. African Americans point out that some churches provide buses to take parishioners to vote immediately, so barring early voting on Sunday might have a discriminatory impact.

Those seeking to reduce the early voting period note that most of the votes come closer to the election, with only light turnout weeks before election day. Another justification stresses the cost of maintaining voting sites when few people take advantage of the opportunity.

## Alabama Legislative Black Caucus v. Alabama

The issues of performance and also, implicitly, of the race-party nexus were addressed by the high court in 2015. In its most recent redistricting case, the Supreme Court remanded a challenge to the latest round of redistricting of the Alabama legislature for further hearing.[45] The Alabama Legislative Black Caucus and the Alabama Democratic Conference attacked the plan for increasing the concentrations of African Americans in some of the state's majority-black districts.

As stated in Justice Stephen Breyer's majority opinion, "The Caucus and the Conference basically claim that the State, in adding so many new minority voters to majority-minority districts (and to others), went too far."[46] In short, the appellants criticized the plans for packing blacks into the twenty-seven house and eight senate districts that had black majorities. The state justified its actions based on its interpretation of Section 5, which was still in place at the time the plans were devised. The districts in question were underpopulated, and in meeting the one person–one vote mandate the state added blacks.

Behind the arguments offered in court lie the political motivations of the actors. In 2011, Republicans had just taken over the Alabama house, having gained twenty-three seats in the 2010 GOP wave to give them sixty-six of the 105 seats. For the first time, Republicans had complete control over redistricting, and they devised plans intended to protect their dominance—certainly not a unique strategy. They packed the most loyal Democrats into a minority of districts while distributing Republicans more efficiently so as to control several districts with small but reliable majorities. Democrats—and the bulk of Alabama's Democratic legislators are African Americans—wanted to distribute their numbers to maximize the number of seats in which they could be competitive, just as the Black Caucus had in Georgia in 2001 in the plan that led to *Georgia v. Ashcroft*.

The Alabama trial court carried out statewide analyses of the house and senate plans as plaintiffs had requested. In sending the case back for further consideration, the Supreme Court directed that the inquiry focus on individual districts and not each plan as an entity. Plaintiffs should have asked the trial court to assess the likelihood that each majority-minority district would continue to have a sufficient minority population to elect the minority-preferred candidates.

A related criticism directed at the trial court took it to task for joining what the Supreme Court characterized as "Alabama's mechanical interpretation of § 5 [which] can raise serious constitutional concerns." The state and the trial court, like many before them, interpreted Section 5 to mean that any decrease in the black concentration in a majority-black district could trigger a DOJ objection on the grounds of retrogression. Although Congress had not interpreted retrogression to mean that there could be no diminution in minority-population concentrations if that could be avoided, it had specifically overruled *Ashcroft* in the course of extending the Voting Rights

Act in 2006. Dramatic reductions in black populations in some Georgia senate districts in *Ashcroft* had not endangered black candidates' ability to win, even in districts that had razor-thin black majorities, yet Congress found these to be contrary to the intent of the Act.[47]

The majority opinion in *Alabama* acknowledges that it may be asking legislatures to hit the sweet spot when drawing minority districts. "The law cannot lay a trap for an unwary legislature, condemning its redistricting plan as either (1) unconstitutional racial gerrymandering should the legislature place a few too many minority voters in a district or (2) retrogression under §5 should the legislature place a few too few." But the Court provides no precise guidance beyond the squishy advice that the legislature "should have asked: 'To what extent must we preserve existing minority percentages in order to maintain the minority's present ability to elect their candidate of its choice?'" The old retrogression test as frequently applied was clear-cut: if the legislature reduced the minority concentration in a majority-minority district, the plan was unacceptable. At an earlier time DOJ and many courts applied a different test but one equally clear: minority districts needed to have at least 65 percent minority population.

In making the district-by-district assessment demanded by the Supreme Court, multiple questions must be asked: What are the turnout rates for minorities and nonminorities? How cohesive is each group? To what extent do participation rates vary between presidential and off-year elections? What is the makeup of the electorate in the Democratic primary? Perhaps most important, how much margin for error will be tolerated in assessing the likelihood of minority success? Reducing a black percentage from 70 to 65 percent may not imperil the ability of African Americans to elect their preferences, but what about dropping the black percentage to 57 or 53 percent? Should the legislature honor an incumbent's request to have a larger minority concentration? Should the legislature include more minority voters, ceterus paribus, if the minority incumbent is near retirement or has been drawn out of the district since a new minority candidate would lack the personal following of an incumbent? In a community in which a some whites vote Democratic, would a state be obligated to reduce a district's minority population below the 50 percent threshold if evidence indicated that a majority-white district nonetheless would elect a black, since the black vote controlled the Democratic primary?

Our previous discussion of the work of David Epstein and his colleagues has bearing on this part of the problem too. In southern congressional districts, Epstein and his colleagues show the point at which African Americans had an even chance of electing their preference required a black VAP of about 40 percent.[48] Can majority districts be justified if using these remedies results in needless packing of the black vote?

The Supreme Court's admonition to conduct a functional assessment of each minority district adds to the time required to develop a new plan. That will not be a problem in most states, but in Louisiana, Mississippi, and Virginia, each of which has a substantial black population and which holds state elections in odd-numbered years, the legislature may have to work overtime in 2021 to get plans in place for elections scheduled for later that year.

At the rehearing of the Alabama case, will the state contend that it relied not on race but primarily on partisanship when assigning precincts to districts? In *Easley v. Cromartie*, North Carolina successfully defended one of its iterations of the "I-85 district" made famous in *Shaw v. Reno* by asserting that the basis for placing precincts in the district was their support for Democratic candidates and not the racial makeup of the precincts.[49] In approving this district, which plaintiffs argued was the product of a racial gerrymander, as they did in the Alabama case, the Supreme Court recognized the strong correlation between race and support for Democratic candidates in the South but accepted the state's claim that its primary motivation was party advantage and not race.[50]

The Supreme Court held that equalizing populations among districts cannot be the predominant factor in a redistricting plan since that is constitutionally required. At the new trial, Alabama may try to offer other explanations, including, as in *Cromartie*, placing an emphasis on partisan motives. But if on rehearing the state fails to convince the Court that race was not the predominant factor when drawing the challenged districts, the upshot may be significant advantage for Democrats in states in which they control the redistricting process. Packing members of the opposition into as few districts as possible so that they waste votes by winning by overwhelming margins is a standard redistricting practice. Democrats will continue to be able to carry out that ploy. But if when Republicans attempt the same move they are called for a racial gerrymander—and since African Americans are the most loyal Democrats it is precincts in which they live that a GOP cartographer would cluster together— they will be denied one of gerrymandering's most effective tools.

Racial minorities, but not other groups in society, will have been given a right to maximize their influence by receiving the most effective distribution of their numbers.

## Empirical Evidence

As the litigation over these new issues continues, a growing body of empirical evidence has emerged that will allow future courts to rely on data rather than speculation about the benefits or consequences of the proposed changes. Lorraine Minnite, the leading researcher into the incidence of voter fraud, finds little evidence of the voter impersonation that photo IDs are designed to prevent. She does not have comparable data when exploring the impact photo ID laws may have in keeping people from voting, although she concludes that it exceeds the number of cases of potential fraud that are thwarted. Minnite hypothesizes, "Voter identification laws are too new and too different for statistical analysis to be of much help, and even if we had more elections in which to test for an effect, it is not clear that a small negative impact of 1, 2, or 3 percentage points is detectable given the data and analytical tools that we have."[51] Others have taken on the challenge to determine the magnitude of the impact.

Photo ID laws have been in place for several election cycles now, so their impact can begin to be assessed. Evidence of such impact comes from two sources. Survey research has found very few individuals who have been kept from voting because they lacked photo IDs. Steven Ansolabehere has reported that fewer than 0.2 percent of prospective voters were turned away because they lacked a photo ID.[52] An analysis of the impact of Georgia's photo ID law concluded that it reduced turnout by about 0.4 percent.[53] Ansolabehere's survey data also show that the small number of people turned away cannot be attributed to those lacking an ID not going to the polls. Of 4,000 people questioned, just seven said they stayed home because of the ID requirement. This is not surprising, since almost everyone believes that they have an ID that allows them to vote. A Pew Research Center survey found that 98 percent of respondents believed that they possess the necessary documents for voting.[54] A survey done in conjunction with the challenge to the Texas ID requirement found that 97.2 percent of respondents believed they had an appropriate document.[55]

Before- and after-turnout data from states that have implemented photo ID laws provide an alternative to survey research for assessing the consequences of these requirements. The bulk of the evidence does not find the drop in overall or minority turnout that opponents of photo IDs have anticipated. The post-election surveys conducted by the Census Bureau show that turnout rates by African Americans increased in Indiana and Georgia in 2008, the first presidential election in which photo IDs were needed, when compared with 2004. The increase might be partially the result of the presence of Barack Obama on the ballot, but the increase in the two states with the most demanding photo ID laws at that time outpaced the increase nationwide. Moreover, when black turnout for 2010, when Obama did not appear on the ballot, is compared with 2006, increases in Georgia and Indiana exceeded the national figure. Georgia is one of the handful of states that collect information on the race/ethnicity of registrants. In 2008 the share of the state's votes cast by African Americans rose to an unprecedented 30.5 percent, up from 25.4 percent four years earlier. Black turnout dropped in the 2010 midterm to 28.2 percent, but that was 4 points above the 2006 figure. The 2014 midterm saw African Americans cast 28.6 percent of Georgia's votes, the largest share for blacks in a Georgia midterm.[56]

Less evidence exists on the impact of shortening the time for early voting. Georgia reduced the forty-five days available in 2008 to twenty-one days and saw total turnout slip from 3,934,388 (75.7 percent of registrants) to 3,908,500 (72.9 percent of registrants) in 2012. The drop in Georgia was in keeping with national trends that saw 2.25 million fewer votes cast, a decline of 3.4 points in terms of voting age population.[57] Prior to the 2014 election, North Carolina reduced the early voting period from seventeen to ten days, although it expanded the hours available during the week before the election, and eliminated the possibility of registering and casting a ballot on the same day. In another change, election officials asked for photo IDs but allowed voters without an acceptable document to cast a ballot. Experts testifying on behalf of the DOJ effort to block these changes had predicted that minority turnout would suffer. Despite having seven fewer early voting days, the number of ballots cast before election day 2014 increased by one-fifth over 2010 to 1,152,989. North Carolina, like Georgia, gathers information on voter race or ethnicity at the time of registration, and a post-election audit showed that black turnout increased by almost 100,000 over 2010 and that the share of all ballots cast by blacks increased by 1.3 percentage points.[58]

Data coming from states that have adopted photo ID laws and shortened the period for early voting will allow further analysis. But on the basis of what he has seen thus far, Robert Popper, former deputy chief of the Voting Section in the Obama Justice Department, concluded, "It is becoming harder to ignore the data suggesting that the 'voter suppression' narrative is a myth."[59]

Concerns about the consequences of the Supreme Court decision striking down Section 4, along with recent state actions requiring photo IDs or shortening early voting periods, all illustrate probability neglect, a concept introduced in chapter 5. For members of minority groups that in the past have faced obstacles to participation, the fear that recent changes will impede the way to the ballot box more than offsets the probability that a return to some status quo ante could actually occur.

Advocates on both sides of the debate encourage probability neglect. Those urging adoption of a photo ID requirement warn that in its absence elections could be undermined by the casting of illegal ballots. In a close election just a handful of ballots could change the outcome. Al Franken (D-Minn.) defeated Sen. Norm Coleman in 2008 by just 312 votes. In 2014, Martha McSally won in Arizona's 2nd District, the closest U.S. House race, by 167 votes. The 1976 New Hampshire Senate contest was so close that a do-over was ordered after the secretary of state awarded the Democrat a ten-vote victory but the GOP election commission ruled the Republican candidate had won by two votes. Although every election year produces a few nail-biters, examples of voter impersonation—the type of fraud that a photo ID would prevent—have proven elusive.

Those opposed to photo ID laws warn that large numbers of eager voters will be turned away at the polling station. Thus far plaintiffs have provided little evidence of voters barred from the ballot box because they could not provide a photo ID. Instead, a growing body of data show that even groups thought to be most at risk to a photo ID demand, African Americans, are participating at higher rates *after* a state changes its laws.

Both sides in the arguments over photo IDs, reduced periods of early voting, and the consequences of eliminating preclearance have incentives to paint pictures far starker than reality. Fanning the flames of fear that political access grudgingly extended to minorities over the past half-century could be retracted may stimulate greater turnout, which could tip the balance in hotly contested elections. These fears may also encourage financial support for groups opposing the changes. Raising the alarm that elections are about to be stolen by those not entitled to vote can also serve as a mobilizing event. Since the competing fears have become touchstones for the opposing political parties, they are likely to continue being trumpeted regardless of what the evidence shows.

## CONCLUSION

This is a story without a happy ending for those who seek a restoration of the old Voting Rights regime, at least for the near term at the time of this writing. Despite the existence of myriad voting issues in the United States, the ability to craft a credible and effective national voting law to address the issues we describe here is impeded by politics. The ability to craft a restoration of a national regulatory regime to restore old authority is impeded both by both politics and by a change in the constitutional interpretation regime at the Supreme Court that precludes any action by Congress that is an affront to the Court's vision of federalism.

As we move forward into this new environment, the Department of Justice and progressive advocates for voting rights confront a very different playing field. The burden of proof has shifted away from suspect jurisdictions, and the cost structure of achieving success is now much higher. But we also have entered the next stage of an experiment that has potentially great costs for individual rights. By removing the old regulatory regime, we will see what previously suspect states and localities do, and how the courts in turn treat claims made under Sections 2 and 3 of the Act. Did the treatment take? Is the emergency over? Or do we follow the closing of the books on the second Reconstruction with the return of a new Jim Crow era? We cannot answer these questions now, for to do so is only to speculate. But we can observe that the political and judicial environment has never been more disposed to weigh against national government action against emergent states' rights arguments and policies at any time in the past century.

# Notes

## INTRODUCTION

1. In 1883 the Court struck down the Civil Rights Act of 1875 (sometimes called the Enforcement Act). Congress had passed that act as an enforcement mechanism to prevent discrimination in public accommodations (*The Civil Rights Cases* 109 U.S. 3). Many of the provisions of the stricken law were reenacted eight decades later in the Civil Rights Acts of 1964 and 1968.

## 1. CONDITIONS GIVING RISE TO THE VOTING RIGHTS ACT

1. *Guinn v. U.S.*, 238 U.S. 347 (1915). The *Lochner* era court was willing to overturn state laws that presented a clear and unambiguous violation of the Fifteenth Amendment.

2. *Smith v. Allwright*, 321 U.S. 649 (1944).

3. Charles S. Bullock III, Scott Buchanan, and Ronald Keith Gaddie, *The Three Governors Controversy* (Athens: University of Georgia Press, 2015), chap. 3.

4. Data provided by M. V. Hood III. These data were used by Hood, Quentin Kidd, and Irwin Morris to create Figure 2.7 in *The Rational Southerner* (New York: Oxford University Press, 2012).

5. In 1957, Thurmond was a Democrat; he switched to the GOP in 1964 to back Barry Goldwater's presidential bid.

6. Quoted in Dan T. Carter, *The Politics of Rage* (New York: Simon & Schuster, 1995), 102.

7. *U.S. v. Raines*, 172 F. Supp. 552 (M.D. Ga. 1959); Rev'd 362 U.S. 17 1960, 189 F. Supp. 121 (M.D. Ga. 1960).

8. U.S. Commission on Civil Rights [U.S.C.C.R], *Voting: 1961 Commission on Civil Rights Report* (Washington, D.C.: U.S. Government Printing Office, 1961), 29–30.

9. U.S.C.C.R, *Report of the United State Commission on Civil Rights, 1959* (Washington, D.C.: U.S. Government Printing Office, 1961), 67.

10. U.S.C.C.R, *Voting 1961*, 84–85.

11. Alternative figures appear at ibid., 33, where the Commission on Civil Rights reports the increase in black registration going from eighty-two to 133. Even accepting the higher figure of 133 black registrants, less than 4 percent of the potential black electorate had signed up to vote.

12. *U.S. v Alabama*, 171 F. Supp. 720 (M.D. Ala.); Affd 267 F. 2d 808 (5th Cir. 1960).

13. Washington, D.C.: U.S. Government Printing Office, 1961), *Voting 1961*, 86.

14. U.S.C.C.R, *Report, 1959*, 78.

15. Ibid., 75–78.

16. Ibid., 75–76.

17. A third suit, *U.S. v. McElveen*, 177 F. Supp. 355 (E.D. La. 1959), 180 F. Supp. 10 (E.D. La. 1960) involved Washington Parish. As a result of the *McElveen* case, 1,377 blacks who had been previously registered but were unable to reregister had their names restored to the voter rolls.

18. Donald R. Matthews and James W. Prothro, *Negroes in the New Southern Politics* (New York: Harcourt, Brace and World, 1966), 149.

19. Ibid., 115.

20. V. O. Key, Jr., *Southern Politics* (New York: Knopf, 1949).

21. U.S.C.C.R, *Voting 1961*, 136, 69–70.

22. U.S.C.C.R, *Report, 1959*, 98, 105–106.

23. Ibid., 34.

24. Ibid., 61, 20, 34.

25. U.S.C.C.R, *Voting 1961*, 33–34.

26. Ibid., 80.

27. Ibid., 44, 49–52.

28. Ibid., 56–57.

29. Ibid., 64.

30. U.S.C.C.R, *Report, 1959*, 60.

31. Ibid., 63.

32. U.S.C.C.R, *Voting 1961*, 91–92.

33. Matthews and Prothro, *Negroes*, 303–304.

34. U.S.C.C.R, *Voting 1961*, 36–37; for economic intimidation in Louisiana, see 67.

35. In the fascinating chronicle of black political emergence in majority-black McIntosh County, Georgia, none of the three black leaders was dependent upon whites for income. Melissa Fay Greene, *Praying for Sheetrock* (New York: Addison-Wesley, 1991).

36. Matthews and Prothro, *Negroes*, 44, 73, 78.

37. U.S.C.C.R, *Civil Rights '63* (Washington, D.C.: U.S. Government Printing Office, 1963), 30, 15.

38. Ibid., 14–15, 32–35.

39. U.S.C.C.R, *Voting 1961*, 22.

40. Figures for Texas are unavailable.

41. For recitation of murders of those seeking to exercise the franchise in Georgia, see Donald L. Grant, *The Way It Was in the South: The Black Experience in Georgia* (Athens: University of Georgia Press, 1993).

42. *South Carolina v. Katzenbach*, 383 U.S. 301 (1966).

43. Smith v. Allwright, 321 U.S. 649 (1944).

. 44. Harrell R. Rodgers, Jr., and Charles S. Bullock III, *Law and Social Change: Civil Rights Laws and Their Consequences* (New York: McGraw-Hill, 1972), 27.

45. U.S.C.C.R, *Political Participation* (Washington, D.C.: Government Printing Office, 1968) 224–225.

46. Matthews and Prothro, *Negroes*, 331.

47. *Allen v. State Board of Elections*, 393 U.S. 544 (1969).

48. *City of Mobile v. Bolden*, 446 U.S.1 55 (1980).

49. Hatch and DOJ quoted in Walter Isaacson, "Pondering the Voting Rights Act," *Time*, May11, 1981.

50. *Thornburg v. Gingles*, 478 U.S. 30 (1986).

51. For a detailed discussion of the impact of Section 2 on representation on local governing bodies in southern states covered by Section 5, see Chandler Davidson and Bernard Grofman, eds., *Quiet Revolution in the South: The Impact of the Voting Rights Act, 1965–1990* (Princeton, N.J.: Princeton University Press, 1994).

52. *Miller v. Johnson*, 51 U.S. 900 (1995).

53. *Hays v. Louisiana*, 936 F. Supp. 367 (W.D. La. 1996); *Johnson v. Mortham*, 915 F. Supp. 1529 (N.D. Fla. 1995); *Moon v. Meadows*, 952 F. Supp. 1141 (E.D. Va. 1996); *Bush v. Vera*, 517 U.S. 952, 116 S. Ct. 1941 (1996).

54. *Beer v. United States*, 425 U.S. 130 (1976); *Reno v. Bossier Parish School Board*, 428 U.S. 320 (1999).

55. *Vieth v. Jubelirer*, 541 U.S. 267 (2004).

## 2. IMPLEMENTING THE ACT

1. Rick Pildes and Dan Tokaji, "What Did VRA Preclearance Actually Do? The Gap between Perception and Reality." Election Law Blog, Accessed August 19, 2013, at http://electionlawblog.org/?p=54521.

2. Justin Levitt, "Section 5 as Simulacrum," *123 Yale L. J. Online* 151 (2013), Loyola-LA Legal Studies Paper 2013–17.

3. *Allen v. State Board of Elections*, 393 U.S. 544 (1969).

4. Quoted in Walter Isaacson, "Pondering the Voting Rights Act," *Time*, May 11, 1981.

5. See, for example, Pamela S. Karlan, "Testimony of Professor Pamela S. Karlan, Stanford Law School, on the Continuing Need for Section 5 Preclearance," *Election Law Journal* 5 (2006): 338.

6. Sen. Patrick Leahy (D-Vt.), *Congressional Record*, July 20, 2006, S 8008.

7. Preclearance data throughout this review of states, unless noted otherwise, are drawn from Luis Ricard Fraga and Maria Lizet Ocampo, "The Deterrent Effect of Section 5 on the Voting Rights Act: The Role of More Information Requests," presented at the symposium Protecting Democracy: Using Research to Inform the Voting Reauthorization Debate, Washington, D.C., February 9, 2006.

8. James Blacksher, Edward Still, Nick Quinton, Cullen Brown, and Royal Dumas, "Voting Rights in Alabama 1982–2006," RenewtheVRA.org, July 2006, 8, 13–14.

9. U.S. Commission on Civil Rights, *Political Participation* (Washington, D.C.: Government Printing Office, 1968), 223–227.

10. *Georgia v. Reno*, 881 F. Supp. 7 (D.D.C. 1995).

11. *Miller v. Johnson*, 51 U.S. 900 (1995).

12. *Beer v. United States*, 425 U.S. 130 (1976).

13. John R. Dunne, "Remarks of John R. Dunne," *Cardozo Law Review* 14 (1993): 1128.

14. *Reno v. Bossier Parish School Board*, 428 U.S. 320 (1999).

15. Nina Perales, Louis Figueroa, and Criselda G. Rivas, "Voting Rights in Texas, 1982–2006," RenewtheVRA.org, June 2006, 16.

16. Jonel Newman, "Voting Rights in Florida 1982–2006," RenewtheVRA .org, March 2006, 4.

17. "From Selma to *Shelby County:* Working Together to Restore the Protections of the Voting Rights Act": Hearing before the S. Comm. on Judiciary (July 17, 2013).

18. Much of the data in this Section come from Ellen Katz and The Voting Rights Initiative, VRI Database Master List (2006), www.votingreport.org. We acknowledge and thank Professor Katz and her research team for their efforts in gathering and archiving these data. Katz team figures are augmented by information on unreported decisions tabulated by the National Commission on the Voting Rights Act, *Protecting Minority Voters: The Voting Rights Act at Work, 1982–2005* (Washington, D.C.: Lawyers' Committee for Civil Rights Under Law, 2006).

19. National Commission on the Voting Rights Act, *Protecting Minority Voters*.

20. *NAACP v. Fordice*, 252 F.3d 361 5th Cir. (2001); *Magnolia Bar Association, Inc., v. Roy Noble Lee, et al.*, 994 F.2d 1143 (1993).

21. *Jordan v. Winter, 604 F. Supp. 807* (N.D. Miss. 1984).

22. *Buskey v. Oliver*, 565 F. Supp. 1473 (M.D. Ala. 1983).

23. *Wesch v. Hunt*, 785 F. Supp. 1491 (S.D. Ala. 1992).

24. *Gadsden County*, 691 F.2d 978.

25. *Johnson v. Bush*, 405 F.3d 1214 (2005); *De Grandy*, 512 U.S. 997 (1994); *Martinez v. Bush*, 234 F. Supp. 2d 1275 (2002).

26. Supplemental declaration of Dr. Peyton McCrary in *Shelby County v. Holder*, 811 F. Supp. 2d 424 (2011).

27. *Major v. Treen*, 574 F. Supp. 340 (1983).

28. *Thornburg v. Gingles*, 478 U.S. 30 (1986).

29. McCrary declaration, *Shelby County v. Holder*, 811 F. Supp. 2d 424 (2011).

30. *Holder v. Hall*, 512 U.S. 874 (1994).

31. *Sumter County*, 775 F.2d 1509 (1985); *Brooks*, 158 F.3d 1230 (1998).

32. *Jeffers v. Clinton*, 730 F. Supp. 196, 1989.

33. *Smith-Crittenden County*, 687 F. Supp. 1310, 1988; *West*, 786 F. Supp. 803, 1992.

34. *Democratic Party of Arkansas*, 902 F.2d 15 (1990).

35. *Taylor v. Haywood County*, 544 F. Supp. 1122 (W.D. Tenn. 1982); *Rural West Tennessee African-American Affairs Council, Inc v. Sundquist*, 209 F.3d 835 (6th Circ.); *Rural West Tennessee African-American Affairs Council, Inc. v. Sundquist*, 116 S. Ct. 42 (1995).

36. *Dean*, 555 F. Supp. 502 D.R.I. 1982; *Marks-Philadelphia*, 1994 WL 146113 E.D. Pa. 1994; *Town of Cicero* 2000 WL 34342276 N.D. Ill.; *Arakaki* 314 F.3d 1091 9th Cir. 2002.

37. Jurisdictions in Virginia that bailed out between 1984 and 2006: City of Fairfax, and the City of Fairfax School; Frederick County, including the Frederick County School Board the Towns of Middletown and Stephens City; and the Frederick County Shawneeland Sanitary District; Shenandoah County, Virginia including the Shenandoah County School Board, the Towns of Edinburg, Mount Jackson, New Market, Strasburg, Toms Brook, and Woodstock, the Stoney Creek Sanitary District, and the Toms Brook-Maurertown Sanitary District; Roanoke County, including the Roanoke County School Board and the Town of Vinton; City of Winchester; City of Harrisonburg, including the Harrisonburg City School Board; Rockingham County, including the Rockingham County School Board and the Towns of Bridgewater, Broadway, Dayton, Elkton, Grottoes, Mt. Crawford, and Timberville; Warren County, including the Warren County School Board and the Town of Front Royal; Greene County, including the Greene County School Board and the Town of Standardsville; Pulaski County, including the Pulaski County School Board and the Towns of Pulaski and Dublin; Augusta County, including the Augusta County School Board and the Town of Craigsville; City of Salem; and Troutville.

38. Essex County, including the Essex County School Board and the Town of Tappahannock; Middlesex County, including the Middlesex County School

Board and the Town of Urbanna; Amherst County, Virginia, including the Town of Amherst; Page County, including the Page County School Board and the Towns of Luray, Stanley, and Shenandoah; and Washington County, including the Washington County School Board and the Towns of Abington, Damascus, and Glade Spring.

39. Towns of Antrim, Benton, Boscawen, Millsfield, Newington, Pinkham's Grant, Rindge, Stewartstown, Stratford, and Unity.

40. City of Manassas Park; Rappahannock County, including the Rappa-hannock County School Board and the Town of Washington; Bedford County, including the Bedford County School Board; City of Bedford; Culpeper County, including the Culpeper County School Board and the Town of Culpeper; James City County; City of Williamsburg, including the Williamsburg-James City County School Board; King George County, including the King George County School Board; Prince William County, including the Prince William County School Board and the Towns of Dumfries, Haymarket, Occoquan, and Quantico; Wythe County, including the County School Board and the Towns of Rural Retreat and Wytheville; Grayson County, including the County School Board and the Towns of Independence, Fries and Troutdale; Craig County, including the Craig County School District and the Town of New Castle; Carroll County, including the Carroll County School District and the Town of Hillsville; and City of Falls Church, and the Falls Church City Public School District.

41. Evidence of widespread local discriminatory behavior can also result in the bail-in of an entire state, as happened in Arkansas.

42. Los Angeles County, Calif.; Escambia County, Fla.; Thruston County, Neb.; Bernalillo County, N.M.; Buffalo and Charles Mix Counties, S.D.; and Chattanooga, Tenn.

## 3. A COMPARATIVE ANALYSIS OF THE IMPACT OF THE VOTING RIGHTS ACT IN THE SOUTH

1. In Charles S. Bullock III and Ronald Keith Gaddie, *The Triumph of Voting Rights in the South* (Norman: University of Oklahoma Press, 2009), we argued that Section 5 constituted a natural experiment. This chapter's analysis represents the cumulative comparative analysis for that experiment. Readers inter-ested in the deeper context of voting rights progress in the individual states of the South should consult chapters 1–11 of that work.

2. Douglas Rae, *The Political Consequences of Electoral Laws* (New Haven, Conn.: Yale University Press, 1971); Arend Lijphart, *Patterns of Democracy: Govern-ment Forms and Performance in Thirty-Six Countries* (New Haven: Yale University Press, 1999), especially chap. 8; David M. Farrell, *Electoral Systems: A Compara-tive Introduction* (New York: Palgrave, 2001), especially chap. 7.

3. Andrew Gelman and Gary King, "Estimating Incumbency Advantage without Bias," *American Journal of Political Science* 34 (1990): 1142–1164.

4. The Census Bureau did not release its report on the 2006 election until 2008.

5. Bullock and Gaddie, *Triumph*, chap. 12.

6. For all of these comparative analyses we rely on Spearman's rho to test for significant changes in terms of black voter progress across the South. Spearman's rho calculates the similarity or dissimilarity of two rank orderings. The Spearman's rho computed using the pre–Voting Rights Act ranking and the 2004 ranking from ibid., table 12.1, is -.406. This indicates a degree of reversal in the rank orderings of the two different periods of time, although the relationship is not statistically significant ($p = .12$, one-tailed test).

7. The Spearman's rho of .636 ($p = .018$, one-tailed test) calculated between the 2004 rankings for blacks and whites shows a striking similarity between the relative registration rates of the two races across the eleven states.

8. Angus Campell, Philip Converse, Warren Miller, and Donald Stokes, *The American Voter* (New York: J. Wiley and Sons, 1960); Sidney Verba and Norman Nie, *Participation in America* (New York: Harper and Row, 1972); Sidney Verba, Norman Nie, and J. Kim, *Participation and Political Equality* (New York: Cambridge, 1978); Raymond Wolfinger and Steven Rosenstone, *Who Votes?* (New Haven, Conn.: Yale University Press, 1980); Jan E. Leighley and Jonathan Nagler, "Class Bias in Turnout: The Voters Remain the Same," *American Political Science Review* 86 (1992): 725–736; Jan E. Leighley and Jonathan Nagler, "Individual and Systemic Influences on Turnout: *Who Votes?* 1984," *Journal of Politics* 54 (1992): 718–740.

9. Katherine Tate, "Black Political Participation in the 1984 and 1988 Presidential Elections," *American Political* Science Review 85 (1991): 1159–1176; Peter W. Wielhouwer, "Releasing the Fetters: Parties and the Mobilization of the African American Electorate," *Journal of Politics* 62 (2000): 206–222.

10. See Bullock and Gaddie, *Triumph*, 379–385.

11. States would invariably have higher index scores if the denominator reflected the size of the pool of potential justices rather than the voting age population. Service on a state's highest court requires not simply that one be an adult but that one also be an attorney. It is highly likely that African Americans constitute a smaller share of the bar than of the voting age population.

12. The *Southern Political Report* (2006) shows North Carolina not having a black justice, but governor Mike Easley subsequently named an African American to a vacancy.

13. Richard L. Engstrom and Michael McDonald, "The Election of Blacks to City Councils," *American Political Science Review* 75 (June 1981): 344–354.

14. Chandler Davidson and Bernard Grofman, eds., *Quiet Revolution in the South* (Princeton, N.J.: Princeton University Press, 1994).

15. Since the data on black local officials come from the 2001 survey done by the Joint Center for Political and Economic Studies, the VAP figures are from the 2000 census. For the congressional, state legislator, and supreme court membership, citizen voting age estimates from 2012 are used.

16. Bullock and Gaddie, *Triumph*, 339.

17. $p = .021$, one-tailed test.

18. David Lublin, *The Paradox of Representation* (Princeton, N.J.: Princeton University Press, 1997).

## 4. THE VRA, MR. OBAMA, AND THE 2008 AND 2012 PRESIDENTIAL ELECTIONS IN THE SOUTH

1. To minimize front loading, the Democratic Party had authorized four states to conduct their presidential selection contest early. Iowa was given the position of first caucus state, with New Hampshire maintaining its tradition of being the first primary state. To increase the diversity of states participating early in the process, South Carolina was designated as the second primary state and Nevada would be the second caucus state. Florida and Michigan "jumped the line," with Florida holding an unsanctioned primary on January 29, four days before South Carolina's vote. The Democratic Party threatened not to seat the delegates chosen in the unsanctioned primaries but ultimately relented once Obama's nomination was secured.

2. Morrison's quote appeared in a 1998 *New Yorker* essay.

3. Charles S. Bullock III, "Barack Obama and the South," *American Review of Politics* 31 (Spring 2010): 3–24.

4. "Rep. Lewis Switches to Obama," *Los Angeles Times*, February 28, 2008.

5. Shailagh Murray, "For Black Superdelegates, Pressure to Back Obama," *Washington Post*, March 3, 2008, A1.

6. This section draws on Bullock, "Barack Obama," 10–11.

7. Linear regression is a common statistical technique for estimating the relationship between an outcome (dependent variable) and one or more explanatory (independent) variables. The technique tests the linear "fit" of explanatory variables to the outcome. It does so by creating an estimate of how an increase in value of the explanatory variable results in a corresponding change of the value in the outcome. So, for example, if votes for a Democratic candidate are more likely among racial minority voters in an electorate, then increasing the minority vote share should produce a linear increase in the Democratic candidate vote share.

8. Estimate of total, black, and white vote shares for southern Democratic U.S. Senate and gubernatorial candidates in 2008:

|  | Total Vote | Black vote | White vote |
|---|---|---|---|
| Intercept | -30.86 | -21.41 | 1.82 |
| Obama % | 1.72** | 1.18 | 1.16** |
| Incumbency | 3.15 | 4.54* | 5.66 |
| Adjusted R2 | .62 | .18 | .73 |
| N | 11 | 11 | 11 |

$*p < .05$
$**p < .01$

9. The response of the Obama share of the white vote to the size of the African American and Latino share of turnout:

|  | White vote share |
|---|---|
| Intercept | 52.41** |
| African American % | -1.12** |
| Latino % | -.29 |
| Adjusted R² | 49 |
| N | 11 |

**Significant at a .01 level, two-tailed test.

10. The Voter News Service did not take exit polls in the District of Columbia and nineteen states: Alaska, Arkansas, Delaware, Georgia, Hawaii, Idaho, Kentucky, Louisiana, Nebraska, North Dakota, Oklahoma, Rhode Island, South Carolina, South Dakota, Tennessee, Texas, Utah, West Virginia, and Wyoming. Marjorie Connelly, "Election Exit Polls Are Eliminated in 19 States," *New York Times*, October 4, 2012.

## 5. THE 2006 DEBATE AND RENEWAL OF THE ACT

1. Bullock's telephone interview with Blum on September 9, 2013, is the source of the Blum quotations unless otherwise indicated.

2. Morgan Smith, "One Man Standing against Race-based Laws," *New York Times*, February 23, 2012.

3. Michael Barone and Grant Ujifusa, *The Almanac of American Politics, 1994* (Washington, D.C.: National Journal, 1993), 1251.

4. Ibid., 1252.

5. Hurd's Louisiana case became *U.S. v Hays*, 515 U.S. 737 (1995).

6. On appeal to the Supreme Court the case became *Bush v. Vera*, 517 U.S. 952 (1996).

7. Joan Biskupic, "Special Report: Behind U.S. Race Cases, a Little-Known Recruiter," Reuters.com, December 4, 2012.

8. David C. Huckabee, "Congressional Districts: Objectively Evaluating Shapes," CRS Report for Congress, May 24, 1994.

9. Craig Washington survived Blum's general election challenge in the 1992 general election but succumbed to Democratic primary challenger Sheila Jackson Lee in 1994.

10. *Shaw v. Reno*, 509 U. S. 630 (1993); *Miller v. Johnson*, 515 U.S. 900 (1995).

11. Smith, "One Man Standing."

12. Charles S. Bullock III and Ronald Keith Gaddie, *The Triumph of Voting Rights in the South* (Norman: University of Oklahoma Press, 2009).

13. Krissah Thompson, "Edward Blum Defies Odds in Getting Cases to Supreme Court," *Washington Post*, February 25, 2013.

14. Edward Blum, *The Unintended Consequences of Section 5 of the Voting Rights Act* (Washington, D.C.: American Enterprise Institute, 2007). The quotes in this paragraph appear on p. 7 of the monograph.

15. Abigail M. Thernstrom, *Who's Votes Count? Affirmative Action and Minority Voting Rights* (Cambridge, Mass.: 20th Century Fund, 1987).

16. Blum, *Unintended Consequences*, 19.

17. Richard H. Pildes, "What Does the Court's Decision Mean?" *Election Law Journal* 12 (2013): 318.

18. *Congressional Record* 152, no. 91 (Thursday, July 13, 2006), H5148.

19. Ibid., H5144.

20. Ibid., H5162.

21. Ibid., H5150.

22. Bryan Tyson, who served on the staff of Lynn Westmoreland at the time of the VRA renewal, interviewed by Bullock on September 11, 2013.

23. *Georgia v. Ashcroft*, 539 U.S. 461 (2003); *Beer v. U.S.*, 425 U.S. 30 (1976).

24. Norwood was a retired dentist. Westmoreland, a home builder in the booming Atlanta suburbs, had not completed college.

25. Brian Robinson, former press secretary to Lynn Westmoreland, personal interview by Bullock, October 17, 2013.

26. Carl Hulse, "Rebellion Stalls Extension of Voting Rights Act," *New York Times*, June 22, 2006.

27. *City of Boerne v. Flores*, 521 U.S. 507 (1997).

28. Testimony of Professor Richard L. Hasen, presented to the Senate Judiciary Committee, May 9, 2006, accessed at www.judiciary.senate.gov/imo/media/doc/Hasen%20Testimony%20050906.pdf.

29. Testimony of Professor Samuel Issacharoff testimony, presented to the Senate Judiciary Committee, May 9, 2006, accessed at www.judiciary.senate.gov/imo/media/doc/Issacharoff%20Testimony%20050906.pdf.

30. *South Carolina v. Katzenbach*, 383 U.S. 334 (1966). After *Shaw*, Ellen Katz, who has extensively researched Section 2 cases, came to a conclusion much like Issacharoff's. She noted that with the striking down of Section 4, "Whatever happens, and a good deal of it may be ugly, it will not rise to the level of what prompted [the] statute in the first place." Katz, "What Was Wrong with the Record?" *Election Law Journal*, 12, no. 3 (2013): 329.

31. Nathaniel Persily, "The Promise and Pitfalls of the Voting Rights Act," *Yale Law Journal* 117, no. 2 (2007): 105–183.

32. Lynn Westmoreland, "Georgia Has Changed for the Better, and the Voting Rights Act Should Too," *The Hill*, June 7, 2006.

33. Mark Niesse, "Changed Voting Act Could Affect Isle Elections," *Star Bulletin*, June 30, 2006.

34. Raymond Hernandez, "After Challenges, House Approves Renewal of Voting Rights," *New York Times*, July 14, 2006.

35. This second dichotomous variable is, essentially, Level 2 after representatives whose districts fall into Level 3 have been eliminated.

36. Sen. Barack Obama, floor statement to the United States Senate, July 20, 2006, *Congressional Record*, S7984.

37. Sen. Jeff Sessions, floor statement to the United States Senate, July 20, 2006 *Congressional Record*, S7986.

38. Senate Report 109-295, "Fannie Lou Hamer, Rosa Parks, Coretta Scott King, and Cesar E. Chavez Voting Rights Act Reauthorization and Amendments Act of 2006, July 26, 2006.

39. Unattributed quotes here and below come from Bullock's interviews with Senate staffers promised anonymity.

40. The differing perspectives of some Republican senators and House Republicans from the same states materialized again in the context of the decisions to close down the government at the beginning of the 2014 fiscal year. Republican senators, with a notable exception of Ted Cruz (R-Tex.), displayed less enthusiasm for the government shutdown. In contrast, several Republican House members, especially those who either had or eagerly sought Tea Party support, viewed the shutdown not as an indication of a dysfunctional legislature but rather as a reason to celebrate a victory. Extensive survey research showing that the public overwhelmingly blamed Republicans for the shutdown and viewed that action negatively was not representative of the constituents of these conservative Republicans, who believed, probably correctly, that their constituents supported the shutdown even if no tangible benefits accrued from that action.

41. Yuval Rottenstreich and Christopher C. Hsee, "Money, Kisses, and Electric Shocks: On the Affective Psychology of Risk," *Psychological Science* 12 (May 2001): 185–190.

42. Cass R. Sunstein, "Terrorism and Probability Neglect," *Journal of Risk and Uncertainty* 26 (2003): 121–136.


## 6. PUSHBACK

1. Arend Lijphart, *Patterns of Democracy* (New Haven, Conn.: Yale University Press, 1999), 52.

2. For a recent overview of the potential sources of the southern realignment, see Ronald Keith Gaddie, "Realignment," in Charles S. Bullock III and Mark J. Rozell, eds., *The Oxford Handbook of Southern Politics* (New York: Oxford University Press, 2012); Alan I. Abramowitz and Kyle L. Saunders, "Ideological Realignment in the U.S. Electorate," *Journal of Politics* 60, no. 3 (1998): 634–652; Kyle L. Saunders and Alan I. Abramowitz, "Ideological Realignment and Active Partisans in the American Electorate," *American Politics Research* 32, no. 3 (2004): 285–309; Charles S. Bullock III, Donna R. Hoffman, and Ronald Keith Gaddie, "The Consolidation of the Southern White Vote," *Political Research Quarterly* 58 (2005): 231–243; Charles S. Bullock III, Donna R. Hoffman, and Ronald Keith Gaddie, "Regional Variations in the Realignment of American Politics, 1944–2004," *Social Science Quarterly* 87 (2006): 494–518; Earl Black and Merle Black, *The Rise of the Southern Republicans* (Cambridge, Mass.: Belknap, 2002).

3. In 1956, Louisiana voted for Eisenhower as a result of dissatisfaction over Democratic positions on the offshore oil production that contributed significantly Louisiana's economy.

4. Charles S. Bullock III and Mark J. Rozell, "Introduction: Southern Politics and the Twenty-First Century," in Bullock and Rozell, eds., *The New Politics of the Old South*, 3rd ed. (Lanham, Md.: Rowman and Littlefield, 2007), 15.

5. *Georgia v. Ashcroft*, 539 U.S. 461 (2003). Prior to *Ashcroft*, redistricting scholar Richard H. Pildes had anticipated the outcome: "At the same time, that functional approach might suggest that there is no impermissible 'retrogression' under Section 5 of the VRA if a jurisdiction recasts a safe district of the 1990s into a coalitional district in the 2000s, as long as the evidence shows that the coalitional district will afford an equal opportunity to elect." Pildes, "Is Voting-Rights Law Now at War with Itself? Social Science and Voting Rights in the 2000s," *North Carolina Law Review* 80 (2002): 1568.

6. Earl Black and Merle Black, *Politics and Society in the South* (Cambridge, Mass.: Harvard University Press, 1989); Black and Black, *Rise of the Southern Republicans*; Alexander Lamis, *The Two-Party South* (New York: Oxford University Press, 1986); Bullock and Rozell, *New Politics*. But see also David Ian Lublin, *The Republican South: Democratization and Partisan Change* (Princeton, N.J.: Princeton University Press, 2007). Lublin directs readers to the prominent role of social and economic forces beyond race that helped propel the rise of the southern Republicans.

7. Robert Dallek, *Lyndon B. Johnson: Portrait of a President* (New York: Oxford University Press, 2005), 170.

8. Reg Murphy and Hal Gulliver, *The Southern Strategy* (New York: Scribner, 1971).

9. Earl Black and Merle Black, *The Vital South* (Cambridge, Mass.: Harvard University Press, 1992); Black and Black, *Rise of Southern Republicans*. Also see Warren Miller and Merrill Shanks, *The New American Voter* (Cambridge, Mass.: Harvard University Press, 1996); Bullock, Hoffman, and Gaddie, "Consolidation" and "Regional Variations."

10. See, for example, Lublin, *Republican South*.

11. M. V. Hood III, Quentin Kidd, and Irwin L. Morris, *The Rational Southerner: Black Mobilization, Republican Growth, and the Partisan Transformation of the American South*. (New York: Oxford University Press 2012).

12. Warren E. Miller and J. Merrill Shanks, *The New American Voter* (Cambridge: Harvard University Press, 1996), 142–143.

13. Seth McKee, "The Past, Present, and Future of Southern Politics," *Southern Cultures* 18, no. 3 (2012): 95–117.

14. Charles S. Bullock III and Ronald Keith Gaddie, *The Triumph of Voting Rights in the South* (Norman: University of Oklahoma Press, 2009).

15. Charles S. Bullock III and Ronald Keith Gaddie, "What If the Courts Have to Handle Section 5 Reviews—Lots of Them?" *James* 7 (February–March 2011): 10, 12, 21.

16. Hans A. von Spakovsky, *Abusing the Voting Rights Act*, National Review Online, February 23, 2011, www.nationalreview.com/articles/260303/abusing-voting-rights-act-hans-von-spakovsky.

17. Bullock and Gaddie, "What If the Courts?"

18. Ibid.: "Three-judge panels, which include one court of appeals judge, review preclearance submissions. The District of Columbia Court of Appeals has 9 judges (plus 2 vacancies) while the DCDC has 18 judges and three vacancies. There are also five senior judges on the appellate bench in DC. If hundreds (or thousands) of jurisdictions doubted the fairness of DOJ and went to court, the limited number of judges would quickly become overwhelmed. DOJ's resources would also be stretched as its attorneys respond to interrogatories, depose opposition witnesses, review expert reports, prepare their own witnesses to testify, and participate in trials. The judicial system could not cope should even a small fraction of the preclearance jurisdictions go to court. A single preclearance trial, involving a three-judge tribunal, would take several days if both expert and lay witness testimony are involved. Even a 'paper trial' using affidavits and deposition examination would consume trial court time. Further, because preclearance evaluations are unique to each jurisdiction, it would be nearly impossible to consolidate cases. To avoid the potential of a judicial log-jam, DOJ attorneys would be well-served to signal to submitting authorities that they can expect treatment free of partisan overtones if they follow the administrative route to preclearance."

19. Although a few Virginia jurisdictions had bailed out of Section 5, we treat the state here as still being fully covered.

20. U.S. Commission on Civil Rights, *Redistricting and the 2010 Census: Enforcing Section 5 of the Voting Rights Act* (Washington, D.C.: U.S. Commission on Civil Rights, 2012).

21. Quoted in Robert Barnes, "States Line Up to Challenge Stringent Section Voting Rights Provision," *Washington Post*, February 9, 2012.

22. Letter from Loretta King, Acting Assistant Attorney General to James P. Cauley III, denying Kinston, N.C., request to change from partisan to nonpartisan elections, August 17, 2009, copy accessed at https://www.cir-usa.org/legal_docs/kinston_v_holder_dojletter.pdf.

23. Greg Stohr, "Voting Rights for Blacks in '65 Face Court Challenge," *Bloomberg*, September 17, 2012.

24. *Georgia v. Ashcroft*, 539 U.S. 461 (2003); *Reno v. Bossier Parish School Board*, 528 U.S. 320 (2000).

25. Northwest Austin Municipal Utility District Number One was created in 1987 to deliver basic city services to part of Travis County, Texas. The district has a five-member board and it conducts elections, but it does not engage in voter registration. All of Texas is subject to Section 5 (see chap. 8). The MUD applied for bailout and asked that the constitutionality of Section 5 be reconsidered if it were denied bailout. The case was designed to test the constitutionality of Section 5.

26. *City of Rome v. United States*, 446 U.S. 156 (1980).

27. Opinion of Justice Thomas, dissenting, *NAMUDNO v. Holder*, 557 U.S. 214–215 (2009).

28. Among the parties filing briefs in support of the *NAMUDNO* were several pro–limited government groups and individuals including the Mountain States Legal Foundation, Pacific Legal Foundation Center for Equal Opportunity and Project 21, Southeastern Legal Foundation, Georgia governor Sonny Perdue, Abigail Thernstrom, and Goldwater Institute. Alabama governor Bob Riley's filing supported neither party but appeared sympathetic toward the plaintiff-appellant's perspective.

29. Opinion of the Court, Justice Roberts, *NAMUDNO v. Holder*, 557 U.S. 193, 194 (2009).

30. *South Carolina v. Katzenbach*, 383 U.S. 301 (1966); *Allen v. State Board of Elections*, 393 U.S. 544 (1969); *City of Rome v. United States*, 446 U.S. 156 (1980).

31. *League of United Latin American Citizens v Perry*, 548 U.S. 399.

32. *NAMUDNO v. Holder*, 557 U.S. 193, 199 (2009).

33. Ibid.

34. Ibid., 8–9.

35. Ibid., 9.

36. Ibid., 16–17.

37. Ibid., 1–3.

38. Ibid., 5 note 1.

39. Ibid., 15.

40. Ibid., 17–18.

41. Bullock and Gaddie, *Triumph*, 355.

## 7. *SHELBY COUNTY* AND EQUAL SOVEREIGNTY

1. Bullock's telephone interview with Blum on September 9, 2013, is the source of the Blum quotations unless otherwise indicated.

2. Telephone interviewed conducted by Bullock on October 10, 2013.

3. Unless otherwise noted, quotes from Ellis come from Bullock's interview with him on September 24, 2013.

4. Letter from Acting Assistant Attorney General Grace Chung Becker to Dan Head, August 25, 2008, copy accessed at www.justice.gov/crt/about/vot/sec_5/pdfs/1_082508.pdf.

5. *National Federation of Independent Business v. Sebelius*, 132 S. Ct. 2566 (2012).

6. Ibid., 44.

7. See, for example, Lee Epstein and Jack Knight, *The Choices Justices Make* (Washington, D.C.: CQ Press, 1998); Forrest Maltzman, James F. Spriggs, and

Paul J. Wahlbeck, *Crafting Law on the Supreme Court: The Collegial Game* (Cambridge: Cambridge University Press, 2000).

8. For a review of this literature, see Thomas M. Keck, "Party, Policy, or Duty: Why Does the Supreme Court Invalidate Federal Statutes," *American Political Science Review* 101, no. 2 (2007).

9. Rogers M. Smith, "Political Jurisprudence, the 'New Institutionalism,' and the Future of Public Law," *American Political Science Review* 82, no. 1 (1988): 95.

10. *Federalist Papers*, No. 78.

11. Robert McCloskey, *The American Supreme Court* (Chicago: University of Chicago Press, 2010), 13.

12. See, for example, Keith E. Whittington, "'Interpose Your Friendly Hand': Political Supports for the Exercise of Judicial Review by the United States Supreme Court," *American Political Science* Review 99, no. 4 (2005): 583–596; Mark A. Graber, "The Nonmajoritarian Difficulty: Legislative Deference to the Judiciary," *Studies in American Political Development* 7 (Spring 1993): 35–73.

13. *U.S. v. Lopez*, 514 U.S. 549 (1995); *U.S. v. Morrison*, 529 U.S. 598 (2000).

14. *Gonzales v. Raich*, 545 U.S. 1 (2005); *U.S. v. Comstock*, 130 S. Ct. 1949 (2010).

15. *Parents Involved in Community Schools v. Seattle School Dist. No. 1*, 551 U.S. 701 (2007).

16. *Gonzales v. Carhart*, 550 U.S. 124 (2007).

17. *District of Columbia v. Heller*, 554 U.S. 570 (2008); *McDonald v. Chicago*, 561 U.S. 3025 (2010).

18. *Seminole Tribe v. Florida*, 517 U.S. 44 (1996).

19. *Alden v. Maine*, 527 U.S. 706 (1999); *City of Boerne v. Flores*, 521 U.S. 507, 520 (1997). See also Jack M. Balkin and Sanford Levinson, "Understanding the Constitutional Revolution," 87 *Virginia Law Review* 8 (2001).

20. *Citizens United v. Federal Election Commission*, 558 U.S. 310 (2010).

21. *Roe v. Wade*, 410 U.S. 113 (1973); *Planned Parenthood of Southeastern Pennsylvania v. Casey*, 505 U.S. 833 (1992). "As applied challenges" are challenges to a law that might have some constitutional use or basis but which might be invalid as applied in a particular case or given a particular set of facts.

22. *District of Columbia v. Heller*, 554 U.S. 570 (2008); *McDonald v. Chicago*, 561 U.S. 742 (2010).

23. Jeffrey Toobin, *The Oath: The Obama White House and the Supreme Court* (New York: Doubleday, 2012), 165.

24. Transcripts of Oral Arguments, *Citizens United v. Federal Election Commission*, No. 08–205, March 24, 2009, at 29.

25. *Austin v. Michigan Chamber of Commerce*, 494 U.S. 652 (1990); *McConnell v. Federal Election Commission*, 540 U.S. 93 (2003). This effectively meant that the Court was considering a facial challenge to the Bipartisan Campaign Reform Act.

26. Transcripts of Oral Arguments, *Citizens United v. Federal Election Commission* at 65.

27. Ibid., 91.

28. *Shelby County v. Holder*, 133 S. Ct. 2612 (2013) at 2622.

29. Ibid., 2618–2619.

30. Ibid., 2619.

31. Ibid., 2621.

32. Ibid., 2622.

33. Ibid.

34. *NAMUDNO v. Holder*, 557 U.S. 193, 203 (2009).

35. 133 S. Ct. 2631, quoting *Blodgett v. Holden*, 275 U.S. 142, 148 (1927).

36. 133 S. Ct. 2631.

37. Ibid., 2632–2633.

38. Ibid, 2635, the last quoting H.R. Rep. No. 109–478 (2006), 6.

39. 133 S. Ct. 2612 at 2636–2637, and quoting Akhil Amar, *America's Constitution: A Biography* (New York: Random House, 2010), 361, 363, 399.

40. 383 U.S. 301, 324.

41. 133 S. Ct. 2612 at 2638.

42. James Blacksher and Lani Guinier, "Free at Last: Rejecting Equal Sovereignty and Restoring the Constitutional Right to Vote in *Shelby County v. Holder*," *Harvard Law and Policy Review* 80 (2014).

43. *Dred Scott v. Sandford*, 60 U.S. 393 (1857).

## 8. THE VOTING RIGHTS ACT AFTER *SHELBY COUNTY*

1. *South Carolina v. Katzenbach*, 383 U.S. 301 (1966).

2. *Shelby County v. Holder*, 811 F. Supp. 2d 505.

3. *Shelby County v. Holder*, 570 U.S. 18 (2013).

4. H. Amdt. 1 to H.R. 9, House Report 109-554, July 12 2006.

5. Charles S. Bullock III and Ronald Keith Gaddie, *The Triumph of Voting Rights in the South* (Norman: University of Oklahoma Press, 2009). Data for 1996 were not readily available for this analysis, so we rely on a more conservative estimate of exclusion under the Norwood amendment standard.

6. Samuel Issacharoff, "Is Section 5 of the Voting Rights Act a Victim of Its Own Success?" *Columbia Law Review* 104 (2004): 1710–1731.

7. Roberts quoted in "Was Chief Justice John Roberts Right about Voting Rates in Massachusetts, Mississippi?" Politifact.com, March 5, 2013, www. politifact.com/truth-o-meter/statements/2013/mar/05/john-roberts/was-chief -justice-john-roberts-right-about-voting-/.

8. Bernard Grofman, "Devising a Sensible Trigger for Section 5 of the Voting Rights Act," *Election Law Journal* 12, no. 3 (2013): 333.

9. Peyton McCrary, "Supplemental Declaration of Dr. Peyton McCrary," in *Shelby County v. Holder*, C.A. No. 1: 10-cv-00651-JDB, U.S. District Court, District of Columbia, 2011.

10. Grofman, "Devising a Sensible Trigger," 335.

11. Ibid., 335–336.

12. This paragraph draws from "A Flawed Attempt at Protecting *Minority* Voters' Rights: Voting Rights Act Amendment of 2014 (H.R. 3899, S. 1945)," Factsheet No. 139, Heritage Foundation, March 14, 2014.

13. Personal communication with Christopher Coates, March 26, 2014.

14. Travis Crum, "Note: The Voting Rights Act's Secret Weapon, Pocket Trigger Litigation and Dynamic Preclearance," 119 *Yale L. J. Online* 1992, 2010–15 (2010); see also Shelby County v. Holder, 679 F.3d 848, 881 (D.C. Cir. 2012); Travis Crum, "Voting Blogs: An Effects-Based Pocket Trigger? Voting News, July 9. 2013, http://thevotingnews.com/an-effects-test-pocket-trigger-travis-crumelection-law-blog.

15. *United States of America v. State of Texas*, S.D. of Texas, filed August 22, 2013.

16. Richard H. Pildes, "What Does the Court's Decision Mean?" *Election Law Journal* 12, no. 3 (2013): 317–318.

17. Nathaniel Persily, "The Promise and Pitfalls of the New Voting Rights Act," *Yale Law Journal* 117 (2007): 178.

18. Bruce E. Cain, "Moving Past Section 5: More Fingers or a New Dike?" *Election Law Journal* 12, no. 3 (2013): 338–340.

19. A collection of essays from the University of Arkansas's Diane D. Blair Center documents the consistent economic policy differences between blacks and whites in several southern states: see Todd G. Shields and Shannon G. Davis, eds., *The New South Consortium: The Status of Women and Minorities in the New South* (Tallahassee, Fla.: FSU Institute of Government, 2008).

20. See, for example, V. O. Key, Jr., *Southern Politics* (New York: Knopf, 1949); Alexander Heard, *A Two-Party South* (Chapel Hill: University of North Carolina Press, 1952).

21. Earl Black and Merle Black, *The Rise of the Southern Republicans* (Cambridge, Mass.: Belknap, 2002); David Ian Lublin, *The Republican South: Democratization and Partisan Change* (Princeton, N.J.: Princeton University Press, 2007).

22. Black and Black, *Rise of the Southern Republicans.*

23. Kyle L. Saunders and Alan I. Abramowitz, "Ideological Realignment and Active Partisans in the American Electorate," *American Politics Research* 32, no. 3 (2004); Shields and Davis, *New South Consortium.*

24. Pub. L. No. 97–205, 96 Stat. 134, at 42 U.S.C. § 1973(a) (1982).

25. *Bush v. Vera*, 517 U.S. 952, 983 (1996); see also Issacharoff, "Is Section 5 of the Voting Rights Act?" 1717.

26. David Epstein and Sharyn O'Halloran, "Measuring the Electoral and Policy Impact of Majority-Minority Voting Districts," *American Journal of Political Science* 43, no. 2 (1999): 369.

27. David T. Canon, *Race, Redistricting, and Representation: The Unintended Consequences of Black Majority Districts* (Chicago: University of Chicago Press, 1999).

28. Christian R. Grose, *Congress in Black and White: Race and Representation in Washington and at Home* (New York: Cambridge University Press, 2011), 83.

29. *Georgia v. Ashcroft*, 539 U.S. 461 (2003).

30. Although DOJ claims that it never had a 65 percent rule, that was its threshold in *Busbee v. Smith*, 549 F. Supp 494 (D.D.C. 1982) and is referenced in other court opinions of the period; see also *United Jewish Organizations of Williamsburgh v. Carey*, 430 U.S. 144 (1977).

31. The replacement of African American members of Congress in Memphis and New Orleans by a white Democrat and a Vietnamese-American Republican, respectively, was not due to reducing black concentrations in these districts.

32. Expert report of David Epstein, *Georgia v. Ashcroft*, 195 F. Supp. 2d 25 (D.D.C. 2002) (No. 01-2111), 16–17; David Epstein and Sharyn O'Halloran, "Measuring the Electoral and Policy Impact of Majority-Minority Voting Districts," *American Journal of Political Science* 43 (1999): 367–395.

33. A majority vote requirement exists for nominations in Alabama, Arkansas, Georgia, Louisiana, Mississippi, Oklahoma, South Carolina, and Texas and a 40 percent threshold determines nominations in North Carolina. Many municipalities across the nation also have a majority vote requirement for election.

34. In states in which both the Senate and gubernatorial contests were polled, the results tend to be quite similar. In Texas, however, the Democratic candidate for governor, Wendy Davis, beat Greg Abbott (R) 55–44 percent among Hispanics.

35. See, for example, *Vieth v. Jubelirer*, 541 U.S. 267 (2004), on partisan gerrymandering; *Cox* v. *Larios*, 542 U.S. 947 (2004), on population equality and partisan gerrymandering; and *Easley v. Cromartie*, 532 U.S. 234 (2001), for racial gerrymandering under the beard of partisan gerrymandering.

36. Open Secrets reports that Nunn raised more than $14.25 million, and with five weeks remaining Carter's fundraising report filed with the Georgia Ethics Commission showed him having raised almost $7 million.

37. Pew Research Center, "Broad Support for Photo ID Voting ID Requirements," October 11, 2012; Pew Hispanic Center, "Hispanic Voters Support Obama by 3–1 Ratio, but Are Less Certain than Others about Voting," October 11, 2012.

38. *Crawford v. Marion County Election Board*, 553 U.S. 181 (2008).

39. See DOJ letters from Thomas E. Perez to C. Havird Jones, Jr. (S.C.), December 23, 2011, and to Keith Ingram (Tex.), March 12, 2012, accessed at www.justice.gov/crt/records/vot/obj_letters/.

40. *South Carolina v. U.S.*, Civil Action No. 12-203 (D.D.C., 2013).

41. Adam Liptak, "Courts Strike Down Vote ID Laws in Wisconsin and Texas," *New York Times*, October 9, 2014.

42. John Harwood, "Voting Restrictions: Key Variable in Midterms," *Atlanta Journal- Constitution*, September 4, 2014, A5.

43. *Florida v. U.S.*, Case No. 1:11-cv-01428 (D.D.C., 2011).

44. Adam Liptak, "Supreme Court Blocks an Order to Restore a Unique Week of Early Voting in Ohio," *New York Times*, September 30, 2014, A14.

45. *Alabama Legislative Black Caucus v. Alabama* 575 U.S. ____ (2015). The Court also sent back down a similar case from Virginia: *Cantor, et al. v. Personhuballah, et al.* docket number No. 14-518. The three-judge federal panel rejected Virginia's 3rd congressional district as an unconstitutional racial gerry-mander. The panel split 2–1. The commonwealth was given until September 1, 2015, to remedy the defect, though attorneys for Virginia indicated they would appeal again to the Supreme Court. At the time of this writing the issue was unresolved.

46. Although not a factor in this litigation, the appellants had criticized Alabama for adopting a policy of keeping population deviations among districts to less than 1 percent. The appellants had wanted some majority-minority districts to be underpopulated since that would "stretch" the black population, that is, allow for its distribution among a greater number of districts.

47. The black incumbent in one of the districts made much whiter lost but the cause was malfeasance. He was subsequently convicted in federal court of more than 130 offenses. A black candidate regained this seat in the next election.

48. Report of David Epstein in *Georgia v. Ashcroft*, 539 U.S. 461 (2003); Charles Cameron, David Epstein, and Sharyn O'Halloran, "Do Majority-Minority Districts Maximize Substantive Black Representation in Congress?" *American Political Science Review* 93 (March 1999), 804.

49. *Easley v. Cromartie*, 532 U.S. 234 (2001); *Shaw v. Reno*, 509 U.S. 630 (1993).

50. The Supreme Court found party to have been a stronger explanation than race despite the question posed by the top staff member involved with redistricting, who, noting that he had added the Greensboro black population to the district, asked the Senate committee chair by e-mail who he should remove to bring the district back in line with the equal population requirement. The trial court had found that e-mail strong evidence that race was the predomi-nant factor.

51. Lorraine C. Minnite, *The Myth of Voter Fraud* (Ithaca, N.Y.: Cornell University Press, 2010), 126.

52. Stephen Ansolabehere, "Effects of Identification Requirements on Voting: Evidence from the Experiences of Voters on Election Day," *PS*, January 2009, 129.

53. M. V. Hood III and Charles. S. Bullock III, "Much Ado about Nothing: An Empirical Assessment of the Georgia Voter Identification Statute," *State Politics and Policy Quarterly* 12 (2012): 394–414.

54. Pew Research Center, "Broad Support for Photo ID."

55. Expert report of Matt A. Barreto and Gabriel R. Sanchez, filed in *Veasey v. Perry*, Case 2:13-cv-00193 (2014).

56. Figures from the reports complied by the Georgia Office of the Secretary of State and posted on its website except for 2014, which come from Kristin Torres, "White Voters Dominated Georgia Midterm Election," *Atlanta Journal-Constitution*, December 17, 2014, B2.

57. National figures from the American Presidency Project, www.presidency.ucsb.edu.

58. Robert D. Popper, "The Vote Suppression Myth Takes Another Hit," *Wall Street Journal*, December 29, 2014, A13.

59. Ibid.

# Index